CONTEXTS OF THE BILL OF RIGHTS

Edited by

STEPHEN L. SCHECHTER and

RICHARD B. BERNSTEIN

New York State Commission
on the
Bicentennial of the United States Constitution
Albany, New York

©New York State Commission on the
Bicentennial of the United States
Constitution, 1990
Albany, New York

Printed in the United States of America

Library of Congress Cataloging in Publication Data

Contexts of the Bill of Rights / edited by Stephen L. Schechter and
    Richard B. Bernstein.
        p.   cm.
    Includes bibliographical references.
    ISBN 0-945660-04-9
    1. Civil rights—United States—History.   2. United States. Constitution.
1st–10th amendments—History.   I. Schechter, Stephen L., 1945–
II. Bernstein, Richard B., 1956–   .   III. New York State Commission
on the Bicentennial of the United States Constitution.
KF4749.C648   1990
342.73 '085—dc20   90-5550
[347.30285]   CIP

Contents

Foreword   v
   by Chief Judge Sol Wachtler, Chairman
   New York State Bicentennial Commission

Editors' Introduction: Restoring the Contexts of the   ix
   Bill of Rights
   by Stephen L. Schechter and Richard B. Bernstein

The U. S. Bill of Rights in Historical Perspective   3
   by Donald S. Lutz

The Making of the Bill of Rights: 1787–1792   18
   by John P. Kaminski

The Bill of Rights: A Bibliographic Essay   65
   by Gaspare J. Saladino

Appendix

Augustine Davis   110
   by Thomas E. Burke

The RATIFICATIONS of the New Foederal Constitution,   112
together with the AMENDMENTS, PROPOSED BY THE
SEVERAL STATES (1788)
   Printed by Aug. Davis

Author–Editor Index to Bibliographic Essay   147

Index   152

Contributors   158

New York State Commission on the Bicentennial of the U.S. Constitution

Hon. Mario M. Cuomo
Governor

Hon. Sol Wachtler
Chief Judge of the
State of New York
Chairman

Hon. Domenick L. Gabrielli
Vice-Chairman

COMMISSIONERS

Hon. Beatrice S. Burstein
Antonia M. Cortese
Edward B. Flink, Esq.
Hon. Kenneth P. LaValle
Hon. Michael McNulty
Dr. Joseph S. Murphy
Hon. Mark Alan Siegel
Hon. Thomas Sobol
Dr. Robert J. Spitzer
Hon. Moses M. Weinstein
Hon. Clifford R. Wharton, Jr.

Stephen L. Schechter
Executive Director

Paul J. Scudiere
Administrative Officer

Foreword

HON. SOL WACHTLER

Chief Judge, New York State Court of Appeals,
and *Chairman*, New York State Commission
on the Bicentennial of the United States Constitution

The Bill of Rights was the crowning achievement of the first Congress to meet under the Constitution. While not detracting from the pivotal role of Representative James Madison of Virginia, recent scholarship on the origins of the Bill of Rights makes clear that these constitutional provisions are solidly rooted in the constitutional development of the seventeenth and eighteenth centuries on both sides of the Atlantic Ocean. In particular, our renewed appreciation of the traditions of rights and constitutional government in the colonies and (after 1776) states compels us to conclude that the states were active, though forgotten, partners in the creation of federal constitutional guarantees of individual liberty. Moreover, in light of recent developments in federal constitutional law under the U.S. Bill of Rights, many judges and legal scholars have shifted their jurisprudential focus to state constitutional guarantees.

It is therefore especially appropriate for the New York State Commission on the Bicentennial of the United States Constitution to commemorate the two hundredth anniversary of the framing of the Bill of Rights. As a complement to the Commission's sponsorship of exhibitions and public-education programs on the Bill of Rights and as a lasting contribution to historical scholarship on the Bill of Rights, we are proud to present the essays collected in these pages.

Donald S. Lutz, whose previous books are landmark works in the study of American constitutional thought in the Revolutionary period,[1] begins with an incisive discussion of the changing meanings of rights and declarations of rights in the eighteenth century. In the process, he rightly emphasizes the influence of the Americans' political experience during the colonial period and the theory and practice of constitution making in the states during the first years of the Revolution. Lutz stresses the political—as opposed to legal—character and uses of state declarations of rights to highlight both the continuities and the divergences between the states' experience and the framing and adoption of the federal Bill of Rights in 1789–1791.

Complementing Lutz's analysis of the intellectual history of bills of rights is John P. Kaminski's fine essay describing the politics of the controversy over a federal bill of rights between 1787 and 1791. Kaminski's account draws on the extensive primary sources surviving from the ratification controversy and the tantalizing surviving materials from the deliberations of the First Congress and the state legislatures on the proposed Bill of Rights. He delineates the complex and conflicting motives of the advocates of a bill of rights during the ratification struggle, and of those who actually pressed for constitutional amendments once the new government was in operation. Whereas he demolishes the conventional view of James Madison as a sincere and disinterested advocate of protecting individual liberty, he still demonstrates the extraordinary challenge facing Madison and his colleagues, and Madison's generally successful efforts to win adoption of his proposals.

Finally, Gaspare J. Saladino's thoughtful and comprehensive historiographical essay surveys the vast scholarly literature seeking to understand the origins—and original meanings—of the Bill of Rights. Saladino's review encompasses not only publications examining the Bill of Rights as a whole, but the growing bodies of scholarship focusing on individual amendments and clauses. In light of the strong linkages between the concerns of judges, litigants, and legal scholars and those of constitutional historians, Saladino's essay shows the clear connections between the growing importance of a given guarantee in the Bill of Rights and the growth of scholarly interest in the origins and purposes of that provision. Saladino's essay thus enables us to track the parallel courses of evolution—in constitutional law and in constitutional scholarship—of the Bill of Rights and its individual provisions.

The introductory essay by Stephen L. Schechter and Richard B. Bernstein proposes useful and persuasive contexts in which the reader may set the essays by Lutz, Kaminski, and Saladino. First, they show that the challenge of reconciling age-old understandings of individual rights as protections against government with the literally revolutionary conception of popular self-government is a constant theme of American constitutional development. Second, they outline the influence that the early state constitutions' declarations of rights and the nascent system of constitutional federalism exerted on the framing of the federal Bill of Rights. (This point is underscored by the inclusion, in the appendix to this volume, of the text of Augustine Davis's valuable 1788 compilation of amendments proposed by the state ratifying conventions, a source on which James Madison relied in framing his draft amendments for submission to the First Congress.) Finally, they introduce the reader to perhaps one of the most exciting developments in American constitutional law—the rediscovery of state constitutional law as a source of protection for individual liberty. One need not be a state appellate judge to recognize the far-reaching consequences of the renewed vigor of interpretation and application of state constitutional provisions by courts and litigants, and their study by legal scholars, historians, and political scientists. This development can only be cause for celebration.

Especially in light of the extraordinary recent developments in the nations of eastern Europe, such questions—and the ways in which the American political builders of the eighteenth century resolved them— are of abiding interest. The scholars whose illuminating and useful essays are collected in this book have performed a public service.

---

¹Donald S. Lutz, *Popular Consent and Popular Control: Whig Political Theory in the Early State Constitutions* (Baton Rouge: Louisiana State University Press, 1980); Donald S. Lutz, *The Origins of American Constitutionalism* (Baton Rouge: Louisiana State University Press, 1988).

Editors' Introduction: Restoring the Contexts of the Bill Rights

Two hundred years ago, the American people engaged in a long process of political experimentation to find the best means of governing themselves. The capstone of this process was the framing and adoption of the first ten amendments to the Constitution of the United States—what we now call the Bill of Rights. On the occasion of its bicentennial, these essays consider the origins of the Bill of Rights, using complementary interpretative strategies in the service of common themes.

The most obvious of the themes shared by these essays is the restoration of the contexts of the Bill of Rights. Donald S. Lutz restores its *intellectual* context, by analyzing the changing ideas about rights in colonial, Revolutionary, and early national American political thought and culture. John P. Kaminski restores its *political* context in his admirable narrative of the emergence of the Bill of Rights from the constitutional controversies of 1787–1792. Gaspare J. Saladino restores its *historiographical* context, surveying the voluminous literature, both in history and in lawyers' legal and constitutional history, on the origins of the Bill of Rights and the individual amendments composing it.

Three other less obvious themes merit discussion: the paradox of rights and popular government; federalism and the state roots of the Bill of Rights; and the renewed appreciation of the states as sources of rights. This introduction considers each of these themes in turn.

I. THE PARADOX OF RIGHTS AND POPULAR GOVERNMENT

The history of the federal Bill of Rights may be understood as the working out of a paradox: how to protect the rights of the people against the powers of a government created of, by, and for the people.[1] This paradox originated at the same time that the Bill of Rights was drafted and adopted; it therefore provides a useful context for analyzing the development of American understandings of constitutional rights.

Until the American Revolution, Western political thought assumed that all societies were divided into two hostile camps, one entitled to govern and the other obliged to obey. In British Colonial America, this assumption gave rise to what historians have called the "deferential society," in which the "better sort" governed a largely passive people, or common sort.[2] The written Bill of Rights was a key consequence of the Anglo-American view that rights were concessions made, willingly or reluctantly, by the sovereign power to the people. Eighteenth-century Americans believed that such great documents of human liberty as Magna Carta had been wrested from government by the exertions of the people.[3]

Most Americans of the 1780s and 1790s who took part in or thought about politics believed, with varying degrees of satisfaction, that their revolution had established that the people could and should govern themselves. At the same time, they had only begun to work out the consequences of the Revolution for the theory and practice of popular government. James Madison of Virginia identified one such consequence with epigrammatic terseness: "In Europe, charters of liberty have been granted by power. America has set the example . . . of charters of power granted by liberty."[4] This conceptual reversal of the relationship between liberty and power posed a disturbing problem for the idea and purpose of a bill of rights: If such written guarantees of liberty previously had been extracted from grudging sovereigns adverse to the people, what role were they to play when the people were their own sovereigns? Indeed, what need is there for a bill of rights, for is it not illogical to maintain that the people would take away their own liberties?

In 1787–88, those Federalists unwilling to amend the Constitution to recognize and protect individual rights often invoked this argument. As described by John Kaminski in this volume, they made other arguments as well, including citation of the sorry record of violations of rights by governments throughout human history, even those with written declarations of rights. This latter argument is the source of a famous, but often misunderstood, phrase coined by James Madison— "parchment barriers." Madison meant by this term the futility of enumerating rights in written form when such lists have no inherent power to restrain governments bent on violating them. He explained to Thomas Jefferson in October 1788: "[E]xperience proves the inefficacy of a bill of rights on those occasions when its controul is most needed. Repeated violations of these *parchment barriers* have been committed by overbearing majorities in every State."[5]

Such arguments had greater force in 1787–88 than we may realize today. Both Donald Lutz's essay in this volume and the recent work of Robert C. Palmer have shown that declarations of rights originally were not legally enforceable limitations on government power; rather, they were political documents, enshrining the people's values at the heart of the polity and providing the citizenry with a means to evaluate the performance of their elected officials.[6] Government officials could ignore such political guidelines, however, with virtual impunity from popular reaction and even with popular approval. In *The Federalist No. 48*, for example, Madison noted the many violations of the Pennsylvania Constitution of 1776 catalogued by the 1783 report of the state's council of censors—abuses that had been, and continued to be, tolerated by the people of the state:

> The conclusion which I am warranted in drawing from these observations is that a mere demarcation on parchment of the constitutional limits of the several departments is not a sufficient guard against those encroachments which lead to a tyrannical concentration of all the powers of government in the same hands.[7]

These and other arguments against the need for a federal bill of rights did not prevail for two reasons, one political and the other a mixture of politics and constitutional principle. First, their opponents had the upper hand; as the ratification campaign progressed, Federalists gradually were forced to a fallback position, pledging to work for constitutional amendments protecting individual rights against the general government as the price of ratification (and as a way to fend off more sweeping proposed amendments that would have gutted the new government). Second, some Federalists began to recognize that there might be good and substantive reasons for the people to seek to limit their own powers as exercised by and through the government they had created. Thomas Jefferson made this case most strongly in his series of letters to James Madison. As he chided Madison, "a bill of rights is what the people are entitled to against any government on earth, general or particular, and what no government should refuse, or rest on inference."[8]

Jefferson's correspondence with Madison on this question is remarkable for many reasons, but particularly because, taken together, his letters represent a key juncture in changing American conceptions about rights.[9] The author of the Declaration of Independence, the paradigmatic expression of the American theory of popular government, provided in the passage quoted above a classic statement of the traditional understanding of rights as a people's defense against government. In this correspondence, Jefferson also offered a solution to the problem of protecting the people's rights against the people's government, pointing out that one powerful argument for a declaration of rights is "the legal check which it puts into the hands of the judiciary."[10] Thus, a declaration or bill of rights enables one branch of the people's government to protect the people against violations or abuses by other branches.

Under the traditional view, the controversy over adding a bill of rights to the United States Constitution in 1787–1791 evidenced the people's profound interest at that time in the nature and extent of individual rights and the theory and practice of popular government. However, as Kaminski notes (citing the work of Kenneth R. Bowling), the sincerity of the Antifederalists' calls for a bill of rights, and of Madison's determination to give them one, may be questionable: what was at stake in the amendments controversy, at least as much as protecting liberty at the federal level, was whether other amendments cutting back on the Constitution's grants of federal power over taxation and interstate and foreign commerce would be proposed or rejected. Antifederalists charged that Madison's proposed bill of rights was simply a "tub to the whale," distracting the people from the need to restrict the dangerous powers conferred by the Constitution to the United States.

Under either reading of the controversy, once the first ten amendments became part of the Constitution, they lost whatever hold they may have had on the public mind. Even the scattered attempts to invoke the federal Bill of Rights in its first decades (for example, during the crisis over the Sedition Act of 1798) did not win general support— in part because the issues (for example, the constitutionality of the Sedition Act) were not as clear-cut to the contending parties as they may seem to us; in part because they were entangled with other issues (for example, questions of state *versus* federal authority) obscuring the issues of rights.

At least as important a cause for the general neglect of the Bill of Rights as those noted above was its still-problematic character— whether it was a catalogue of principles of free government or of legally enforceable constitutional limitations on federal power. It may be significant evidence as to the prevailing view of the purpose of the Bill of Rights in 1798–1800 that no defendant prosecuted under the 1798

Sedition Act sought to appeal his conviction to the U.S. Supreme Court (although that may only indicate contemporary lawyers' recognition that the Federalist-dominated Court was unlikely to overturn such convictions). It is also arguable that the electorate's repudiation of Federalists in the 1800 presidential and congressional elections may have been an instance of the voters' use of the federal Bill of Rights as a standard for deciding whether those holding political power should be permitted to retain it.

The U.S. Supreme Court's 1833 decision in *Barron v. Baltimore* sheds additional light on this historical problem.[11] In his last major constitutional opinion, Chief Justice John Marshall held for the Court that a Baltimore resident could not invoke the Fifth Amendment's due process and takings clauses against the Baltimore city government; the Fifth Amendment—and the rest of the Bill of Rights—limited only the powers of the federal government, not the states. Marshall had no trouble maintaining this position, especially as Congress in 1789 had rejected Madison's proposed amendment depriving the states of power to limit individual freedoms of religion, speech, and press. Furthermore, the Court's decision evoked little reaction in the political or legal communities, or from the citizenry at large—principally because an individual had little contact with government in any event, and such contacts were nearly always with state and local governments, whose actions were governed by state constitutions.

Thus, for more than half its history, the U.S. Bill of Rights had little actual effect on the legal and political life of the United States, except as a symbol of rights and as a pattern for bills of rights included in new or revised state constitutions. At the same time, both in the development of state constitutional law, statutory law, and common law, as well as in the political discourse of the time, rights were constant subjects of controversy at the level of the states.

By contrast, the twentieth century has witnessed a major transformation in popular and legal understandings of the Bill of Rights—one that, until the past decade, has obscured the importance of state protection of individual rights. This transformation has at least four sources.

First, groups previously excluded from what Henry Adams once called the "political population" have demanded recognition and protection of their rights. Such movements as the civil rights movement of the 1950s and 1960s and the women's rights movement of the 1970s and 1980s exemplify the continuing diversification and democratization of American society and public life. Even when they have not achieved all their goals, they still have posed stark challenges to the existing legal and political order—challenges predicated on claims of individual rights.[12]

Second, the growing interconnectedness of the nation through improved methods of transportation and communication has made certain that issues that earlier were regarded as local are now legitimate concerns of national politics and federal law. For example, many federal laws protecting civil rights, such as the Civil Rights Act of 1964 and the Public Accommodations Act of 1964, are grounded in the Constitution's grant of federal power to regulate interstate commerce. Similarly, the rise of a national news media to serve a national political and cultural community has ensured that issues of free speech and press, and issues of privacy, are national issues as much as state or local.

Third, the participation of the United States in the Second World War, and the presentation of American involvement in that war as a fight for liberty and democracy, coincided with several national anniversaries, among them the bicentennial of the birth of Thomas Jefferson and the sesquicentennial of the adoption of the Bill of Rights.[13] Emphasis on Jeffersonian ideals of liberty (as reinterpreted by scholars of the New Deal period) and on the Bill of Rights, combined with the stark evidence of the Nazis' brutal violations of individual rights and common decency, helped further to fix the importance of the Bill of Rights in the American public mind—even though, at the same time, the United States government interned more than 150,000 Japanese-Americans, both native-born and naturalized citizens, in the single most sweeping violation of individual rights under the color of United States law.[14]

Fourth, in response to these developments and to the flood of rights litigation in the federal courts in the past four decades, judges, legal scholars, and lawyers have developed methods of constitutional reasoning and models of constitutional law emphasizing the need to protect rights.[15] This development has implicated not only the federal Bill of Rights, but—perhaps even more important—the Fourteenth Amendment, through which federal courts have applied many of the protections of the Constitution's first ten amendments to limit the powers of state and local governments to infringe individual rights.[16] (One consequence of the startling growth of litigation over federal constitutional rights is the tidal wave of legal and historical investigations of the origins and original understandings of the Bill of Rights and its individual provisions. Gaspare Saladino's sensitive and comprehensive historiographical essay ably examines this vast literature.)

All these forces have helped cement American national identity and the American national political community; they also have had profound effects on American understandings of governmental power and individual rights.

Neither the invention of popular government under a written constitution nor the growth of what recent historians have called "rights consciousness"[17] dispelled the belief that government was the enemy of the people, and the corollary belief that rights were the people's defense against government. The idea of the adversarial relationship between the people and their government has persisted and grown even stronger with the increase in the size of government, the scope of governmental activities and responsibilities, and the corresponding growth in the distance (real or perceived) between the people and their government. Indeed, the existence of legally enforceable rights has become more, not less, important with the growth of popular distrust of government—so much so that we may say that the distrust of government and the importance of rights have grown together, and at roughly the same rate.

In sum, the paradox of the people's government and the people's rights is alive and well in the two-hundredth year of the federal Bill of Rights.

II. FEDERALISM AND RIGHTS PROTECTION: STATE ROOTS OF THE U.S. BILL OF RIGHTS

The Constitution of the United States did not spring magically into existence at the Federal Convention of 1787, but rather was the product of decades of intellectual ferment and political change. The delegates to the Federal Convention drew on a rich heritage of political experience and constitutional thought, encompassing the history of England, the republics of classical antiquity and the Renaissance, and the nearly two centuries of political experience amassed by the colonists of British North America. Of particular interest to the Framers of the federal Constitution were the state constitutions adopted between 1776 and 1784; the most notable of these for their influence on the Constitution of the United States were the New York Constitution of 1777 and the Massachusetts Constitution of 1780.[18]

This is also the case with the U.S. Bill of Rights. The idea of a written declaration of rights was invented by George Mason and his colleagues at the Virginia Convention of 1776, the body that framed the Virginia Constitution of 1776 and the Virginia declaration of rights. To be sure, not every state constitution adopted in the Revolutionary period included a declaration or bill of rights, and, as noted in Part II of this introduction and in Donald Lutz's essay, the "ought" or

"should" language of the state declarations of rights is far removed
from the "shall" language of the federal Bill of Rights. Nonetheless,
the federal constitutional guarantees were shaped by the experience of
state constitution makers in drafting, and state governments in admin-
istering, their constitutions and declarations of rights.

In addition, the lists of recommendatory amendments compiled
by many of the state ratifying conventions (and collected in pamphlet
form by Augustine Davis, whose compilation is reprinted here) drew
extensively on these same state constitutional provisions. As Madison
used the Davis pamphlet as one of his principal sources in drafting his
proposed version of constitutional amendments in 1789, the states' constitutions exerted indirect, as well as direct, evidence on the framing of
the federal Bill of Rights.

The federal Bill of Rights was a catalogue of rights which had been
infringed both by colonial governments and by the British government,
both in the British Isles and in America. It also listed rights that state
constitution-makers had wanted to recognize and to protect, in whatever
fashion, against the powers of their new-fashioned state governments.[19]

Just as important as the question of roots or origins is the recognition that the structures of rights recognized by state constitutions and
the political principles enshrined in those constitutions shaped the
development of federal constitutional guarantees of liberty. Two examples, both of which are discussed in Kaminski's essay, will suffice:

When, at the Federal Convention of 1787, George Mason of Virginia and Elbridge Gerry of Massachusetts urged the preparation of
a declaration of rights, Roger Sherman of Connecticut invoked the
states' bills of rights as sufficient security for liberty. Mason responded
that the federal Constitution would be paramount to state bills of rights.
His answer, while ignored at the time, prophesied the problems of
federalism that would preoccupy generations of judges and constitutional scholars.

In 1789, during the debates over the framing of the federal Bill of
Rights, representatives from New England states opposed Madison's proposed guarantee against religious establishments. Madison agreed to the
insertion of the word "national" in his amendment to make clear that
the federal government would have no power to create a national
religious establishment *or* to disturb whatever arrangements the several
states had arrived at with regard to church-state relations.

These examples could be multiplied indefinitely, but their common
theme is clear: In determining what rights should be protected against
the powers of the general government, the Framers of the U.S. Bill of
Rights had to keep in mind the parallel—or even clashing—systems of

rights protection in the states and the novel and as yet imperfectly understood system of constitutional federalism.

Federalism was implicated in the creation of the U.S. Bill in two distinct, almost complementary ways:

First, the advocates of adding a bill of rights to the proposed Constitution sought to limit the powers of what, for them, was an untried and threatening creature: a general government which was to coexist with the state governments and operate directly on individual citizens alongside the operations of the state governments, perhaps in areas traditionally regarded as barred to the states—those defined by state declarations of rights or state constitutions' rights-protecting provisions. It is a commonplace of historians' and political scientists' discussions of federalism that the politicians of the 1770s and 1780s were wrestling with the age-old idea that *imperium in imperio* (a state within a state) was impossible. The system of federalism that we see as inherent in the Constitution actually took decades to evolve; it is likely that none of the Framers of the Constitution could have predicted its ultimate shape or course of development.[20] Thus, the demand for a federal bill of rights was as much a demand for certain basic restraints on this untried system's potential to invade the sphere of state authority and the limits on that authority as a demand to protect individual rights.

Second is a point related to—in many ways a special case of—the first. As illustrated by the quarrel in the U.S. House of Representatives in 1789 over the effect of a federal bill of rights on state religious establishments, many Americans were suspicious of the ways in which provisions of the U.S. Constitution dealing with rights might interfere with or even preempt analogous state arrangements. The idea that the federal Bill of Rights would limit only the general government and not the states was one part of the eventual solution to this problem. The other part was the development, over the succeeding two hundred years, of the idea that the federal Bill of Rights (provisions of which were applied by the courts through the Fourteenth Amendment to limit the powers of state and local government) represented a "floor" of rights protection below which state and local governments could not fall. The idea of a federal "floor," however, did not—and does not—prevent state and local governments from giving more protection to individual rights than does the federal Constitution. We turn now to examine this subject.

III. NOT THE ONLY GAME IN TOWN: THE RENEWED APPRECIATION OF STATES AS SOURCES OF RIGHTS

The Bill of Rights has acquired parity with the Constitution and the Declaration of Independence as symbols of human liberty. Indeed, the late Richard B. Morris used to grumble that modern constitutional law's focus on rights, and on judicial review as the primary means to protect rights, made most Americans think that the Constitution consisted *only* of the Bill of Rights.

The extraordinary symbolic importance of the U.S. Bill of Rights has obscured state constitutions, statutes, and common-law doctrines as sources of protection of individual rights. In part, this problem is rooted in the civil rights struggles of the 1950s and 1960s: Opponents of federal civil-rights laws and lawsuits invoking federal constitutional guarantees sought the shelter of doctrines of federalism and "states' rights." At the same time, an activist Supreme Court freely invoked federal constitutional authority for decisions upholding individual liberties against state constitutional provisions, statutes, and common-law doctrines.

With the shift in the Supreme Court in the direction of a more conservative federal constitutional jurisprudence, many scholars and litigators have rediscovered state constitutional law as a means to protect rights. Justice William J. Brennan, Jr., of the U.S. Supreme Court has repeatedly urged this step, as have many other jurists and legal scholars.[21]

One source of this movement to revive state constitutional law is pragmatic: the Supreme Court may not review a case from a state court on federal constitutional grounds if the lower court includes in its decision "adequate and independent state grounds" for its holding.[22] Thus, if the New York Court of Appeals rules in a state criminal appeal that a defendant's conviction must be overturned because the prosecution violated her rights under the U.S. Constitution *and* the New York state constitution, the Supreme Court cannot disturb the ruling, for the New York court is the highest court authorized to interpret its own state constitution. The doctrine of "adequate and independent state grounds" is particularly useful for those claiming protection for a right under comparable federal and state constitutional provisions when the state's courts read the state provision more broadly than the federal provision.

Another source of the renewed interest in state constitutional law is the realization that state constitutions are often more specific and versatile guides to an individual's constitutional rights than the U.S.

Bill of Rights. For example, although the U.S. Bill of Rights does not explicitly mention the right to privacy, many state constitutions do. Thus, if the U.S. Supreme Court continues to restrict the federal constitutional right to privacy first identified in *Griswold v. Connecticut*,[23] lawsuits seeking to protect individual privacy rights increasingly will be filed in state courts and will invoke state constitutional guarantees.

This may well be our future; indeed, the future may well be here already. If this is the case, then we will have come a long way from the constitutional and legal culture of the 1950s and 1960s. Invocation of state constitutional law will no longer seem a disingenuous and disreputable brand of collaboration with the forces of segregation and discrimination, as they were when "states' rights" was the rallying cry of the opponents of the civil rights movement, or a reflexive response by conservatives to creative uses of federal power to solve social problems. Rather, state constitutional law will become a new and versatile tool in the reconciling of our legal systems with the continuing diversification and democratization of American life.

On a more theoretical level, a reinvigorated state constitutional jurisprudence may well bring with it a badly needed breathing space for the U.S. Constitution and for the dissonant and cranky brawling ground of modern constitutional theory. That is, it could relieve the strain on the conceptual and theoretical frameworks of American constitutional law—by siphoning off those constitutional problems not readily fitting into the federal Constitution, and, consequently, by limiting those occasions when intractable constitutional problems compel judges to engage in what their critics call impermissible judicial activism (or, in the language of slogans, "when judges make law instead of interpreting and applying law").

To be sure, a reinvigorated state constitutional law would not still the calls for uniform national understandings about fundamental rights—understandings that could only be grounded in an extant provision of the federal Constitution newly interpreted or in a new-fashioned amendment to the Constitution. Nonetheless, it might revive the interest of the general public in political, legislative, and judicial arenas other than the national ones—spheres of governance which exert comparable, if not equally powerful, influences on their daily lives. And, it might well revive the sense that state constitutions are truly part of the Constitution of the United States—an idea evoked powerfully in the context of the 1770s and 1780s in Donald Lutz's *The Origins of American Constitutionalism*.[24]

Such a revival, in sum, would restore to the American people the elements out of which they could construct a reinvigorated constitutional and political culture. It would not, of course, guarantee that development, but such are the challenges of constitutional self-government.

Stephen L. Schechter
Richard B. Bernstein

NOTES:

[1]In 1943, Henry Steele Commager summed up this paradox in the arresting phrase "majority rule and minority rights." See Henry Steele Commager, *Majority Rule and Minority Rights* (New York: Oxford University Press, 1943).

[2]On "deference," see, e.g., John B. Kirby, "Early American Politics—The Search for Ideology: An Historical Analysis and Critique of the Concept of 'Deference,' " *Journal of Politics* 32 (1970): 808–838; Joy B. Gilsdorf and Robert R. Gilsdorf, "Elites and Electorates: Some Plain Truths for Historians of Colonial America," in David H. Hall, John M. Murrin, and Thad W. Tate, ed., *Saints and Revolutionaries: Essays on Early American History* (New York: W.W. Norton, 1984), 207–244; and Ronald P. Formisano, "Deferential-Participant Politics: The Early Republic's Political Culture," *American Political Science Review* 68 (1974): 473–487.

[3]On this point, see generally A.E. Dick Howard, *The Road from Runnymede: Magna Carta and American Constitutionalism* (Charlottesville, Va.: University Press of Virginia, 1968).

[4]James Madison, "On Charters," *National Gazette*, January 19, 1792 in William M. Hutchinson, William M. E. Rachal, and Robert A. Rutland, ed., *The Papers of James Madison*, 15 vols. to date (vols. 1–8, Chicago: University of Chicago Press, 1962–1975; vol. 9–, Charlottesville: University Press of Virginia, 1977– [hereafter cited as *Madison Papers*]), XIV, 191–192 (quote at 191).

[5]James Madison to Thomas Jefferson, October 17, 1788, in *Madison Papers*, XI, 295–300 (esp. 297–300) (emphasis added). See also *The Federalist No. 48* (J. Madison), quoted in text at note 7, for an analogous metaphor.

[6]Robert C. Palmer, "Liberties as Constitutional Provisions: 1776–1791," 55–148 in William E. Nelson and Robert C. Palmer, *Liberty and Community: Constitution and Rights in the Early American Republic* (New York: Oceana Publications, 1987) (New York University School of Law Linden Studies in Legal History).

[7]*The Federalist No. 48* (J. Madison).

[8]Thomas Jefferson to James Madison, December 20, 1787, in *Madison Papers*, X, 335–339.

[9]See the following letters as published in *Madison Papers:* Jefferson to Madison, December 20, 1787, in X, 335–339; Jefferson to Madison, February 6, 1788, in X, 473–475; Jefferson to Madison, July 31, 1788, in XI, 210–214; Jefferson to Madison, November 18, 1788, in XI, 353–355; Jefferson to Madison, March 15, 1789, in XII, 13–16. Madison's replies are contained in Madison to Jefferson, October 17, 1788, in XI, 295–300; Madison to Jefferson, December 8, 1788, in XI, 381–384; Madison to Jefferson, May 27, 1789, in XII, 185–186. Madison reported his introduction of amendments on the floor of the House to Jefferson, Madison to Jefferson, June 14, 1789, in XII, 217–218, and Madison to Jefferson, June 30, 1789, in XII, 267–272. Jefferson's reaction is in Jefferson to Madison, August 28, 1789, in XII, 360–365. The best available analysis of the collaboration between Jefferson and Madison is still Adrienne Koch, *Jefferson and Madison: The Great Collaboration* (New York: Knopf, 1950). This well-written book is more admiring than analytical, however.

[10]Thomas Jefferson to James Madison, March 15, 1789, in *Madison Papers*, XII, 13–16. For a rare instance of agreement between Jefferson and Hamilton, compare the letter cited above with the following passage from *The Federalist No. 78:*

> The complete independence of the courts is peculiarly essential in a limited Constitution. By a limited Constitution, I understand one which contains certain specified exceptions to the legislative authority; such, for instance, as that it shall pass no bill of attainder, no *ex post facto* laws, and the like. Limitations of this kind can be preserved in practice no other way than through the medium of courts of justice, whose duty it must be to declare all acts contrary to the manifest tenor of the Constitution void. Without this, all the reservations of particular rights or privileges would amount to nothing.

[11]32 U.S. (7 Peters) 243 (1833).

[12]See, e.g., Taylor Branch, *Parting the Waters: America in the King Years, 1954–1963* (New York: Simon and Schuster, 1988); David Garrow, *Bearing the Cross: Martin Luther King and the Southern Christian Leadership Conference* (New York: Morrow, 1986); and Richard Kluger, *Simple Justice* (New York: Knopf, 1975) [African–Americans]; Cynthia Harrison, *On Account of Sex* (Berkeley, Calif.: University of California Press, 1988) [women].

[13]On these subjects, see Merrill D. Peterson, *The Jefferson Image in the American Mind* (New York: Oxford University Press, 1960); Trevor Colbourn, ed., *Fame and the Founding Fathers: Essays of Douglass Adair* (New York: W.W. Norton, 1974).

[14]The definitive treatment of the law and history of the Japanese internment is Peter Irons, *Justice at War* (New York: Oxford University Press, 1985).

[15]The literature is enormous. See, e.g., Laurence H. Tribe, *American Constitutional Law*, 2d ed. (Mineola, N.Y.: Foundation Press, 1988); Michael J. Perry, *The Constitution, the Courts, and Human Rights* (New Haven: Yale University Press, 1982); Archibald Cox, *Freedom of Expression* (Cambridge, Mass.: Harvard University Press, 1981); Archibald Cox, *The Role of the Supreme Court in American Government* (New York: Oxford University Press, 1976). For recent attacks on these approaches to constitutional law, see, e.g., Robert H. Bork, *The Tempting of America* (New York: Free Press/Macmillan, 1990); Christopher Wolfe, *The Rise of Modern Judicial Review* (New York: Basic Books, 1986); and Raoul Berger, *Government by Judiciary: The Transformation of the Fourteenth Amendment* (Cambridge, Mass.: Harvard University Press, 1978).

[16]For a challenging reinterpretation of the original context, framing and adoption, and early judicial history of the Fourteenth Amendment, see William E. Nelson, *The Fourteenth Amendment: From Political Principle to Judicial Doctrine* (Cambridge, Mass.: Harvard University Press, 1988); for an expert and reliable survey of the massive historical, legal, and jurisprudential literature on the amendment, see id., 1–12 and sources cited.

[17]See the essays collected in David Thelen, ed., *The Constitution and American Life* (Ithaca, N.Y.: Cornell University Press, 1988), 135–374. This valuable and illuminating collection was originally published as a special issue of the *Journal of American History* commemorating the bicentennial of the Constitution, *Journal of American History* 74, no. 3 (1987).

[18]See generally, Donald S. Lutz, *The Origins of American Constitutionalism* (Baton Rouge, La.: Louisiana State University Press, 1988); Richard B. Bernstein with Kym S. Rice, *Are We to Be a Nation? The Making of the Constitution* (Cambridge, Mass.: Harvard University Press, 1987); Forrest McDonald, *Novus Ordo Seclorum* (Lawrence, Kans.: University Press of Kansas, 1985); Donald S. Lutz, *Popular Consent and Popular Control: Whig Political Theory in the First State Constitutions* (Baton Rouge, La.: Louisiana State University Press, 1980); and Willi Paul Adams, *The First American Constitutions* (Chapel Hill, N.C.: University of North Carolina Press, 1980). Henry Steele Commager, *The Empire of Reason: How Europe Conceived and America Realized the Enlightenment* (New York: Anchor Press/Doubleday, 1977), is particularly good on the exchange of ideas and controversy over politics and constitution making between the Old and New Worlds.

[19]For further discussion of the points raised in this section, see Lutz, *Origins of American Constitutionalism*; Robert A. Rutland, *The Birth of the Bill of Rights 1776–1791* (1955; rev. ed., Boston: Northeastern University Press, 1983), and Bernard Schwartz, *The Great Rights of Mankind* (New York: Oxford University Press, 1977).

[20]Leading works on the problem of federalism in the Revolutionary and Confederation periods include: Jack N. Rakove, *The Beginnings of National Politics: An Interpretive History of the Continental Congress* (New York: Knopf, 1979); Peter S. Onuf, *The Origins of the Federal Republic* (Philadelphia: University of Pennsylvania Press, 1983); and Jack P. Greene, *Peripheries and Center* (Athens, Ga.: University of Georgia Press, 1986). See also Richard B. Morris, "The Forging of the Union Reconsidered: A Historical Refutation of State Sovereignty over Seabeds," *Columbia Law Review* 74 (1974): 1054–93; [Eric M. Freedman] "Note: The United States and the Articles of Confederation: Drifting toward Anarchy or Inching toward Commonwealth?" *Yale Law Journal* 88 (1978): 142–66.

[21]One indication of this is the growth of interest in state constitutions in the scholarly legal periodicals. A superb recent example is "Symposium: The Emergence of State Constitutional Law," *Texas Law Review* 63 (1985): 959–1318. An article often cited as the root of this movement is William J. Brennan, Jr., "State Constitutions and the Protection of Individual Rights," *Harvard Law Review* 90 (1977): 489.

[22]See the discussion in Paul Bator, David Shapiro, Paul Mishkin, and Herbert Wechsler, ed., *Hart and Wechsler's "The Federal Courts and the Federal System"*, 2nd ed. (Mineola, N.Y.: Foundation Press, 1973), 962–979; see also, Tribe, *American Constitutional Law*, 155–156, 162–173, and sources cited.

[23]381 U.S. 479 (1965).

[24]Lutz, *Origins of American Constitutionalism, passim*.

Contexts of
The Bill of Rights

The U.S. Bill of Rights in Historical Perspective

DONALD S. LUTZ

The University of Houston

The English and American Background

Americans are justifiably proud of their national Bill of Rights. Along with the Declaration of Independence and the Constitution itself, the Bill of Rights has been so widely admired and emulated that its impact has been world-wide and of major historical importance. Indeed, in an age sensitive to the ratio of imports to exports, the idea of human rights, the nature and basis of those rights, and the practice of placing rights in a constitution or document of political foundation are worth noting as among the most important and successful of American exports. If, as is likely, these documents and ideas are what Americans will be most praised for in future generations, it would seem reasonable that Americans today should have a working understanding of them. The bicentennial celebration has as its aim the wide dissemination among the American public of just such a working knowledge, and the time has come to become more familiar with the Bill of Rights.

As with the Declaration of Independence and the Constitution, the first thing to get clear about the Bill of Rights is that it was neither the sudden, original, spontaneous product of a few minds, nor an updated American version of the Magna Carta. The Bill of Rights had a long historical pedigree, but that pedigree lay substantially more in documents written by those on American shores than in England.

One simple way of demonstrating the relative influence of Magna Carta on the Bill of Rights is a simple count of overlapping provisions. The Bill of Rights has twenty-eight separate rights listed in its ten amendments. Of these twenty-eight rights, only four are also found in Magna Carta. Looking at it from the other direction, only four of the sixty-three provisions in Magna Carta ended up in the Bill of Rights. The overlap is not impressive. As it turns out, neither the function nor the content of the two documents were similar, and thus we must look elsewhere for most of the Bill of Right's pedigree.

We need not look far. Americans who argued most vigorously for adding a bill of rights to the Constitution were the same people who emphasized the importance of state governments and their respective constitutions, and it is in these state constitutions that we find the bills of rights that form the immediate background to the national Bill of Rights. Almost every one of its twenty-eight rights was found in two or three state constitutions, and most of them in five or six of the state documents.[1] Furthermore, the state bills of rights usually contained a more extensive listing than did the national version. For example, Maryland's 1776 document listed more than fifty rights in forty-two sections, Massachusetts' document listed at least fifty-eight rights in thirty sections, and New Hampshire listed even more in the thirty-eight sections to its 1784 document.[2] Virginia (1776) and Pennsylvania (1776) each listed thirty rights in sixteen sections, and came closest to duplicating the content of the national Bill of Rights.[3]

Where did these state bills of rights come from? They came from bills of rights written by American colonists. Because of English preoccupation with internal political disorder from 1640 to 1688, and then with French competition from 1700 to 1760, the colonists were left with a surprisingly high level of political independence. In addition to writing what amounted to functional constitutions between 1620 and 1775, the colonists also wrote many bills of rights, and these colonial documents stood as background to the state bills of rights.[4] Examples are the New York Charter of Liberties and Privileges (1683), the Laws and Liberties of New Hampshire (1682), William Penn's Charter of Liberties (1682), the General Laws and Liberties of Connecticut (1672), the Maryland Toleration Act (1649), Laws and Liberties of Massachusetts (1647), and the Massachusetts Body of Liberties (1641).[5] This last document, adopted a century-and-a-half before the American national Bill of Rights, contained all but three of the twenty-eight rights found in the national document.

These colonial bills of rights were not compilations of English common law any more than was the national Bill of Rights. When James Madison proposed the Bill of Rights in 1789 he said that there were too many differences with common law to warrant comparison:

> [The] truth is, they [the British] have gone no farther than to raise a barrier against the power of the Crown; the power of the

Legislature is left altogether too indefinite. Although I know whenever the great rights, the trial by jury, freedom of the press, or liberty of conscience, come in question [in Parliament] the invasion
of them is resisted by able advocates, yet their Magna Charta does
not contain any one provision for the security of those rights, respecting which the people of America are most alarmed . . . those
choicest privileges of the people are unguarded in the British Constitution. But although . . . it may not be thought necessary to provide limits for the legislative power in that country, yet a different
opinion prevails in the United States.[6]

The Massachusetts Body of Liberties (1641), which contains all but
three of the Bill of Rights' twenty-eight rights, was also written almost
a half century before the English Bill of Rights (1689), which has no
more overlap with the American Bill of Rights than does Magna Carta.
Furthermore, as Madison says, no English document before the American Bill of Rights limits the legislature as well as the executive. English
documents limit the actions only of the Crown, whereas the American
Bill of Rights says, "Congress shall make no law . . ."

Where, then, do the rights in the 1641 Massachusetts Body of Liberties and later colonial documents come from? It is interesting that
these colonial documents frequently cite the Bible to justify their various
provisions. However, there is no more a listing of rights in the Bible
than there is in the writings of Locke, Hume, or Montesquieu. Basically, American notions of rights developed from their own political experience as colonists, an experience significantly affected by the peculiar
and historically important conditions in which they found themselves.[7]

First of all, these were a religious people. In attempting to lead ex-
emplary lives they were acutely sensitive to human relationships being
based upon God's laws as expressed in the Bible, and there is in the
Bible a strong sense of fairness and a respect for all individuals that
easily leads to community rules that look like what we now call rights.
Furthermore, the religion these people professed emphasized certain
things supportive of a rights orientation.

All humans were viewed as being made in the image and likeness
of God, and thus a certain equality in value should be accorded every
person. Those in government were thus not of a different order from
those they governed, and did not have inherent prerogatives or rights
different from others. A fundamental equality lay in every person's ability to say yes or no to God's grace on his or her own. From this came
the ability to give or withhold consent for human laws, and in turn the

notion that government should rest upon the consent of those governed was a straightforward deduction.

These tendencies were reinforced by the belief in the ability of each individual to read the Bible and have an independent relationship with God. Not only was there no justification for a priestly caste—each person had to be viewed as having an independent conscience. Government could not interfere in this fundamental independence. Also, since God's law was accessible to every person's understanding, so should the human law which was supposed to be in conformity with God's law. There should be no need for a priestly caste, called lawyers, to interpret human law. The process for making and enforcing human laws was thus seen as susceptible to codification, a codification that would treat everyone the same and be understandable to all. These codifications were the first American bills of rights.

In addition to religion, the desperate situation of colonists isolated in pockets scattered along a thousand-mile coastline put a high premium upon cooperation if all were to survive. The earliest colony, in Virginia, initially tried a military style of organization, but this soon gave way to a system of eliciting cooperation by treating people well. Thus, early bills of rights, to the extent they were honored, were an effective and efficient means for producing order, stability, cooperative behavior, and economic progress.

Finally, the status of American colonies as economic enterprises, especially as seen from England, tended to emphasize economic output rather than political control as the primary consideration. That a loose political control produced the most economic output only enhanced the sense colonists had of running their own lives. A confluence of circumstances led Americans to require, develop, and expect a set of rights not found in England, and this set of rights was characterized by a breadth, detail, equality, fairness, and effectiveness in limiting all branches of government that distinguished it from English common law.

As one telling example we might consider the case of William Penn. Because of his Quaker religion he suffered through a trial in England which would be shocking to us today, even though it was in conformity with English common law. When he came to America and founded the colony of Pennsylvania, Penn not only granted religious freedom, something lacking in England, he also handed down a comprehensive bill of rights that prohibited the kinds of experiences he had encountered in English courts. It is noteworthy that he succeeded in largely duplicating the codes of rights developed earlier and elsewhere in the colonies, probably because he consulted the codes of Massachusetts, Connecticut, Maryland, and Virginia when composing his own. English common law did form part of the background to our bills of rights, but in America the common law breathed a powerful air of equality and independence that transformed it into a profoundly different American version.

Contrasting English and American Notions of Liberty

The American view of rights was distinguished from that in Britain by two important conceptual differences. One fundamental difference lay in the English notion of liberty as opposed to the American notion developed during the colonial era. In England the concept of liberty had two quite contradictory meanings. One meaning had to do with the general condition of men based upon natural law, or a condition of all Englishmen based upon their common legal and constitutional past. The second meaning had to do with the medieval idea of a hierarchy of liberties which varied according to an individual's or a group's station and purpose in life. Parliament had certain liberties, as did the monarch. The aristocracy had certain liberties, commoners had others. For example, the property rights of aristocratic women were much broader than women not of the aristocracy. Also, certain localities often had special liberties granted by charter. A given town might contain in its charter liberties not found elsewhere, or a shire or locality might retain special liberties as a result of a connection by marriage to the Crown at some time past. A freeman could, by moving to a new town or locality, alter his liberties.

In this sense, liberty was an exemption from normal obligations or punishments. Frequently, the distribution of liberties was related to the distribution of property—a holdover from the feudal system of fiefs. In a broader sense, this notion viewed liberty as submission to duly constituted authority as opposed to submission to force. It was not, however, submission to government erected by consent. Indeed, under this notion a man was not considered as being deprived of liberty because he was denied self-government. Magna Carta assumed this second notion of liberty, as did much of English common law.

With no aristocracy in America, essentially cut off from the remnants of feudal relationships in England, populated by a people largely holding to dissenting Protestant theology with the implications noted above, and faced with problems of survival that required cooperation rather than contention over relative rights, the American colonies failed to include this second British notion of liberty in their political development, at least to any significant degree. The governing boards back in

England, many of the British-trained lawyers in America, and certainly the Crown-appointed governors of the colonies still had a strong sense of liberty of the second type, but there was no room or prudential basis for it in America. American bills of rights, then, did not include this second notion of liberty, but worked from the first. The Massachusetts Body of Liberties did not look like Magna Carta, and the national Bill of Rights did not look like the English Bill of Rights (1689). The absence of this conflicting view of liberty was a major reason for the differences.

There was another basic source of differences, and this, too, stemmed from the religious background and tenuous situation of most colonists. When we look at the earliest colonial documents of political foundation, like the Mayflower Compact (1620), the Pilgrim Code of Law (1636), and Fundamental Orders of Connecticut (1639), we find that among other things they usually involve the self-creation of a people—in the double sense of forming a new people, and then of laying out the common values, interests, and goals which bind them as a people.[8] These self-defining or self-creating people were in the habit of providing in later documents updated versions of their fundamental, shared values, and it is such lists of shared values that evolved into what we now call bills of rights.

It made sense for a religious people to cite the Bible in a bill of rights. Since the Bible was central to what they shared, the values they held could be justified by identifying where in the Bible they were enunciated or implied. As the population became more diverse and less religious, the biblical references might disappear, but not the tendency for bills of rights to be full of more than legalistic rights, and to use admonitory language rather than legally binding terminology. Consider for example the following typical excerpts from state bills of rights:

XV. That the freedom of the press is one of the great bulwarks of liberty, and therefore ought never to be restrained. [North Carolina, 1776][9]

VI. That the legislative, executive, and judicial powers of government, ought to be forever separate and distinct from each other. [Maryland, 1776][10]

IX. All elections ought to be free; and all the inhabitants of this commonwealth, having such qualifications as they shall establish by their frame of government, have an equal right to elect officers, and to be elected, for public employments. [Massachusetts, 1780][11]

XIV. That a frequent recurrence to fundamental principles, and a firm adherence to justice, moderation, temperance, industry, and frugality are absolutely necessary to preserve the blessings of liberty and keep government free . . . [Pennsylvania, 1776][12]

These may strike some people as peculiar statements for a bill of rights, yet they are all from state bills of rights, and are typical of the language rather than exceptional. One can see clearly from the use of "ought" and "should" instead of "shall" and "will" that the language is admonitory rather than capable of being legally enforced. One can also easily see how these bills of rights are statements of shared values and fundamental principles rather than a simple listing of prohibitions on governmental action. We are here a long way from common law.

Contending Views of Rights in 1789

In 1789, on the eve of the writing of America's Bill of Rights, there were the following contending positions in the Anglo-Saxon world on the nature of rights: One was associated with the common–law view of liberty derived from medieval society and embodied in Magna Carta. In this view the Crown was limited by the rights associated with the aristocracy in the feudal hierarchy, and was attached to the distribution of property. Even though this was the stronger of two strains in common law, it was not part of the American notion of rights.

A second position on rights was associated with the other common-law view of liberty—that all Englishmen possessed from their common legal and constitutional past a set of rights that protected them from an arbitrary Crown, especially in the operation of the court system. This position had been read into Magna Carta even though it was not there, most notably by Sir Edward Coke. In Coke's view, the common law protected all Englishmen against royal prerogative. Since this view was used primarily by Parliament in its struggle with the Crown, rights were not seen as limiting Parliament. Since Americans lacked an aristocracy upon which to rest the first version of common law, the second version was dominant in the colonies. However, this view gave them no basis for resisting Parliament in its attempts to tax the colonies, which left them either the older version of common law, which the Glorious Revolution in England had rendered anachronistic, or alternatively that Americans had to identify a different grounding for rights from that found in the common law.

Fortunately, the colonists had available a view of rights that they had been more or less using for one hundred fifty years, and that was undergirded by both theology and rationalist philosophy. In this third position, all human law had to be judged in terms of its conformity with God's will, which served as a higher law. By implication all branches of government, including the legislature, were limited by this higher law. Since there was no group of men with a special ability to determine God's will or the meaning of the Bible, all men had an equal role in determining whether or not a given human law was in conformity with God's will. A straightforward deduction led to the view that all branches of government were beholden to popular consent; rights were thus defined as the set of guarantees that protected the free and effective operation of popular consent.

Bills of rights, according to this view, were lists of common commitments that both protected the operation of popular consent, and codified what popular consent had already identified as commonly held commitments. The prominence of this view of rights is the only way we can explain the presence of many provisions in bills of rights similar to the following:

> IV. That all power being originally inherent in, and consequently derived from the people: therefore all officers of government, whether legislative or executive, are their trustees and servants, and at all times accountable to them. [Pennsylvania, 1776][13]

Also, preambles to state constitutions frequently had statements similar to the following from the 1780 Massachusetts document.

> The body politic is formed by a voluntary association of individuals; it is a social compact, by which the whole people covenants with each citizen, and each citizen with the whole people, that all shall be governed by certain laws for the common good.[14]

At first blush these last two quotations might appear to be taken from John Locke, but such language was used in America before Locke's *Second Treatise* was published, indeed before Locke was born. The communitarian, popular-consent approach to rights was initially derived from dissenting Protestant theology as it was applied to the design of political institutions in the circumstances of seventeenth- and eighteenth-century North America. This view emphasized the needs of the community rather than the rights of individuals, but it did see all branches of government as limited in their operation by universally shared, unchanging human rights.

The similarity in language to that used by John Locke, Algernon Sidney, and other English political theorists is a measure of the extent to which religion and rationalism reached similar political conclusions in late eighteenth-century America. The terms and concepts of Sidney, Locke, Bolingbroke, Milton, and a host of others were efficiently blended, or often placed side by side, with those of dissenting Protestantism. Most of the examples taken from state bills of rights thus far exemplify either the Protestant covenantal view, or a complete blending of that view with Lockean rationalism. Interspersed with these were other provisions which are lifted more directly from Sidney and Locke. The juxtapositioning and blending of these two sources can be emphasized by examining the opening articles in the bills of rights of the two most prominent state constitutions.

> I. That all men are born equally free and independent, and have certain natural, inherent and inalienable rights, amongst which are the enjoying and defending life and liberty, acquiring, possessing, and protecting property, and pursuing and obtaining happiness and safety.
>
> II. That all men have a natural and unalienable right to worship Almighty God according to the dictates of their own consciences and understanding . . . [Pennsylvania, 1776][15]
>
> Article I. All men are born free and equal, and have certain natural, essential, and unalienable rights; among which may be reckoned the right of enjoying and defending their lives and liberties; that of acquiring, possessing, and protecting property; in fine, that of seeking and obtaining their safety and happiness.
>
> II. It is the right as well as the duty of all men in society, publicly, and at stated seasons, to worship the Supreme Being . . . And no subject shall be hurt, molested, or restrained, in his person, liberty, or estate, for worshipping God in the manner and season most agreeable to the dictates of his own conscience . . . [Massachusetts, 1780][16]

The rationalist version of this third position on rights may be termed Lockean, although the language just cited was probably taken from Algernon Sidney's *Discourses on Government*. The Lockean approach emphasized the rights of the individual rather than the rights of the community, although the difference between the Lockean and covenantal versions was in fact a matter of emphasis, not fundamental difference in this regard. Locke and Sidney also saw all branches of government as limited by rights, a position that was roundly ignored in England during the eighteenth century. What neither the religious nor the rationalist approaches to this position envisioned was having rights legally enforced by the courts rather than by elections, constitutional revision, or armed rebellion. This important step in the development of American bills of rights was still in the future, and to a certain extent would rest upon an accident of history.

Drafting the U. S. Bill of Rights

The American view of rights, derived in part from English common law, undergirded by dissenting Protestant theology, and reinforced by rationalist political philosophy, was essentially developed in the local political arena, and codified at the colony-wide level. Independence in 1776 did not alter the situation in this regard. The articulation, codification, and protection of rights proceeded at the state and local levels. It should not surprise us, then, to learn that it was state and local leaders, not national political leaders, who insisted upon a national bill of rights.

The United States Constitution, as originally written, contained a few rights scattered through the document, but did not have a fully articulated bill of rights. The Federalists, including Madison and Hamilton, felt that a bill of rights at the national level was unnecessary, and perhaps dangerous.[17] In their view, a national bill of rights was unnecessary for two reasons. First, there were extensive bills of rights already in existence at the state level. Second, the political process defined by the national constitution was viewed as so fair, balanced, and limited that it could not impinge upon rights; if it did, the states could always use their own bills of rights to protect their respective citizens. Again, they believed that a national bill of rights was potentially dangerous— also for two reasons. First, any listing was bound to leave out rights that would in the future be considered important, but implicitly would not be protected because they were not listed. Second, since bills of rights were statements of commonly-held values and commitments, and there were differences in these values and commitments from state to state, a national bill of rights would either have to contain the least common denominator, and thus leave out things considered important by many people, or else would have to ignore local and state diversity, thus imposing nationwide standards and values that were, in fact, not held nationwide. In either case, national bill of rights would be dangerous to rights and liberty in the long run.

These arguments did not convince the opponents to the proposed Constitution, and opposition centered most vociferously upon the lack of a bill of rights. James Madison promised at a critical point in the national debate that if the Constitution were ratified he personally would see that a bill of rights was added. True to his word, but not to his feelings, Madison did initiate and carry through congressional approval for the Bill of Rights, but it was perhaps the most lukewarm introduction in political history. The *Annals of Congress*, the early version of the Congressional Record, reports Madison as, in effect, saying again that a national bill of rights is unnecessary and dangerous, but since he had promised one, here it was. Debate was brief and desultory. It was passed in order to move on to what was viewed as more important matters, such as congressional salaries and the drafting of the first federal revenue bills. Ironically, it was in the state ratification process that controversy arose concerning the Bill of Rights originally proposed by the states.

Originally, when the Constitution was being ratified by the states, various state conventions proposed dozens of rights for inclusion in the document, the list of rights tending to vary from state to state. James Madison, mindful of his own words on the dangers of looking to the least common denominator, nevertheless produced a list of only nine rights. These nine, along with the suggestions from the states, were given to a select committee in the House of Representatives, with one member from each state on the committee. The House produced a list with seventeen articles, which the Senate reduced to twelve. A conference committee worked out the differences, and on October 2, 1789, a proposed bill of rights was sent to the states for ratification.

It was assumed at the beginning of congressional action that the bill of rights would either be placed as a list at the beginning of the Constitution, as was the case with state bills of rights, or scattered through the body of the Constitution proper as Madison proposed. However, the Connecticut delegation insisted that the rights be appended at the end of the document as a set of explicit amendments to reflect their true status. Placing them at the beginning or in the body of a document ratified only with great difficulty implied the need to go through the entire ratification process again, whereas treating them as amendments did not require having to change any wording in the Constitution *per se*.

Roger Sherman's proposal to place the rights at the end, rather than scattering them throughout the document as Madison wanted, turned out to be fateful, since listing the rights together at the end gave them a prominence and combined status over time that would otherwise have been lost. Placing the Bill of Rights at the end, rather than at the beginning as the states preferred, had an unnoted yet historically important effect on the language of the proposed rights.

The lists of rights proposed by the various states almost all used the admonitory "ought" and "should" rather than the legally enforceable "shall" and "will" with which we are now familiar. Madison, on the other hand, intended placing the rights in the body of the Constitution, so he used the constitutionally proper "shall" and "will " When the House select committee agreed to go along with Sherman's proposal and place the Bill of Rights at the end as amendments, the committee found it necessary to rework the proposed amendments in legally enforceable language, because one cannot effectively amend a "shall"— the language of the Constitution's grants of power to the general government—with an "ought."

Without this change in language occasioned by placement at the end rather than the beginning of the Constitution, it is difficult to see how American rights could have developed as they did, or how the Supreme Court could have emerged as the definer and protector of legal rights. The change in wording was entirely due to the placement of the Bill of Rights, not to anything in American rights theory as of 1789. Later developments in American theories of rights would be heavily affected and conditioned by what amounts to an historical accident.

It took two-and-a-half years for the necessary three-fourths of the states to ratify ten of the twelve proposed amendments to the Constitution, which together are now known as the Bill of Rights. (Massachusetts, Connecticut, and Georgia did not ratify these Amendments until the sesquicentennial celebration of the Constitution in 1939; these final ratifications are best understood as exercises in commemoration and as 1939's embarrassed "corrections" of the deeds of the states' legislatures in 1789.) That the process took so long, that it failed to elicit ratification by all of the states, and that two proposed amendments (one dealing with reapportionment of the House of Representatives, and the other dealing with congressional pay raises) failed to receive the necessary three-fourths support are all indicative of some controversy in state legislatures. Much of the controversy stemmed, as Madison had predicted, from different expectations from state to state. Some wanted more or different rights, some wanted fewer. Perhaps we should be surprised that anything coherent passed at all.

The Bill of Rights Since 1792

Passage of the national Bill of Rights did not really change anything at first. The states were still considered the primary protectors of individual rights. It was not until the World War I era, well over a century later, that the national Bill of Rights was used to protect individual rights.

One major effect of the Bill of Rights during the nineteenth century was to lead drafters of state constitutions to recast the language of their bills of rights into the legally binding form using "shall" and "will." With their longer lists of rights, and strengthened language, most states were ahead of the national government in rights development, although nowhere did the breadth and depth of protection approach what it is now.

Two broad developments have occurred during the twentieth century. The first has been the strengthening of national rights, as interpreted by the Supreme Court, to an unprecedented degree. We have come to take these rights so much for granted that we forget how recently they have been expanded. The second development has been the application of the national Bill of Rights against the states using the due process clause of the Fourteenth Amendment. Both developments were made possible in large part by the legally enforceable language inserted in the national Bill of Rights in 1789.

Scholarship and publicity surrounding the second broad development left the impression that rights at the state level were not well protected, and that the national government had forged ahead in rights protection. This was not completely true. The problem was not lagging rights in the states, but diversity in rights among the states. Many or most states already protected rights at a level required by the Supreme Court, but ten to fifteen states clearly lagged behind. The net effect of federal action has been to establish what is now considered a "floor" in American rights. That minimum guarantee is still exceeded by many states.

Active expansion of rights by the Supreme Court, as much as it was needed, had the effect of temporarily eclipsing the development of rights under state constitutions and laws. That may be changing. In recent years there has been a trend toward "rediscovering" an independent constitutional law at the state level with respect to rights, especially in those states where state bills of rights are stronger and broader in definition than the national Bill of Rights. If this flowering at the state level bears fruit, we may be entering a new era with respect to the Bill of Rights—one which produces a healthy competition in rights protection instead of either state or national dominance, as was the case for most of our history.

Taking an historical perspective toward rights in America has a number of implications for how we think about bills of rights, as well as for how we study and teach them. For one thing, the role of the states needs to be more actively considered, as well as the interaction between state and national bills of rights. Changes in the structure, content, and wording of bills of rights reflect changes in how we conceptualize rights, and these theoretical changes need to be more frankly and explicitly faced.

We now rely primarily upon the courts to protect rights, and this is not a bad thing in itself, but it does have the tendency to focus attention upon litigation, and thus upon rights piecemeal, rather than upon bills of rights and the general principles they embody. Certainly we must think deeply about the preferability of using constitutional amendments instead of court interpretation to expand and codify rights. In fact, this is what still tends to happen at the state level, which is one reason why state constitutions so quickly become lengthy and laden with amendments. Many academics view lengthy constitutions as something to be avoided. Another perspective is that long constitutions indicate that people are still taking the constitution seriously enough to amend it through a political process that engages popular consent. Long constitutions may thus be an indication of political health.

There still is something to be said for viewing rights as expressions of fundamental commitments by a people, as the grounding for democratic institutions, and thus an essential part of the total political process in a constitutional order. In short, we may be in need of more frequent public debate as we push our frontiers of freedom forward. These are, after all, our rights, and not simply the conclusions of a priestly caste called judges. Judges may be useful guides to our good conscience as a people, but in the end popular consent, and thus popular support, may be a more secure basis for rights.

NOTES:

[1]The state constitutions can be found in Francis N. Thorpe, ed. *The Federal and State Constitutions* (Washington, D.C.: Government Printing Office, 1907), 7 vols.

[2]Thorpe, 1686-1691 (Maryland), 1889-1893 (Massachusetts), and 2453-2457 (New Hampshire).

[3]Thorpe, 3812-3814 (Virginia), and 3082-3084 (Pennsylvania).

[4]These documents are widely scattered, but many can be found in Donald S. Lutz, *Documents of Political Foundation Written By Colonial Americans* (Philadelphia: ISHI Press, 1986).

[5]See Lutz, *Documents of Political Foundation*, 435-442, 403-410, 359-362, 309-314, 255-302, and 189-194.

⁶*Annals of Congress*, Vol. I, 436.
⁷The argument being made here is fully developed in Donald S. Lutz, *The Origins of American Constitutionalism* (Baton Rouge: Louisiana State University Press, 1988).
⁸These documents can be found in Lutz, *Documents of Political Foundation*, 65–66, 105–112, and 135–142.
⁹Thorpe, 2788.
¹⁰Thorpe, 1687.
¹¹Thorpe, 1891.
¹²Thorpe, 3083.
¹³Thorpe, 3082.
¹⁴Thorpe, 1889.
¹⁵Thorpe, 3082.
¹⁶Thorpe, 1889.
¹⁷See e.g. *The Federalist No. 84* (Hamilton), in Alexander Hamilton, John Jay, and James Madison, *The Federalist* (New York: Modern Library, 1937), 555–561.

BIBLIOGRAPHY

The following are suggested readings for those wishing to pursue the general topic of rights in America, or the Bill of Rights in particular.

Zechariah Chafee, Jr., ed., *Documents on Fundamental Human Rights: The Anglo-American Tradition* (New York, 1963).

Donald S. Lutz, *The Origins of American Constitutionalism* (Baton Rouge, Louisiana, 1988).

Gilman Ostrander, *The Rights of Man in America, 1606–1861* (Columbia, Missouri, 1960).

Bernard Schwartz, ed., *The Bill of Rights: A Documentary History* (New York, 1971).

Bernard Schwartz, *The Great Rights of Mankind: A History of the Bill of Rights* (New York, 1977).

The Making of
the Bill of Rights:
1787–1792

JOHN P. KAMINSKI
University of Wisconsin–Madison

The Role of Government in Protecting Rights

From 1763 until 1788, Americans debated the nature of government and how best to preserve liberty. Never before or since have the American people so seriously and persistently carried on a public debate. Midway through this debate, most Americans had come to realize that their liberties were insecure within the British Empire, and therefore believed that independence must be obtained.

In declaring their independence, Americans expressed the importance of government in protecting the rights of individuals. In June 1776 the Virginia revolutionary convention adopted a new state constitution and preceded it with a declaration of rights that maintained

> That all Men are by Nature equally free and independent, and have certain inherent Rights, of which, when they enter into a State of Society, they cannot by any Compact, deprive or divest their Posterity; namely, the Enjoyment of Life and Liberty, with the Means of acquiring and possessing Property, and pursuing and obtaining Happiness and Safety.

A month later, the delegates to the Second Continental Congress meeting in Philadelphia pronounced the same self-evident truths "That all men are created equal, that they are endowed by their Creator with certain unalienable Rights, that among these are Life, Liberty and the pursuit of Happiness.''

Once they declared their independence, Americans adopted state constitutions that created governments that would not endanger their liberties—governments with real power lodged in state assemblies and little authority placed in the upper houses of the legislatures and the new state governors. On the federal level, the Articles of Confederation created a Congress with no power over individuals. States—not people—were represented in Congress, and Congress had only limited power over the states. Article II set the ground rules for the new federal–state relationship:

> Each state retains its sovereignty, freedom and independence, and every Power, Jurisdiction and right, which is not by this confederation expressly delegated to the United States, in Congress assembled.

A decade after independence was declared, many Americans believed that the Articles of Confederation had failed. Something had to be done to limit the state legislatures and invigorate Congress. Without a strengthened general government, the union of the thirteen states would disintegrate into internecine warfare or anarchy, which would eventually lead to despotism. Republicanism and the principles of the Revolution, many believed, were hanging by a thread.

The delegates to the Constitutional Convention did not assemble in the spring of 1787 to protect the rights of Americans from the powers of their general government. Most delegates had two other purposes in mind: they wanted to strengthen the powers of their general government by amending the Articles of Confederation or by creating an entirely new constitution with a federal government armed with coercive power over the states and their citizens. Equally important, the delegates wanted to limit the powers of the state governments that were dominated by popularly elected assemblies which enacted legislation demanded by the majority of voters but that all-too-often violated the rights of the minority. Focused on these goals, it is not surprising that the Constitutional Convention failed to propose a federal bill of rights. Only through strengthening the powers of responsible government and restricting the licentiousness of the people and state assemblies would the principles of the Revolution be preserved.[1]

The Constitutional Convention

Throughout the Constitutional Convention, various individual rights were incorporated into the new draft constitution. Not until late in the Convention, however, was a full-scale bill of rights considered. On September 12, George Mason, author of the Virginia Declaration of Rights, stated that he "wished the plan had been prefaced with a Bill of Rights." Such a written protection, Mason asserted, would "give great quiet to the people; and with the aid of the State declarations, a bill might be prepared in a few hours." Elbridge Gerry of Massachusetts agreed and proposed that a committee be appointed to draft a bill of rights. Roger Sherman of Connecticut, speaking for most of the delegates, objected to such a committee. He favored protecting the rights of the people where necessary, but believed that a federal bill of rights was superfluous, because the state bills of rights were not repealed and were thus sufficient. Still believing that their prime purpose was to strengthen the general government—not to restrict it—the delegates defeated the motion for a committee to draft a bill of rights by a vote of ten states to none.[2]

The decision to omit a federal bill of rights almost proved fatal to the new Constitution. Opponents of the Constitution, called Antifederalists, used the omission of a bill of rights incessantly as proof that a conspiracy was afoot to subvert the principles of the Revolution and deprive Americans of their dear-bought rights. Backed into a corner, supporters of the Constitution, called Federalists, were forced to devise arguments to explain the omission—arguments that convinced few Antifederalists that the Constitution did not need a bill of rights. Throughout the year-long debate (1787–1788) over the ratification of the Constitution, the lack of a federal bill of rights remained the single most important issue.

The Debate in the Confederation Congress

When the Constitutional Convention adjourned on September 17, 1787, it sent the Constitution to the Confederation Congress in New York City requesting that the new form of government be forwarded to the states for their ratification. Congress read the Constitution on September 20 and assigned the 26th for its consideration.

Federalists overwhelmingly controlled Congress, but the handful of Antifederalist delegates took the lead against the Constitution. Nathan Dane of Massachusetts asked that the Constitution be sent to the states with the acknowledgment that the delegates to the Constitutional

Convention had violated their instructions as well as the Articles of Confederation. Federalists opposed Dane, arguing that the Constitution should be sent to the states with congressional approbation.

Richard Henry Lee of Virginia proposed that the Constitution be forwarded to the states with an accompanying bill of rights. In introducing his bill of rights, Lee maintained that

> It having been found from Universal experience that the most express declarations and reservations are necessary to protect the just rights and liberty of mankind from the silent, powerful, and ever active conspiracy of those who govern—And it appearing to be the sense of the good people of America by the various Bills or Declarations of rights whereon the governments of the greater number of the States are founded, that such precautions are proper to restrain and regulate the exercise of the great powers necessarily given to Rulers—In conformity with these principles, and from respect for the public sentiment on this subject it is submitted That the new Constitution . . . be bottomed upon a declaration, or Bill of Rights, clearly and precisely stating the principles upon which this Social Compact is founded.[3]

Lee proposed that freedom of religion, freedom of the press, the right to assemble, and the right to petition be protected. In judicial matters, he wanted due process of law guaranteed as well as the right to jury trials of the vicinage (region) in both criminal and civil cases. Excessive bail and fines, cruel and unusual punishments, and unreasonable searches and seizures were to be prohibited. Federal elections should be free and frequent, while standing armies in peacetime were to be prohibited unless approved by a two-thirds majority in both houses of Congress.

After considerable debate, both sides agreed on September 28 to send the Constitution to the states with neither approbation nor disapprobation, and to strike the debate over the Constitution—including Lee's bill of rights from the journals. Federalists, who could have easily outvoted their adversaries, were thereby able to hide from the public the fact that Congress was divided over the Constitution. Federalists wanted the states to act on the Constitution as written by the Constitutional Convention. If Congress amended the new Constitution, James Madison asserted, there would be two plans before the states. "Some will accept one & some another, this will create confusion."[4] Antifederalists, on the other hand, were able to deny the Constitution the endorsement of Congress. They knew that the debate over a federal bill of rights would soon erupt in the press where they would try to convince the public of the necessity of restrictions on federal power.

The Antifederalists' Opening Salvos

Immediately upon the adjournment of the Constitutional Convention, Antifederalists began their campaign against the Constitution's omission of a bill of rights. George Mason gave Elbridge Gerry a copy of his objections to the Constitution which began with a thunderous "There is no Declaration of Rights." Mason met with Philadelphia Antifederalists and let them make copies of his objections. Before long, Mason's objections circulated throughout the country in manuscript form.[5] Between November 21 and 23, the objections were independently printed in three newspapers in Boston, Massachusetts, and in Alexandria and Winchester, Virginia. Within two months, Mason's objections were reprinted nationwide in more than twenty-five newspapers, in several pamphlet anthologies, in the Philadelphia *American Museum*, a nationally circulated magazine, and as broadsides that were enthusiastically distributed by Antifederalists.[6]

Richard Henry Lee sent copies of the amendments he had proposed in Congress to correspondents in Massachusetts, Pennsylvania, and Virginia.[7] In writing to Samuel Adams, the old revolutionary who was now president of the Massachusetts senate, Lee suggested that

> The corrupting power, and its insatiable appetite for increase, hath proved the necessity, and procured the adoption of the strongest and most express declarations of that *Residuum* of natural rights, which is not intended to be given up to Society, and which indeed is not necessary to be given for any good social purpose.[8]

By the end of September 1787, the Antifederal minority of the Pennsylvania assembly publicly asked its constituents whether they were willing to give up freedom of the press and trial by jury and "whether in a plan of government any declaration of rights should be prefixed or inserted."[9] "Centinel," the most prominent Pennsylvania Antifederal essayist, answered the assemblymen's questions by asking his readers to compare the Pennsylvania Declaration of Rights with the new federal Constitution before they surrendered their "great and valuable privileges up forever." "All the blessings of liberty and the dearest privileges of freemen," he asserted, were "now at stake" and depended on their actions.[10]

In New York, "Brutus" led the fight. In reviewing the natural rights philosophy espoused by many Americans and used to justify independence from Great Britain, "Brutus" argued that

> The common good . . . is the end of civil government, and common consent, the foundation on which it is established. To effect this end, it was necessary that a certain portion of natural liberty should be surrendered, in order, that what remained should be preserved: how great a proportion of natural freedom is necessary to be yielded by individuals, when they submit to government, I shall not now enquire. So much, however, must be given up, as will be sufficient to enable those, to whom the administration of the government is committed, to establish laws for the promoting the happiness of the community, and to carry those laws into effect. But it is not necessary, for this purpose, that individuals should relinquish all their natural rights. Some are of such a nature that they cannot be surrendered. Of this kind are the rights of conscience, the right of enjoying and defending life, &c. Others are not necessary to be resigned, in order to attain the end for which government is instituted, these therefore ought not to be given up. To surrender them, would counteract the very end of government, to wit, the common good. From these observations it appears, that in forming a government on its true principles, the foundation should be laid . . . by expressly reserving to the people such of their essential natural rights, as are not necessary to be parted with.[11]

These principles, "Brutus" asserted, were fundamental and were embodied "in all the constitutions of our own states . . . when the pulse of liberty beat high" just a decade earlier. Now, however, "Brutus" was astonished "that this grand security, to the rights of the people, is not to be found" in the proposed Constitution. Federalists were clearly on the defensive; they needed an explanation for their failure to produce a bill of rights.

James Wilson's Explanation

During the first week of October 1787, Pennsylvanians campaigned for their elections to the state assembly. On October 6, James Wilson, Pennsylvania's most prominent lawyer who had a decade earlier signed the Declaration of Independence, gave the first public explanation of the new Constitution by a former delegate to the Constitutional Convention. Wilson, one of the most influential delegates to the Convention, faced the issue squarely. Americans, he asserted, had to understand the basic difference between state constitutions and the Constitution of the United States.

> When the people established the powers of legislation under their separate governments, they invested their representatives with every right and authority which they did not in explicit terms reserve; and therefore upon every question, respecting the jurisdiction of the house of assembly, if the frame of government is silent, the jurisdiction is efficient and complete. But in delegating foederal powers, another criterion was necessarily introduced, and the congressional authority is to be collected, not from tacit implication, but from the positive grant expressed in the instrument of union. Hence it is evident, that in the former case every thing which is not reserved is given, but in the latter the reverse of the proposition prevails, and every thing which is not given, is reserved.

Once Antifederalists realized this important distinction, Wilson felt that they would accept the omission of a federal bill of rights. Furthermore, Wilson argued, a federal bill of rights would be dangerous because it would imply that the federal government had "some degree of power" in every area, even though no specific powers were delegated.[12] James Madison agreed with Wilson, explaining in a letter to Thomas Jefferson that he favored a bill of rights if one could be written without giving the federal government enormous powers by implication.[13]

Federalists throughout America adopted Wilson's theory of reserved powers as the "official" explanation for the lack of a federal bill of rights. Antifederalists attacked it. "Agrippa," printed in the *Massachusetts Gazette* on January 14, 1788, called the reserved power theory "a mere fallacy, invented by the deceptive powers of mr. Wilson." "Cincinnatus," written by Arthur Lee of Virginia who was then serving in New York City as a member of the Confederation's Treasury Board, accused Wilson of sophistry. His quaint conundrum was, in essence, "a distinction without difference." Why should Americans accept Wilson's "play on words," when a real safeguard could easily have been incorporated into the new Constitution just as it had been in the Articles of Confederation? Why, they asked, was this important provision stipulating the federal-state relationship omitted from the new Constitution? Why was this vital relationship left to assumption and interpretation?[14]

Antifederalists found Wilson's argument flawed by the prohibitions on the federal government incorporated in the Constitution itself. Richard Henry Lee told Samuel Adams that every one of the constitutional restrictions on Congress "proves the Rule in Conventional ideas to be, that what was not reserved was given."[15] Thomas Jefferson, serving in Paris as U.S. minister to France, wrote James Madison that Wilson's theory was "a gratis dictum, opposed by strong inferences from the body of the instrument."[16] "Federal Farmer," the most influential Antifederal pamphleteer, asserted that "the 9th and 10th Sections in Art. 1. in the proposed constitution, are no more nor less, than a partial bill of rights." He encouraged his readers to extend this guarantee further "as a part of this fundamental compact between the people of the United States and their federal rulers."[17]

Federalists only occasionally came to Wilson's aid with reasoned arguments. More often than not, they merely praised him and accepted his interpretation. "Remarker," in the Boston *Independent Chronicle* on December 27, maintained that "notwithstanding all that hath been said of it," the theory of reserved powers was "perfectly true." The Convention's omission of a bill of rights "was wisdom itself, because it implies clearly that the people who are at once the *source* and *object* of power, are already in full possession of all the rights and privileges of freemen. Let the people retain them forever."

James Madison, writing in *The Federalist No. 44*, attempted to explain why certain rights were explicitly protected in the Constitution, while most others were not. He admitted that bills of attainder and ex post facto laws were already contrary to the social compact theory, principles of sound legislation, and some of the state bills of rights and constitutions. Nevertheless, Madison argued, "additional fences against these dangers ought not to be omitted. Very properly therefore have the Convention added this constitutional bulwark in favor of personal security and private rights." Madison did not explain why it was proper to safeguard these rights but not others. Despite the reserved powers theory, Federalists realized that the lack of a federal bill of rights presented the major obstacle to the ratification of the Constitution.

The First State Ratifying Conventions

Pennsylvania was the first state to call and hold a ratifying convention. Weeks before the convention assembled on November 20, 1787, it was apparent that two-thirds of the delegates supported the Constitution. Consequently, the outcome of the convention was never in doubt. Because Federalists did not wish to give the impression of "cramming the Constitution down the throats of their opponents,'' they allowed Antifederalists almost a month to debate the Constitution.

Federalists maintained that the Constitution had to be adopted *in toto* or rejected completely. The convention had no authority to propose amendments or ratify conditionally. Federalists called for a complete adoption of the Constitution to revive the economy, restore America's honor, and preserve the Union. The lack of a federal bill of rights, they argued, presented no danger. Quite the contrary—a bill of rights would endanger liberties because all rights could not be enumerated. What would happen to those rights that were omitted? Would they be forfeited? James Wilson again led the Federalist argument:

> A bill of rights annexed to a constitution is an enumeration of the powers reserved. If we attempt an enumeration, everything that is not enumerated is presumed to be given. The consequence is, that an imperfect enumeration would throw all implied power into the scale of the government; and the rights of the people would be rendered incomplete.[18]

Federalist Thomas McKean, chief justice of the Pennsylvania supreme court, argued that bills of rights were first written to protect the liberties of the people from all-powerful feudal kings. A bill of rights had no place in a republic where the people, either directly or indirectly, elected all officeholders. Did the people, asked McKean, need a bill of rights to protect themselves from themselves? No, he answered. If the people were dissatisfied with their government, they possessed the power to alter it; and the new Constitution provided a means of enacting amendments. *The Federalist No. 84*, written by Alexander Hamilton, reiterated this argument. Bills of rights, he declared

> have no application to constitutions professedly founded upon the power of the people, and executed by their immediate representatives and servants. Here, in strictness, the people surrender nothing, and as they retain every thing, they have no need of particular reservations. 'WE THE PEOPLE of the United States, to secure the blessings of liberty to ourselves and our posterity, do *ordain* and *establish* this constitution for the United States of America.' Here is a better recognition of popular rights than volumes of those aphorisms which make the principal figure in several of our state bills of rights, and which would sound much better in a treatise of ethics than in a constitution of government.

Antifederalists were dissatisfied with their opponents' arguments. They pointed to the general welfare clause and the necessary and proper clause to show that Congress possessed unlimited authority under the Constitution. If ever a dispute arose over whether Congress had overstepped its authority, the federal government, armed with the supremacy clause of the Constitution, would make the final decision. How could the states or the people expect fair treatment when their federal rulers possessed all power and were to be the final arbiters in disputed cases?

By the 12th of December, most of the issues in contention had been debated thoroughly. Before taking the final roll call, however, Antifederalist Robert Whitehill submitted petitions from 750 inhabitants of Cumberland County praying that the Constitution not be adopted without a bill of rights. Whitehill then presented a list of fifteen amendments to the Constitution in the form of a bill of rights. The final amendment—a paraphrasing of the second article of the Articles of Confederation—specifically limited Congress to those powers expressly delegated to it in the Constitution. Whitehill moved that the convention adjourn "to some remote day" to give the people time to consider the amendments and to coordinate Pennsylvania's actions with other states. Federalists discarded Whitehill's amendments (refusing even to allow them on the official journals) and voted to ratify the Constitution by a vote of 46 to 23. The minority published its objections, including Whitehill's bill of rights, in newspapers, broadsides, and pamphlets that were circulated throughout the country.

While Pennsylvania's convention debated the Constitution, neighboring Delaware acted quickly. After only three hours of debate, the Delaware convention ratified the Constitution unanimously on December 7. New Jersey and Georgia followed suit on December 18 and January 2 (1788), respectively. Connecticut's convention then ratified by a two-thirds majority on January 9. Minor opposition to the Constitution surfaced in each of these three last states, but delegates operated under the impression that they had to either accept or reject the new form of government in its entirety; therefore amendments were not proposed. The initial phase of the ratification process had been completed with five of the necessary nine states solidly supporting the new Constitution.

A New Strategy:
Massachusetts Ratifies with Proposed Amendments

After Connecticut ratified the Constitution, nationwide attention focused on Massachusetts. As the second-largest state in the Union,

Massachusetts was expected to play a vital role in the ratification struggle. All opinions seemed agreed that rejection by Massachusetts would spell defeat for the new charter. Federalists could not afford to falter.

The Massachusetts ratifying convention met on January 9, 1788. It soon became evident that a sizeable majority of the delegates were Antifederalists. Federalists labored long and hard to change the minds of lukewarm opponents of the Constitution as it stood; but, after three weeks of debate, Federalists realized that they had failed. If a vote were taken, the Constitution would be defeated. This desperate situation called for desperate measures.

Governor John Hancock had been elected president of the Massachusetts convention, but he had been unable to attend the sessions because of a severe attack of the gout. The gout often plagued the governor when he faced difficult political decisions. Many of the governor's friends and enemies alike believed that Hancock was sitting on the sidelines testing the political winds before he made his appearance at the convention.

When Federalists realized that they could not command enough votes to ratify the Constitution, they decided to approach Hancock, their erstwhile political enemy, for assistance. Federalist leaders proposed a series of amendments to the Constitution that they wanted Hancock to present to the convention as his own. The convention would ratify the Constitution unconditionally but would "enjoin it upon their representatives" in the first federal Congress "to exert all their influence" to get the proposed amendments adopted. In return for his assistance, Federalists promised Hancock that they would not challenge his gubernatorial candidacy in the spring. Federalists also suggested that they would back Hancock as the first vice president of the United States. Furthermore, if Virginia refused to ratify the Constitution, George Washington would be ineligible for the presidency. Hancock would be the obvious replacement.

The Federalist bait was tempting. Hancock's gout improved enough to allow him to attend the convention and propose "his" amendments. These amendments convinced a sufficient number of wavering Antifederalists that the Constitution should be adopted and that, with the support of the remaining state conventions, appropriate safeguards would be proposed by Congress and adopted by the state legislatures as provided in Article V of the Constitution.[19]

The immediate response from Federalists nationwide was relief. James Madison wrote George Washington that "The amendments are a blemish, but are in the least Offensive form."[20] To George Nicholas, Madison averred that "the plan of Massts. is unquestionably the Ultimatum of the foederalists.[21] Antifederalists such as Patrick Henry argued that Massachusetts had "put the cart before the horse."[22] After seeing the Massachusetts amendments, Thomas Jefferson changed his mind about the best procedure to follow in ratifying the Constitution.

> My first wish was that 9 states would adopt it in order to ensure what was good in it, & that the others might, by holding off, produce the necessary amendments. but the plan of Massachusetts is far preferable, and will I hope be followed by those who are yet to decide.[23]

As it turned out, Jefferson's wish came true; six of the remaining seven states used the Massachusetts technique of ratifying the Constitution unconditionally while proposing recommendatory amendments. Without this type of ratification, the Constitution never would have been adopted.

Maryland and South Carolina became the seventh and eighth states to ratify the Constitution in April and May 1788, respectively. One more state ratification was needed to adopt the Constitution. As the conventions of Virginia, New Hampshire, and New York began to meet in June, most people presumed that New Hampshire would follow Massachusetts' example, thus providing the ninth ratification. But even if nine states ratified and the Constitution were declared adopted, a viable Union would be unthinkable without New York and Virginia—two states where Antifederalism was strong and demand for a bill of rights was widespread.

Virginia
A Bill of Rights: Now or Later

Most Virginians wanted the Confederation government strengthened, and thus there was a predilection to accept whatever the Constitutional Convention proposed. But after reading the Constitution and listening to the public debate, many Virginians suspected that the delegates to the Constitutional Convention had gone too far. Amendments would be needed to clarify the federal–state relationship and to guarantee the rights of individuals. Most important would be the question of when amendments should be added to the Constitution—before or after the state ratified. On the eve of the elections to the state convention, these apprehensions were eloquently stated by a writer in the *Virginia Independent Chronicle* calling himself "The Impartial Examiner." The "Examiner" asked his fellow Virginians: "can any one think that there is no medium between want of power, and the possession of it in an un-limited degree? Between the imbecility'' of the Articles of Confederation and "the sweeping jurisdiction" of the new Constitution? Couldn't the federal government be given all the requisite power over commerce and foreign affairs but leave the states competent to rule in the every-day concerns of people? Some limitation had to be placed on federal rulers so that personal liberties would be protected. It was this problem that the 170 delegates to the Virginia convention would wrestle with when they met on June 2, 1788.

When the Virginia convention assembled, neither Federalists nor Antifederalists knew for sure which side had a majority. Seemingly, Federalists had elected a few more delegates than their opponents, but no one knew exactly how the fourteen delegates from the District of Kentucky would vote. Only eight states had ratified; therefore, the magnet of an already functioning government would not pull Virginia into the new federal orbit. Despite this uncertainty, Virginians could agree upon one thing. The new government would not survive unless Virginia joined it.

For the next three weeks, Antifederalists, led by Patrick Henry, George Mason, William Grayson, James Monroe, and John Tyler, attempted to demonstrate the dangers inherent in the Constitution; while James Madison, Edmund Pendleton, George Nicholas, Henry Lee, John Marshall, Francis Corbin, and, most importantly, Governor Edmund Randolph countered this Antifederalist phalanx and demonstrated the absolute necessity of the Constitution to preserving the Union and per-petuating the principles of the American Revolution.

Patrick Henry began his onslaught on the Constitution by asking "what right had" the Constitutional Convention "to say *We, the People*, instead of *We, the States*? States," he said, "are the characteristics, and the soul of a confederation. If the States be not the agents of this compact, it must be one great consolidated National Government."[24]

Henry told the convention that the new Constitution proposed a revolution in government.

> Here is a revolution as radical as that which separated us from Great Britain. It is as radical, if in this transition, our rights and privileges are endangered, and the sovereignty of the States be relinquished: And cannot we plainly see, that this is actually the case? The rights of conscience, trial by jury, liberty of the press, all of your immu-nities and franchises, all pretensions to human rights and privileges, are rendered insecure, if not lost, by this change.[25]

Americans, he said, "were wandering on the great ocean of human affairs" with "no landmarks to guide us."[26] He warned his fellow delegates "to be extremely cautious, watchful, [and] jealous of your liberty; for instead of securing your rights, you may lose them forever. If a wrong step be now made, the Republic may be lost forever," for surely the new Constitution would "destroy the State Governments, and swallow the liberties of the people."[27]

Federalists responded that there was "no quarrel between Government and liberty; the former is the shield and protector of the latter. The war is between Government and licentiousness, faction, turbulence, and other violations of the rules of society" established to preserve liberty.[28] "Experience and history" had taught that in forming a government, the powers must be commensurate with the object. Too much power would "subject the people to the depravity of rulers." But because "there can be no liberty without Government," it must be as dangerous to make powers too limited, as too great.[29] That powers once granted could one day be abused was in no way "a sufficient reason against conceding them" in the first place.[30]

Henry, however, saw government as "no more than a choice among evils." If the adoption of the new Constitution was viewed as "a little or a triffling evil," then the convention ought to adopt it. But, he argued, if "its adoption may entail misery on the free people of this country, I then insist, that rejection ought to follow."[31]

James Monroe echoed Henry. "Upon reviewing this Government, I must say, . . . I think it a dangerous Government, and calculated to secure neither the interests, nor the rights of our countrymen." The new Constitution endangered the principles of the Revolution for which Americans had fought so long and hard.[32] Few persons, Monroe stated, would be more willing to bind the American states "together by a stronger or more indissoluble bond, or give the national Government more powers." But Monroe wanted to prevent the new national government "from doing harm, either to States or individuals."[33]

In a pamphlet addressed to his constituents on the eve of the state convention, Monroe outlined his objections to the Constitution. He said that

> We have struggled long to bring about this revolution, we have fought and bled freely to accomplish it, and in other respects braved difficulties almost without a parallel. Why then this precipitation, why this hurry upon a subject so momentous, and equally interesting to us all? Is it to be supposed that unless we immediately

adopt this plan, in its fullest extent, we shall forever loose the opportunity of forming for ourselves a good government? That some wild phrensy or delirium of the brain will seize upon us, and losing all recollection of things past, and abandoning the social ties that bind mankind together, we shall fall into some strange and irretrievable disorder? Or is it not more natural to suppose that perfection in any science, if attainable at all, is to be approached by slow and gradual advances, and that the plan of government now presented for your inspection, though a powerful effort of the human mind, is yet to be improved by a second essay?[34]

The most serious Antifederalist concern in the convention was the lack of a federal bill of rights. Expounding James Wilson's theory to counter this concern, Federalists argued that the Constitution created a federal government of delegated powers. Congress could legislate only when the Constitution authorized it. In all other cases, they pointed out, powers were reserved to the states.

Antifederalists, however, referred to the general welfare clause, the necessary and proper clause, and the supremacy clause of the Constitution. Taken together, these provisions of the proposed Constitution rendered state bills of rights useless in confrontations with the federal government, they argued. George Mason maintained that when the people of Virginia formed their own state constitution, they also adopted a Declaration of Rights. Virginians "would not trust their own citizens, who had a familiarity of interest with themselves."[35] And yet, with the new federal Constitution, Virginians would give up a great part of their rights to a far-off government controlled by a majority of Northerners totally unsympathetic to the South. Mason wanted a clause in the Constitution reserving to the states all powers not delegated to the federal government. Such a clause, he said, existed in the Articles of Confederation, even though the articles provided for a far weaker general government. "Why not then have a similar clause in this Constitution," Mason reasoned. "Unless this were done, many valuable and important rights would be concluded to be given up by implication," and he saw no "distinction between rights relinquished by a positive grant, and lost by implication. Unless there were a Bill of Rights, implication might swallow up all our rights."[36]

Patrick Henry was also dissatisfied with Federalists' arguments against a bill of rights. "A Bill of Rights," he said, "is a favourite thing with" Virginians, and with the people of the other states. If the unlimited, undefined powers of Congress were unchecked by a bill of rights, Henry told the convention that the government of Virginia would be an absurdity. It would give up all its powers over taxation and the military to the general government "without check, limitation, or controul."[37] The people of Virginia would still have their Declaration of Rights, but it would check a

> weakened, prostrated, enervated State Government! You have a Bill of Rights to defend you against the State Government, which is bereaved of all power; and yet you have none against Congress, though in full and exclusive possession of all power! You arm yourselves against the weak and defenceless, and expose yourself naked to the armed and powerful. Is not this a conduct of unexampled absurdity?[38]

In response to an overture from the Antifederal Committee of New York City, an Antifederal committee of the Virginia convention, chaired by George Mason, wrote a letter on June 9 asking the New Yorkers to appoint a delegation from their convention to meet one from Virginia "to agree on the necessary Amendments" to the Constitution. The communication was so secret that it was not entrusted to the mail for fear that Federalists would intercept it. Philadelphia Antifederal printer Eleazer Oswald carried the letter from Richmond to John Lamb, the coordinator of Antifederal activities in New York City. Lamb forwarded the Virginia letter via courier to Governor George Clinton in Poughkeepsie, where the New York convention had just convened.[39] Clinton wrote to Lamb telling him that the Antifederalists in the New York convention had appointed a committee of correspondence chaired by Robert Yates. Clinton said that "It gives me and them sensible Pleasure to learn that the Friends to the Liberties of our Country to the Southward are equally anxious with those who are not ashamed of that unfashionable Name here."[40] A letter from Yates's committee was enclosed, stating that New York Antifederalists were pleased to find the Virginians in agreement with them on amendments that "stand on the Broad Basis of securing the Rights and equally promoting the Happiness of every Citizen of the Union." No final list of amendments had yet been drafted by the New York convention, but a preliminary list was sent.[41] Unfortunately for the opponents of the Constitution, the time to travel between Richmond and Poughkeepsie made serious efforts to coordinate their activities impossible.

Throughout the entire Virginia convention, the overriding issue was whether the delegates would ratify the Constitution with previous, conditional amendments or subsequent, recommendatory amendments. All

of the delegates could agree that the Constitution was not perfect, but
Federalists maintained that the new government should first be established and tested before amendments were proposed and adopted.

Antifederalists objected to their opponents' appeal for future
amendments. Patrick Henry boldly asserted that he would "never agree
to the proposed plan without Amendments." "At present," he argued:

> we have our liberties and privileges in our own hands. Let us not
> relinquish them. Let us not adopt this system till we see them se-
> cured. There is some small possibility, that should we follow the
> conduct of Massachusetts, amendments might be obtained. There
> is small possibility of amending any Government; but . . . shall we
> abandon our most inestimable rights, and rest their security on a
> mere possibility?[42]

Henry continued by asking the delegates whether their

> rage for novelty [was] so great, that you are first to sign and seal,
> and then to retract. Is it possible to conceive a greater solecism?
> . . . You agree to bind yourselves hand and foot—For the sake of
> what?—Of being unbound. You go into a dungeon—For what? To
> get out. Is there no danger when you go in, that the bolts of fed-
> eral authority shall shut you in?[43]

Anyone, Henry asserted, who told him to adopt an avowedly defective
government was obviously "a lunatic." "Reason, self-preservation, and
every idea of propriety, powerfully" urged the convention to adopt the
Constitution conditionally with amendments.[44]

In response to these arguments, James Madison and Edmund Randolph maintained that "previous amendments are but another name
for rejection. They will throw Virginia out of the Union." Randolph
asked his fellow delegates to consider the issue carefully. Many other
states had adopted the Constitution expecting amendments to follow.
Was it not better "to adopt and run the chance of amending it hereafter,
than run the risk of endangering the Union?" The Confederation, he
argued, was destroyed; if the Constitution were rejected, the Union would
be dissolved; "the dogs of war would break loose, and anarchy and
discord would complete the ruin of this country."[45] Adoption of the
Constitution with recommendatory amendments would prevent this
catastrophe, while the unison of sentiments among the adopting states
would assure the passage of subsequent amendments. The issue was sim-

ple and momentous. Would the thirteen states "Unite freely, peaceably, and unanimously, for the security of their common happiness and liberty, or" would everything "be put in confusion and disorder!"[46]

On June 25, after three weeks of intense debate, the convention was ready to decide the issue. First, a vote was taken on a list of amendments proposing both guarantees for individual liberties and alterations in the structure and nature of the federal government. These amendments were defeated by a vote of 88 to 80. The final vote on unconditional ratification then occurred, and the Constitution was ratified 89 to 79.

Over the next two days, a committee drafted and then the convention agreed to recommendatory amendments to the Constitution. It would be left to the first federal Congress to propose necessary amendments that would protect basic human rights, and Virginians would play an important—a decisive—role in obtaining the future Bill of Rights.

New York:
A Trust for the Future

The New York convention met in Poughkeepsie on June 17 with more than two-thirds of its delegates avowedly opposed to the unconditional ratification of the Constitution. New York Antifederalists opposed the Constitution for many of the same reasons espoused elsewhere. New York's opposition also derived, in large part, from the state's peculiar geography. Blessed with an excellent harbor and navigable rivers, the state was able to levy a tariff on imports that freed its landholders from heavy real estate taxes. Since most of the foreign goods consumed in Connecticut and New Jersey were first imported into and taxed by New York, residents of these two states grudgingly paid large sums annually into New York's treasury. Led by Governor George Clinton, New York Antifederalists, thus, saw the new Constitution, which gave Congress alone the power to tax foreign imports, as a threat to the development of their state. This argument was candidly expressed in a letter from state senator John Williams of Washington County:

> You will also observe . . . that the advantage of having property in a maritime state, will be reduced to an equal value with the property where there is no navigation. If this is not taking our liberty, it is certainly diminishing our property, which is equal to it. What hath kept the taxes so low in this state—the reason is obvious, our impost duties. This is a privilege Providence hath endowed us with.

. . . Let our imposts and advantages be taken from us, shall we not be obliged to lay as heavy taxes as Connecticut, Boston, &c. What hath kept us from those burthens but the privileges, which we must lose if the present proposed constitution is adopted.[47]

But New York Antifederalists also feared the lack of protection for their basic rights. Newspapers, broadsides, and pamphlets were filled with articles that stressed the need for a bill of rights. Thus, when the state convention assembled, Antifederalist delegates opposed the Constitution both out of economic self-interest and for reasons of principle.

With an overwhelming majority of delegates opposed to the Constitution, New York Antifederalists bided their time. They allowed debate over each section of the Constitution with the proviso that amendments be proposed and discussed simultaneously. For three weeks the convention debated the major parts of the new government. During that time, word arrived on June 24 that New Hampshire had ratified the Constitution, followed on July 2 of the news of Virginia's ratification. New York Federalists were buoyed. The Antifederal bloc, although outwardly unaffected, began to lose its cohesiveness as a number of various conditional ratification plans were suggested.

On July 2, Thomas Tredwell of Suffolk County eloquently stated the case for a bill of rights—the rock on which the Constitution should have rested. "No other foundation can any man lay, which will secure the sacred temple of freedom against the power of the great, the undermining arts of ambition, and the blasts of profane scoffers." Tredwell warned his fellow Antifederalists to be wary of those who "tend to corrupt our political faith, to take us off our guard, and lull to sleep that jealousy which, we are told by all writers,—and it is proved by all experience,—is essentially necessary for the preservation of freedom." Tredwell lamented

In this Constitution, sir, we have departed widely from the principles and political faith of '76, when the spirit of liberty ran high, and danger put a curb on ambition. Here we find no security for the rights of individuals, no security for the existence of our state governments; here is no bill of rights, no proper restriction of power; our lives, our property, and our consciences, are left wholly at the mercy of the legislature, and the powers of the judiciary may be extended to any degree short of almighty. Sir, in this Constitution we have not only neglected,—we have done worse,—we have openly violated, our faith,—that is, our public faith. . . . The liberties of the country are a deposit, a trust, in the hands of individuals;

. . . which the possessors have no right to dispose of; they belong to our children, and to them we are bound to transmit them.[48]

On July 7, John Lansing, Jr., one of the three Antifederalist leaders in the convention and a former delegate to the Constitutional Convention, read a bill of rights that was "to be prefixed to the constitution." During the next two days, Antifederalists caucused to try to arrive at some consensus. On July 10, Lansing presented the Antifederalists' proposal—ironically, a year to the day after he and fellow New York delegate Robert Yates had left the Constitutional Convention. Three kinds of amendments were suggested: (1) explanatory, (2) conditional, and (3) recommendatory. The first group of amendments included a bill of rights and some explanations of unclear portions of the Constitution. The conditional amendments prohibited Congress from exercising certain military, fiscal, and regulatory powers until after a second constitutional convention had considered these matters. The recommendatory amendments were "numerous and important" and should, they argued, be considered by the first federal Congress.[49]

Federalists denounced the plan as "a gilded Rejection"; Antifederalists said that it was their *"Ultimatum."*[50] Debate over the plan continued for a week as Antifederalist solidarity diminished. On July 17, Melancton Smith, the self-proclaimed Antifederal manager of the convention, proposed that the convention declare the Constitution defective, but that it join the other ten states and ratify. New York, however, would retain the option to withdraw from the Union if Congress refused to call a second constitutional convention within four years to consider amendments. Facing opposition from both Federalists and Antifederalists, Smith withdrew his proposal on July 19.[51]

From July 19 to 23, the delegates considered a new plan for conditional ratification. The proposal called for the Constitution to be ratified "upon condition" that certain amendments, including a bill of rights, be accepted. On the 23rd, however, Samuel Jones of Queens moved that the words "upon condition" be dropped in favor of "in full confidence." Melancton Smith supported the change.

He was as thoroughly convinced then as he ever had been, that the Constitution was radically defective, amendments to it had always been the object of his pursuit, and until Virginia came in, he had reason to believe they might have been obtained previous to the operation of the Government. He was now satisfied they could not, and it was equally the dictate of reason and of duty to quit his first ground, and advance so far as that they might be received into the

Union. He should hereafter pursue his important and favourite object of amendments with equal zeal as before, but in a practicable way which was only in the mode prescribed by the Constitution.[52]

Smith agreed that conditional ratification would only keep New York out of the Union, thus diluting Antifederalists' strength in the first federal Congress. Without New York in the first Congress, a bill of rights would be almost impossible to obtain.

Smith's argument convinced enough Antifederalists to join Federalists in a vote of 31 to 29 to approve Jones's motion. A final effort to obtain a limited-term ratification failed on July 24, and the next day an Antifederalist motion for adjournment was defeated 31 to 28. On July 26, by a vote of 30 to 27, the convention ratified the Constitution with recommendatory amendments—a bill of rights and a list of structural changes to the Constitution. A circular letter to the states recommending the calling of a second constitutional convention to consider amendments was unanimously approved.

Circumstances outside the state—ratification by ten of the other twelve states—had convinced New York Antifederalists that they had to work within the first federal Congress to obtain the necessary safeguards to protect their liberties. Attention focused on the elections to that Congress, which took place in the winter and spring of 1788–89.

The First Federal Elections:
The Debate over a Bill of Rights Continues

Once the Constitution was ratified by nine states, the contest to elect the first federal representatives and senators began. The Confederation Congress passed an election ordinance on September 13, 1788, and two weeks later, on September 30, the Pennsylvania assembly elected its two U.S. senators—the first federal officeholders elected to the new government. By March 1789, when the first federal Congress was scheduled to meet in New York City, all eleven states that had ratified the Constitution had elected their U.S. representatives; New York was the only state that had not yet elected its senators and presidential electors. (Two of Massachusetts' eight representatives were still not chosen.)

The debate during these elections was, in essence, a continuation of the debate over the ratification of the Constitution. Local issues and conflicting personalities played their usual roles in every state, but the key issue in Pennsylvania, Massachusetts, Virginia, and New York continued to be amendments to the Constitution. What kind of amendments would be proposed and how would they be proposed? Would a bill of rights be proposed or would far-ranging structural amendments also be put forth that, if adopted, would change the nature of the new Constitution? Would Congress propose the amendments or would another constitutional convention be called? No one knew the answers to these questions, but some Antifederalists pictured "the first Congress as a second Convention."[53] Therefore, the men elected to serve in the first Congress would play a critical role in shaping the new Constitution.

Pennsylvania

When news of Virginia's ratification arrived in Pennsylvania, Antifederalists called a convention to meet in Harrisburg to propose amendments to the Constitution and to nominate a slate of candidates for the House of Representatives. The convention met from September 3 to 6 and concluded that "every man of true federal principles" would support constitutional amendments that were "essential to preserve the peace and harmony of the Union and those invaluable privileges for which so much blood and treasure have been recently expended."[54] The convention proposed that the state assembly petition the first federal Congress for a constitutional convention, which would propose a broad range of amendments, including a guarantee of every right reserved by the state constitutions "except so far as they are expressly and manifestly yielded or narrowed by the national Constitution."[55] The delegates to the Harrisburg convention also encouraged Antifederal county committees to propose a slate of candidates for the House.

Pennsylvania Federalists countered with their own slate of candidates and a denunciation of any attempt to amend the Constitution immediately. Friends of the Constitution were warned to be wary of Antifederalists who, "having failed in their attempts to prevent" the ratification of the Constitution, were "now busily employed in endeavoring to *overset* it in a constitutional way."[56] Antifederalists, it was said, aim "not to amend but to destroy."[57] The people were told that the Constitution would preserve liberty and establish national greatness, but that its benefits would be lost if Antifederalists were elected to Congress. Pennsylvanians responded by electing seven Federalists and one mild Antifederalist as their first representatives, while both of the state's senators strongly supported the Constitution. James Madison wrote from Philadelphia that the election results secured "the Constitution against the hazardous experiment of a second convention" and would promote conciliatory measures in the first Congress.[58]

Massachusetts

In Massachusetts, Federalists decried those writers who "disseminate doubts, and conjure up spectres to alarm the unwary—to talk of 'Tyranny, Aristocracy, and Daggers in the heart of Liberty.' "[59] Such "amendment mongers," "sticklers for amendments," and "amendmentites" were "false Patriots." Federalists, on the other hand, were men of "integrity, uprightness, and diligence."

Antifederalists urged the people to elect proponents of amendments. They characterized opponents of amendments as men who "neglect to *repair* a *breach* in the walls of a city liable to be beseiged, in order to discover whether the assailants *would* avail *themselves* of the advantage *offered* them. . . . [but] a *lodgment gained behind the breach . . .* would render *after* precaution *unavailable.*"[60] "Honestus" questioned the integrity of those Federalists in the Massachusetts convention who had urged ratification with recommendatory amendments. He asked "Whether the amendments were proposed with an intention of having them adopted, or whether they were artfully introduced to deceive the members of the Convention?" If amendments were not actively advocated in the first federal Congress, "Honestus" contended, the mind of the public would become jealous and they would come to distrust their rulers. This was not the way to inaugurate the new federal government.[61]

The most controversial election in the state occurred in Middlesex County. Antifederalists put forth a reluctant Elbridge Gerry as their candidate, knowing that he would continue his support of amendments to the Constitution. Federalists worked hard to defeat Gerry, arguing that the former delegate to the Constitutional Convention sought to annihilate the Constitution through amendments. Gerry, however, acknowledged that ever since the Revolution, he had been

> anxious for an efficient federal government, with every power for promoting the Welfare; & sufficient *checks* for securing the liberties of the people. This *latter* is what I have contended for, & those who wish to prey on the people by means of a corrupt government are loading me & every one else who opposes them with anathemas for urging Amendments.[62]

In an address to his friends and fellow citizens of Middlesex County, Gerry asserted that

> Every friend to a vigorous government must, as I conceive, be desirous of such amendments, as will remove the just apprehensions

of the people, and secure their confidence in, and affection for, the new government. For to defeat amendments of this description, must be in effect, to defeat the Constitution itself.[63]

Despite the strong Federalist opposition, Gerry was elected, but six of the state's other seven representatives and both of its senators opposed amendments to the Constitution.

Virginia

In late June 1788, Virginia Antifederalists failed in their attempt to ratify the Constitution with conditional amendments. Federalist convention delegates, however, acquiesced in proposing forty recommendatory amendments—twenty structural alterations and a declaration of rights containing twenty specific protections for personal liberties. "Party madness," however, "had not died . . . with the adoption of the Constitution."[64] On the contrary, it was "renewed with double fury" as Antifederalists continued their efforts to obtain amendments in the fall legislative session where they held slim majorities in both houses.

The legislature, dominated by Patrick Henry, pursued three measures aimed at securing the amendments recommended by the state convention. First, the legislature passed circular letters to the states and resolutions to the first federal Congress advocating the call of a second constitutional convention. Only through such a convention, the legislature maintained, would the defects of the Constitution be addressed and appropriate amendments be proposed that would "promote our common interests, and secure to ourselves, and our latest posterity, the great and unalienable rights of Mankind."[65] Second, the legislature elected two Antifederalists—Richard Henry Lee and William Grayson—as U.S. senators while spurning the candidacy of James Madison. Finally, the legislature enacted an election law that favored Antifederalists. In particular, Federalists charged Patrick Henry's forces with "modelling" congressional districts that favored Antifederalist candidates. This tendency—which can fairly be dubbed "Henry-mandering"—was most apparent in the eighth district, where the opposition to James Madison's candidacy was intense because of the perception that he opposed amendments. Madison felt compelled to set the record straight on this important issue:

> I freely own that I have never seen in the Constitution as it now
> stands those serious dangers which have alarmed many respectable
> Citizens. Accordingly whilst it remained unratified, and it was nec-

essary to unite the States in some one plan, I opposed all previous alterations as calculated to throw the States into dangerous contentions, and to furnish the Secret enemies of the Union with an opportunity of promoting its dissolution. Circumstances are now changed: The Constitution is established . . . and amendments, if pursued with a proper moderation and in a proper mode, will be not only safe, but may serve the double purpose of satisfying the minds of well meaning opponents, and of providing additional guards in favour of liberty. Under this change of circumstances, it is my sincere opinion that the Constitution ought to be revised, and that the first Congress meeting under it, ought to prepare and recommend to the States for ratification, the most satisfactory provisions for all essential rights. . . .[66]

When Madison's position on amendments became clear, he successfully defeated James Monroe, the Antifederalist candidate, by a vote of 1,308 to 972 (after a series of public debates between the two men—the texts of which, unfortunately, were not recorded for posterity).[67] Six of the other nine Federalist candidates were also elected to the U.S. House of Representatives. Neither Federalists nor Antifederalists in Virginia had been totally successful, but their actions would have strong consequences in the first federal Congress.

New York

Of the eleven states that ratified the Constitution by the fall of 1788, New York was probably the most divided. Following ratification, Federalists remained outnumbered except in the lower counties, but their opponents had been badly split between "the adopting and non adopting Antis."[68] Supporters of amendments faced the difficult task of restoring their party's unity. Abraham G. Lansing, writing from Albany, told New York Congressman Abraham Yates, Jr., that "our Friends are much better pleased with" the state's ratification than they "had reason to expect—The Bill of Rights which is interwoven with the adoption is considered by the Majority of those to whom I have shewn it as a security against the Encroachment of the Genl. Government."[69] But Yates was not so optimistic. "The case now is simple. All agree that Amendments are Indispensibly necessary—And where we had it in our own power before, the Convention have transferred it to the union at Large . . . this will be an uphill Affair."[70]

On October 30, 1788, a group of Antifederalists from the southern counties of New York organized into the Federal Republican Committee. Led by John Lamb, Melancton Smith, Marinus Willet (chairman), Samuel Jones, and Charles Tillinghast, the committee resolved to send circular letters to other Antifederalists both in New York and in other states seeking their support in calling a general convention to amend the Constitution. On November 4, the letters were approved and authorized to be sent.

The Federal Republican Committee's job was not easy. Many New York Antifederalists had become disillusioned with their leaders, while the strength and ardor of Antifederalists had been sapped nationwide. The Federal Republican Committee first tried to explain the actions of Antifederalists in the New York ratifying convention. No Antifederalist delegate to the convention had changed his attitude toward the Constitution—all believed that the document was dangerous and had to be amended. But circumstances had changed and "it became a political Calculation with" some Antifederalists "to continue in the Union, and trust, for . . . amendments."[71] The Federal Republican Committee pleaded with Antifederalists to understand the reason why the Constitution had been ratified. A united party was now necessary to obtain amendments at the outset of the federal government. The Constitution was adopted, and it was now "the duty of every true friend to his country to acquiesce, and to use their influence to procure" amendments.[72]

Melancton Smith, the leader of the "adopting Antis," wrote Gilbert Livingston, another "adopting Anti," asking: "Is former confidence revived, and old grudges forgotten?" He hoped so "for the sake of the cause," because

> Union among ourselves is the corner Stone upon which our hopes of success in obtaining amendments must be built—The fair promises and pretensions of most of the leading men who were in favour of the new System are mere illusions—They intend to urge the execution of the plan in its present form—No reliance can be placed in any of them—We ought therefore to strive to maintain our union firm and immoveable as the mountains, to pursue the object of amendments with unremmitting ardour and diligence—Men may differ and will, but . . . they [must] unite in the main point.[73]

Antifederalists were warned of the duplicity of Federalists who had promised in the convention "to assist in procuring" a constitutional convention. Such promises, it seemed, "were made with a View to deceive." If amendments were not approved soon, "the liberties of the People will then depend on the arbitrary Decrees of their Rulers."[74] "An entire revolution is about taking place without war or bloodshed," but a newspaper correspondent warned New Yorkers to elect men to the new federal Congress who would support immediate amendments. Eschew those, they warned, who "now say, it is wise and proper to give the government a trial" for ten or twenty years. By that time, amendment supporters agreed, it would be "too late to secure" the liberties of the people.[75]

While the debate over amendments persisted in the newspapers and in private correspondence, the state assembly, on December 22, 1788, appointed a committee to draft an application to Congress to call a convention for proposing amendments. The committee reported on January 29, 1789, and on February 5 the assembly approved the application, hoping that amendments would be proposed and adopted that would "secure to ourselves and our latest posterity, the great and unalienable rights of mankind." The senate concurred two days later.

The statewide split within Antifederal ranks persisted, however, and supporters of amendments were able to elect only two of New York's six federal representatives. Worse yet, after more than six months of debate, the legislature elected two Federalists to the U.S. Senate.

* * * *

Americans, through their state ratifying conventions, had overwhelmingly voted to adopt the new Constitution. Most Americans at the time that their conventions met seemed to want the new form of government amended. But, by the time the first federal elections occurred, the feeling had changed. It was time to implement the new government. Amendments, it seemed, could wait.

Congress Debates and Proposes a Bill of Rights

On March 4, 1789, the new Congress under the Constitution convened. In his inaugural address on April 30, President George Washington recommended that Congress consider possible amendments to the Constitution. Instead of proposing specific amendments, Washington assured himself that Congress would "carefully avoid every alteration which might endanger the benefits of an United and effective Government, or which ought to await the future lessons of experience." On the other hand, he urged that "a reverence for the characteristic rights of freemen, and a regard for the public harmony" should influence Congress' consideration.[76]

Federalists worried that the states might require Congress to call a second general convention to amend the Constitution. Such a convention, proposed by New York's ratifying convention, would be unrestricted in the amendments it could propose. Perhaps, in fact, an entirely new constitution might be recommended as was done by the Federal Convention in 1787. This fear intensified when Virginia on November 20, 1788, and New York on February 7, 1789, adopted petitions to be laid before the new Congress calling for another convention.

On May 4, 1789, James Madison notified his fellow representatives that he intended to introduce amendments to the Constitution later in the month. The next day, Madison's Virginia colleague, Theodorick Bland, presented to the House of Representatives his state's call for a second general convention. (According to James Monroe, "the draft was revis'd and corrected by Bland and partakes of his usual fire and elegance."[77]) The people of Virginia and of the other states believed, this petition declared, that the Constitution endangered "all the great and unalienable rights of freemen." The objections to the Constitution "were not founded in speculative theory, but [were] deduced from principles which have been established by the melancholy example of other nations in different ages." Expected to be busy in setting up the new government, Congress would surely act slowly in making recommendations for amendments. Thus, Virginia felt obliged to have Congress call a second constitutional convention. New York echoed Virginia's request when on May 6 Representative Nathaniel Lawrence presented his state's request for another convention.[78] The House decided to lay both petitions on the table, declaring that only if it should receive nine such petitions (as required by Article V of the Constitution) would the issue of a second convention properly be before the House.

On Monday June 8, 1789, fulfilling the wishes of his state's convention and his election promise to his constituents, and also trying to defuse the Antifederalists' attempt to call a second constitutional convention, Madison asked the House of Representatives to go into a committee of the whole to consider amendments to the Constitution. Opponents of the measure suggested that the House either choose a select committee to consider amendments or that Madison propose his amendments, have them printed and distributed to the members, and then assign a date for later discussion. An immediate consideration of amendments, they contended, appeared to be "premature"; more important matters in setting up the government should first be considered. Even supporters of amendments believed that the time had not yet arrived to consider the subject. Madison reluctantly agreed that it was inopportune for Congress to consider amendments immediately, but he presented his amendments so that they could be submitted to a committee for later debate. However, Madison said, "prudence" dictated that before the end of its first session, Congress submit amendments to the state legislatures.

Madison told the House that he believed that "a great number" of Americans were "dissatisfied" with the Constitution. "On the principles of amity and moderation," he explained, he wished to protect expressly "the great rights of mankind" under the Constitution. Such an act might also convince North Carolina and Rhode Island to join the Union. Above all, however, Madison believed that all power is subject to abuse; therefore, it would be proper to guard more adequately against this potential danger. He agreed that the door should not be opened to "a reconsideration of the whole structure of the Government," but insisted that a consideration of "the security of rights" posed no danger to the new federal government.

Madison thought that the majority of Antifederalists opposed the Constitution because they feared the possible "encroachments on particular rights," especially in those cases where Americans had become accustomed to "safeguards . . . interposed between them and the magistrate who exercises the sovereign power." Consequently, Madison proposed a number of amendments to the Constitution which, taken together, made up a bill of rights. He stated that he never believed that a bill of rights was so essential that the Constitution should be rejected until one was added. He stressed that his amendments would not affect "the structure and stamina of the government" but would be "important in the eyes of many" as the protection they had sought during the ratification debate. Amendments protecting fundamental rights would prove that Federalists were "sincerely devoted to liberty and a republican government." And, while it was true that bills of rights in Great Britain "have gone no farther than to raise a barrier against the power of the Crown" while the power of the legislature is left unchecked, in America the people "have thought it necessary to raise barriers against power in all forms and departments of Government." The great object in Madison's view was "to limit and qualify the powers of Government, by excepting out of the grant of power those cases in which the Government ought not to act, or to act only in a particular mode."

Many people thought these amendments were unnecessary. Noah Webster, writing as "A Free Mechanic" in the *New York Journal*, August 20, 1789, attacked Madison's proposal: "It seems to be agreed on all hands that paper declarations of rights are trifling things and no real security to liberty." But Madison believed that paper declarations would "have a tendency to impress some degree of respect for them, to establish the public opinion in their favor, and rouse the attention of the whole community.''

Ardent Antifederalists throughout the country who had advocated both a bill of rights and significant structural changes to the Constitution denounced Madison's amendments. George Mason characterized Madison as a supporter of ''Milk & Water Propositions'' that would serve as ''a Tub to the Whale,'' that is, a diversion from significant alterations.[79] Other Virginians viewed the amendments ''as an anodyne to the discontented'' or ''as a soporific draught to the restless.''[80] South Carolina Antifederalist Aedanus Burke condemned the amendments in Congress as ''frothy and full of wind, formed only to please the palate.''[81] Representative George Clymer of Pennsylvania likened Madison to ''a sensible physician [who] has given his malades imaginaries bread pills powder of paste &c neutral mixtures to keep them in play.''[82]

Ironically, Madison now answered all those arguments against bills of rights previously put forth by Federalists during the ratification debate. Over and over again, Madison said that Federalist disclaimers against a bill of rights were inconclusive. Furthermore, he averred that a bill of rights incorporated into a constitution would empower the independent judicial tribunals to consider themselves ''in a peculiar manner the guardians of those rights; they will be an impenetrable bulwark against every assumption of power in the legislative or executive.''

Congress divided, sometimes bitterly, over Madison's amendments. Representative James Jackson of Georgia dismissed them as ''theoretical speculation.'' If ''not dangerous or improper,'' Madison's amendments were ''at least unnecessary.'' Representative Elbridge Gerry, on the other hand, felt that it would be ''improper'' to consider Madison's few amendments when there were many other substantial amendments proposed by the state conventions. Antifederalists would lose faith in Congress, Gerry maintained, if only Madison's amendments were considered. On some occasions, Gerry later reported, the intensity of the debate reached the point where congressmen were ready to settle their disagreements with dueling pistols, but cooler heads prevailed.[83] The debate on June 8 ended when Congress agreed that Madison's amendments should at some future date be considered in the committee of the whole.

On July 21, six weeks after Madison had first introduced his amendments, he ''begged the House to indulge him'' in their further consideration. The House voted to send Madison's amendments and all of the other amendments submitted by state ratifying conventions to a select committee composed of one member from each state. A week later, on July 28, the committee reported a list of seventeen amendments—

basically a composite of Madison's amendments—which was ordered to lie on the table. On August 3, Madison again urged the House to take up the amendments, and it was agreed to discuss the committee's report on August 12. Other business occupied the House on the 12th, and thus the discussion was postponed. On the 13th, a lengthy debate occurred on the propriety of considering amendments when other more pressing matters awaited the House's consideration. Madison saw the real danger that amendments would not be proposed during this first session of Congress. He pleaded with the House:

> I admit, with the worthy gentlemen who preceded me, that a great number of the community are solicitous to see the Government carried into operation; but I believe that there is a considerable part also anxious to secure those rights which they are apprehensive are endangered by the present constitution. Now, considering the full confidence they reposed at the time of its adoption in their future representatives, I think we ought to pursue the subject to effect.

The House voted to accede to Madison's wishes, and between August 13 and 24 the amendments were debated first in a committee of the whole and then, after August 18, in the House itself.

At times during this debate, Madison's amendments appeared to be dead because they did not have the support of the necessary two-thirds majority required by Article V of the Constitution. Madison asked President Washington for support. Washington responded by stating that some of the amendments were "importantly necessary" while others, though not essential in his judgment, would be "necessary to quiet the fears of some respectable characters and well meaning Men. Upon the whole, therefore, not foreseeing any evil consequences that can result from their adoption, they have my wishes for a favorable reception in both houses."[84] With Washington's support (which echoed his endorsement of the need to consider amendments in his April 30 inaugural address), the amendments won approval by the House of Representatives.

One important decision that some representatives at the time thought "trifling" was the matter of form. How would amendments be added to the Constitution? Would they be placed at the end of the original document or would they be interspersed throughout, deleting passages of the original Constitution that were no longer applicable and altering others? In a lengthy debate on August 13, 1789, Madison urged the latter, arguing that "there is a neatness and propriety in incorporating the amendments into the constitution itself." The Constitution, he argued, would "certainly be more simple, when the amendments are interwoven into those parts to which they naturally belong, than it will if they consist of separate and distinct parts."[85] Roger Sherman of Connecticut opposed this interweaving, arguing that "We might as well endeavor to mix brass, iron, and clay, as to incorporate such heterogeneous articles."[86] James Jackson supported Sherman's position, urging "that the original constitution ought to remain inviolate, and not be patched up, from time to time, with various stuffs resembling Joseph's coat of many colors."[87] On August 13, Madison's arrangement was approved, only to be overturned finally by a two-thirds vote six days later.

On August 24, 1789, the House of Representatives sent seventeen proposed amendments to the Senate. The Senate read the amendments on the 25th, when Ralph Izard of South Carolina, John Langdon of New Hampshire, and Robert Morris of Pennsylvania treated them "contemptuously." Izard and Langdon unsuccessfully moved to postpone their consideration to the next session, and on September 2 the Senate began its consideration of the amendments. Within three weeks, the Senate had tightened the language and consolidated the amendments into a list of twelve, which the Senate then approved. Significantly, the Senate eliminated the amendment which Madison considered "the most valuable amendment in the whole lot" when it struck out the prohibition on the states from infringing on the freedom of conscience, speech, press, and jury trial. (This omission was invoked by Chief Justice John Marshall in the U. S. Supreme Court's decision in *Barron* v. *Baltimore* [1833] in which the Bill of Rights was declared applicable only to the federal government, not to the states.) After rejecting a host of amendments based on the Virginia ratifying convention's recommendations, the Senate adopted its version of amendments on September 9, 1789.

The House of Representatives received the Senate's amendments on September 10. It agreed to some of the Senate's changes, and on September 21 called a conference committee to settle the differences. The committee—composed of Madison, Sherman, and John Vining of Delaware from the House, and Oliver Ellsworth (Connecticut), Charles Carroll (Maryland), and William Paterson (New Jersey) from the Senate—reported to the House of Representatives on September 23. The following day the House accepted the committee's report (in which the Senate withdrew those changes not approved by the House) by a vote of 37 to 14, and passed a resolution requesting President Washington to transmit copies of the proposed amendments to the eleven states in the Union as well as to North Carolina and Rhode Island. On September 25, the Senate concurred with the House of Representatives. Congress had complied with the provisions of Article V of the Constitution in recommending amendments to the state legislatures. It had acted to satisfy the apprehensions raised by Antifederalists throughout the ratification debate.

The States Adopt the Bill of Rights

On October 2, 1789, President Washington sent the amendments to the states for their approval. Several state legislatures rejected the first two amendments which provided a formula for the apportionment of the House of Representatives and for a restriction on the power of congressmen to enact salary increases for themselves. It took over two years for the other ten amendments—the future Bill of Rights—to be adopted by the necessary three-fourths of the state legislatures. Much of the delay was due to Virginia's reluctance.

State	Date of Adoption
New Jersey	November 20, 1789
Maryland	December 19, 1789
North Carolina	December 22, 1789
South Carolina	January 19, 1790
New Hampshire	January 25, 1790
Delaware	January 28, 1790
New York	February 27, 1790
Pennsylvania	March 10, 1790
Rhode Island	June 11, 1790
Vermont	November 3, 1791
Virginia	December 15, 1791

Since the proposed amendments to the Constitution were discussed in state legislatures in committees of the whole (and these debates are not recorded), little is known about these debates. At first, ten states were needed to adopt the amendments. But, when Vermont entered the Union becoming the fourteenth state in 1791, eleven states were needed to obtain the necessary three-fourths approval. By mid-December 1791 eleven states, the required three-quarters, had adopted ten of the amendments—the Bill of Rights. The actual procedure followed in each state varied.

New York

In New York, the proposed amendments were considered and approved at the second meeting of the thirteenth session of the state legislature held in New York City from January 13 to April 6, 1790. The following chronology of New York's ratification (which exemplifies the pattern followed in many states) is excerpted from the New York State Senate and Assembly journals and the Minutes of the Council of Revision (courtesy of the New York State Library, Division of Manuscripts and Special Collections, Albany, N.Y.), and from Record Group 11 of the National Archives.

January 13, 1790, Wednesday: Governor George Clinton sends a message to the state legislature enclosing the proposed amendments to the federal Constitution.

January 13, Wednesday: The Senate and the Assembly, each in its own committee of the whole, consider the Governor's message and the papers accompanying it.

January 20, 1790, Wednesday: The Senate assigns "Saturday next" for the consideration of the amendments.

January 22, 1790, Friday: The Assembly resolves to consider the amendments in a committee of the whole on "Tuesday next."

January 23, 1790, Saturday: The Senate, agreeable to the order of the day, considers the amendments in a committee of the whole.

January 26, 1790, Tuesday: The Assembly in a committee of the whole chaired by John Watts, Jr. (City and County of New York) considers the proposed amendments. The committee by a vote of 52 to 5 rejects the second amendment: "No law varying the compensation for the services of Senators and Representatives shall take effect, until an election of Representatives shall have intervened." The committee, after agreeing to the other eleven amendments, reports to the Assembly, which reads and agrees to the committee report. The Assembly appoints Rufus King (City and County of New York), Samuel Jones (Queens

County), Jonathan N. Havens (Suffolk County), John Livingston (Columbia County), and Ezekiel Gilbert (Columbia County) as "a committee to report the form of a ratification of the said amendments."

February 4, 1790, Thursday: The Senate committee of the whole reports "that a special committee be appointed, to devise and report a mode for the ratification of the amendments, proposed to be made to the Constitution." The Senate agrees to the report and appoints James Duane (City and County of New York), Ezra L'Hommedieu (Suffolk County), and Philip Livingston (Westchester County).

February 12, 1790, Friday: Assemblyman Samuel Jones brings in a bill entitled "An act ratifying certain articles in addition to, and amendment of the Constitution of the United States of America, proposed by the Congress"; the Assembly reads the bill for the first time and orders a second reading.

February 13, 1790, Saturday: The Assembly, for the second time, reads the bill ratifying the proposed amendments and commits it to a committee of the whole.

February 20, 1790, Saturday: In a committee of the whole, Assemblyman John Smith (Suffolk County) moves that the proposed amendments to the Constitution be approved by legislative resolution rather than as an act. His motion is defeated 49 to 2. (John Smith and Jonathan N. Havens voted in the minority.) The committee of the whole agrees to the bill without amendment and reports it to the Assembly, which reads the bill, agrees to it, and orders it engrossed. [The rationale for Smith's motion is uncertain. He perhaps believed, from a technical perspective, that the ratification of amendments to the federal Constitution should not take the form of an act but should more properly be done by joint resolution. But Smith may have believed that a bill ratifying the amendments would be rejected by the Council of Revision, which, at that time, had two Antifederalists and one Federalist in attendance. A joint resolution of the legislature would not have required Council consideration.]

February 22, 1790, Monday: The Assembly reads the engrossed bill and passes it. James Gordon (City and County of Albany) and Henry Will (City and County of New York) carry the bill to the Senate for its concurrence.

February 22, 1790, Monday: The Senate receives the bill ratifying the proposed amendments, reads it, and orders a second reading.

February 23, 1790, Tuesday: The Senate reads the bill a second time and refers it to a committee of the whole.

February 24, 1790, Wednesday: Senator James Duane reports that the committee of the whole had gone through the bill without amendment. The Senate reads the bill a third time, agrees to it, and orders Lewis Morris (Westchester County) and Peter Schuyler (Montgomery County) to inform the Assembly.

February 24, 1790, Wednesday: The Assembly receives a message informing that the Senate had approved the bill ratifying the proposed amendments to the Constitution. The Assembly orders Christopher Tappen (Ulster County) and Zina Hitchcock (Washington and Clinton Counties) to deliver the bill to the Council of Revision.

February 25, 1790, Thursday: The Council of Revision (Governor George Clinton, Chief Justice Richard Morris, and Associate Justice Robert Yates in attendance) reads the bill and orders a second reading.

February 27, 1790, Saturday: The Council of Revision reads the bill a second time and resolves, in its standard fashion, "that it does not appear improper to the Council that the said Bill" should become law. The Council orders that a copy of its resolution, signed by Governor Clinton, should be delivered to the Assembly by Justice Yates.

February 27, 1790, Saturday: The Assembly receives the message from the Council of Revision.

March 1, 1790, Monday: The Senate receives a message from the Assembly stating that the Council of Revision has approved the bill ratifying the proposed amendments.

March 16, 1790, Tuesday: The Assembly resolves that, if the Senate agrees, Governor Clinton should be "requested to cause an exemplification of the act" ratifying the proposed amendments to the Constitution to be made and to be sent to the President of the United States. Assemblymen Isaac I. Talman (Dutchess County) and John Carpenter (Orange County) deliver this resolution to the Senate.

March 19, 1790, Friday: The Senate receives the message from the Assembly and concurs with the resolution requesting the Governor to prepare an exemplication of the act ratifying the proposed amendments which should be sent to the President of the United States. James Clinton (Ulster County) and Peter Schuyler ordered to inform the Assembly.

March 27, 1790, Saturday: The exemplification of the act ratifying eleven of the proposed amendments to the Constitution is signed by Governor Clinton and has the Great Seal of the State affixed.

April 2, 1790, Friday: Governor Clinton sends a letter to President George Washington enclosing the exemplification of the act ratifying eleven of the proposed amendments to the Constitution.

April 5, 1790, Monday: President Washington sends Congress New York's exemplification of the act ratifying eleven of the proposed amendments to the Constitution.

The Three Non-adopting States:
Georgia, Connecticut, and Massachusetts

Massachusetts, Connecticut, and Georgia were the three states that failed to ratify the amendments. A joint committee of the Georgia legislature reported on December 1, 1789, that it was premature to consider amendments—only "experience" would "point out" "the defective parts of the Constitution."

In Connecticut the assembly rejected the first amendment, but approved the remaining eleven. The council (the state legislature's upper house) approved all twelve. A conference committee reported a bill containing approval of all twelve amendments, which the assembly rejected preferring to "adhere to their former vote."

Governor John Hancock of Massachusetts transmitted the proposed amendments to the legislature on January 14, 1790. Five days later, after requesting permission, Hancock personally addressed the legislature. The approval of the amendments was "very important" because the people of Massachusetts felt assured by their state ratifying convention "that certain amendments would be adopted." Some of the amendments, Hancock declared, would "afford security to the best rights of men in civil society," while others were "very important to that personal security, which is so truly characteristic of a Free Government."[88] The legislators, in response to the governor's message, promised to consider the amendments carefully because they were "anxious that the Whole Body of the People should have the fullest Confidence, that their Rights, & Liberties are secured to them in the general Government by the most explicit declarations, which will have a tendency to give energy to its Authority & Laws."[89]

On January 29, 1790, the Massachusetts senate approved the last ten proposed amendments to the Constitution and appointed a committee to consider other amendments. Four days later the house of representatives rejected amendments one, two, and twelve, but adopted the other nine amendments. The house also appointed members to the joint committee created by the senate to consider additional amendments. A month later the committee, led by Antifederalists Nathan Dane and Benjamin Austin, reported. The committee believed that

> further Amendments in that Constitution are necessary to secure the Liberties of the People, and the blessings of a free and efficient system of Government; and that such Amendments ought now to be attended to, and made so particular, as will have a tendency to preserve the forms of a Federal Republic, and to prevent a consolidation of the States.[90]

The committee recommended that the legislature "suggest . . . several principles of Amendments" to its congressional delegation to be "attended to, as soon as the important business now before Congress, will admit."[91]

The committee believed that much was needed "to define and complete the System." Committee members sought "Amendments, from what they conceive[d] to be the fundamental principles of a free and energetic System of Government for an extensive Community." After examining the Constitution, the committee concluded "that the powers of the general Government, in several instances, are not well defined or limited; that there is not a just line of distinction drawn between them, and the powers of the local Governments."[92]

In concluding its report, the committee recommended twelve specific amendments to the Constitution: Congress should neither establish commercial monopolies nor interfere in federal elections unless a state failed to provide for an election; republican forms of government should be guaranteed to the territories of the United States; Congress should use the regular civil authorities—not the military—to enforce compliance to its laws, and the states should have a veto power over peacetime military policy; the federal government should exercise no power that was not "expressly delegated" in the Constitution, and certain tax sources ought to be specifically reserved for the states, except "as war and other extraordinary exigencies may require"; the federal judiciary should "be more explicitly defined," with jurisdiction specifically distinguished from state courts; the Senate should be divested of executive and judicial powers, and the states should pay the salaries of federal senators and representatives; state legislatures should have the power to recall and replace federal senators; and all senators should be elected at the same time for four-year terms. These amendments, the committee asserted, would "secure the blessings of freedom without injuring the nerves of Government." The committee was certain that the people of Massachusetts "wished for, and expected further amendments, than those which have been recommended" by Congress. These new amendments would "more explicitly" secure liberty.[93]

The committee's report on amendments shocked Federalists. Abigail Adams, the vice president's wife (then residing in New York), was sorry to find her home state "acting a part so derogatory to their Honour and interest." She was pained "to see such a combination to destroy all order, & overthrow the constitution," and she hoped, "for the Honour of the State," that the proposed amendments, "which strike a deadly blow at the vitals of" the Constitution, would "be successfully combatted."[94]

Abigail's son, John Quincy Adams, a law student in Newburyport, deplored the additional amendments as "further evidence of the petty arts which are used by the enemies to the national union to turn the tide of popular opinion against the national government." Adams had been informed that those behind the scheme "never expected that any amendments would be seriously proposed to Congress by our Legislature." The committee report "was intended for a declamation to the people" illustrating the "dangerous tendency of the government."[95]

The committee report was read in the state senate, which ordered copies printed for the senators' use. Other business intervened, however, and the session neared an end. Antifederalists in the senate, sensing the mood of the people, believed it unwise to persist, "lest they should injure their own interest." Thus, the senate refused to take up the committee report.[96]

Some confusion arose over Massachusetts' action on the amendments to the Constitution proposed by Congress. In March 1791, U.S. Secretary of State Thomas Jefferson wrote that "we know that Massachusetts has agreed to the amendments to the constitution, except (as is said) the 1st. 2d. & 12th. articles. The others therefore are now in force. The articles excepted will depend on the other legislatures."[97] In August 1791, after nine states had adopted ten of the twelve amendments proposed by Congress, Jefferson wrote Massachusetts Senator Christopher Gore requesting an authenticated copy of the state's adoption. Massachusetts, according to Jefferson, "having been the 10th. state which has ratified, makes up the three-fourth[s] of the legislatures whose ratification was to suffice."[98] After checking with the secretary of the commonwealth, Gore reported the embarrassing facts to Jefferson. The house had approved nine amendments and the senate ten. The senate then concurred with the house and a joint committee was appointed "to bring in a bill declaratory of their assent." Unfortunately, the committee never reported a bill, and thus Massachusetts officially had adopted none of the proposed amendments.[99] As a fitting climax, Massachusetts joined Connecticut and Georgia in formally adopting the Bill of Rights as part of their sesquicentennial celebrations in 1939.

Virginia

The most serious debate over the proposed amendments occurred in Virginia. On September 28, 1789, Virginia Senators Richard Henry Lee and William Grayson sent Governor Beverley Randolph and the speaker of the House of Delegates copies of Congress' proposed amendments to the Constitution. The senators characterized the amendments as "inadequate to the purpose of real and substantial amendments, and so far short of the wishes of our Country."[100] The senators had tried without success to obtain "those radical amendments proposed" by the Virginia convention. With no other amendments from Congress, Lee and Grayson predicted a "consolidated empire" and the loss of "civil liberty."[101] The amendments would probably "do more harm than benefit."[102]

Lee's and Grayson's letter alienated many Virginians, even "many who were strong Antifoederalists, and had voted against the constitution in the Convention."[103] Some Antifederalists considered it "seditious and highly reprehensible." James Madison believed that it was "well calculated to keep alive the disaffection to the Government."[104] Patrick Henry attempted to get the assembly to commend the senators for their "great vigilance . . . manifested in their letter," but, after he delivered a speech that did not "take well," the commendation "never stirred again."[105]

Governor Randolph sent the amendments to the Virginia legislature on October 19, 1789. Patrick Henry moved that the house of delegates postpone consideration of the amendments to the next assembly. Since the assembly then sitting had been elected before the promulgation of the amendments, the delegates could not properly express the will of the people on the amendments. The people should consider the amendments and then vote for delegates who would represent their feelings on the subject. If the present assembly felt the need, it could "pass a vote of *approbation* along with the postponement, and Assign the reason of referring the *ratification* to their successors." But, James Madison predicted, if the people, many of whom now wanted to give the Constitution a fair chance to operate, especially with George Washington at the helm, believed that Antifederalist leaders were merely biding time in a "war agst. the Genl Government," the move would "recoil" against them.[106] Sensing that "the pulse of the House . . . did not beat with certainty in unison with his own," Henry left the assembly early, and, in mid-November, the delegates, by a large majority, rejected Henry's motion to postpone. A committee of the whole house then approved the first ten amendments from Congress by a large majority, but narrowly defeated the final two amendments by a vote of 64 to 58.[107] Federalist Edmund Randolph led the opposition to these final two amendments arguing that they were ambiguous. Other Federalists feared the effect of the defeat of these last two amendments: "some who have been decided friends to the ten first think it woud be unwise to adopt them without the 11th. & 12th." Whatever the fate of Congress' amendments, most assemblymen believed that Virginia would apply for further amendments, in particular, a provision denying Congress the power to levy direct taxes.[108] On November 30, the assembly considered the report of the committee of the whole, and, after debate, adopted all twelve amendments "by a pretty good Majority."[109] Two days later the committee of the whole reported that the legislature, "in obedience to the will of the people," as expressed by the Virginia convention, ought to apply to Congress for additional amendments to the Constitution. The assembly accepted the report on December 5, 1789, and appointed a ten-man committee "to prepare a representation to the Congress."[110]

The Virginia senate, sitting as a committee of the whole, first considered the assembly's approval of the amendments on December 5. Much uncertainty existed as to the senate's attitude. Some senators wanted to adopt the amendments; others wanted to defeat them; and still others sought to postpone them to the next session. Those who did not want to ratify immediately were "not dissatisfied with the amendments so far as they have gone, but are apprehensive that the adoption of them at this time will be an obstacle to the chief of their pursuit," an amendment prohibiting direct taxation by Congress.[111]

On December 8, the committee of the whole made its report, which the senate adopted. Eight of the proposed amendments were adopted, but numbers three, eight, eleven, and twelve (the future first, sixth, ninth, and tenth amendments) were postponed to the next session. On December 12, the senators favoring postponement explained their position. They asserted that the people of Virginia and the other states would not have ratified the Constitution unless they were confident that significant alterations would be agreed upon. The four postponed amendments, in the judgment of the majority of senators, fell "far short of affording the same security to personal rights, or of so effectually guarding against the apprehended mischief of the government" as similar amendments proposed by the Virginia convention. Although "satisfied of the defects and dangerous tendency of these four articles," the majority was unwilling to reject them, but preferred to postpone their consideration to the next session so that the people would have an opportunity to consider the amendments and then communicate their feelings to the legislature.[112]

On December 14, the minority of the senate registered its objection to the postponement:

> 1st. Because that although the 3d, 8th and 12th of the said amendments come not fully up in form to those proposed by the Convention of this State, in June 1788, we are of opinion they are analogous thereto, and contain important and essential matter, tending further to secure to the States in the Union, and the people their inherent and undoubted political and natural rights, and are calculated the better to secure them against any undue encroachments of the Federal Government.
>
> 2dly. Because that by adopting these amendments, we by no means meant to abandon the prosecution or true constitutional grounds of other amendments, and considered the accepting of such as were at present offered as a measure better calculated to insure others, than either rejecting or postponing the consideration of them.
>
> 3dly. Because the 11th amendment, though not called for by any of the adopting States, we consider as tending to quiet the minds of many, and in no possible instance productive of danger to the liberties of the people, and because the constitution gives a right to Congress to propose, when two-thirds concur, amendments to the State Legislatures for their ratification.[113]

The assembly rejected the senate's postponement. A conference committee met on December 12, but "both houses remain'd obstinate, consequently the whole resolution was lost, and none of the amendments" were adopted.[114] Edmund Randolph, now a member of the assembly, explained that "the most zealous" Federalists thought it best "to let the whole of them rest" rather than approving a partial list. Some Federalists hoped "to throw the odium of rejection on the senate."[115] Other Federalists were disheartened with the failure to adopt the amendments, but James Madison put a positive light on the situation:

> it will do no injury to the Genl. Government. On the contrary it will have the effect with many of turning their distrust towards their

own Legislature. The miscarriage of the 3d. art: particularly [i.e.,
the future first amendment], will have this effect.[116]

Some Antifederalists soon realized that they had made a mistake.
Senator Richard Henry Lee wrote to Patrick Henry telling him that additional amendments would not be forthcoming from Congress during
its present session, and that perhaps the Virginia legislature should have
adopted the amendments already proposed by Congress. Such protections, he declared, would have inculcated on the people's mind that
government was indeed limited and that rulers were always a potential
threat to rights. Additionally, Lee believed that we ought to get "as much
as we can at different times," so that one day most of our rights might
be protected. Consequently, Lee felt that the people ought to be encouraged to elect new federal representatives who would support further amendments to the Constitution.[117]

The year-long struggle over amendments to the Constitution was
nearing a climax. Senators Richard Henry Lee and John Walker (the
replacement for William Grayson, who had died in March 1790 on his
way to Congress) wrote the speaker of the Virginia house of delegates
on August 9, 1790, that

> The Assent of our Commonwealth may, we humbly conceive, secure
> the establishment of principles, that, by being fixed on the minds
> of the people, will be conducive hereafter to arrest the progress of
> power, should it be disposed to exert itself in future times to the
> injury of public liberty.[118]

During early 1791, Congress debated the reapportionment of the
House of Representatives based upon the federal census of 1790. Virginians feared that they might not fare well in this realignment. Consequently, on October 25, 1791, the Virginia assembly adopted the first
amendment proposed by Congress, which dealt with the apportionment
of the House of Representatives. On November 3, the state senate also
accepted this amendment, and the following day, Governor Beverley
Randolph transmitted the ratification to President Washington. This
action overcame the legislature's inertia, and on December 5, 1791, a
senate committee of the whole house endorsed the remaining eleven
amendments. Nine days later, the senate formally adopted the amendments. The next day, December 15, 1791, the assembly concurred, and
a week later Governor Henry Lee sent Virginia's ratification to President Washington. On December 30, the president laid Virginia's ratifica-

tion before Congress. Not until January 18, 1792, however, did the president deliver Vermont's official adoption of the amendments to Congress. With this transmittal, ten amendments to the Constitution had been adopted. On March 1, 1792, Secretary of State Thomas Jefferson notified the state executives that the first ten amendments to the Constitution—the Bill of Rights—had been adopted by three-fourths of the state legislatures and were now part of the Constitution.

NOTES:

[1]James Madison carried this view further than other delegates were prepared to go. On October 24, 1787, he wrote Thomas Jefferson that "A constitutional negative on the laws of the States seems equally necessary to secure individuals agst. encroachments on their rights. The mutability of the laws of the States is found to be a serious evil. The injustice of them has been so frequent and so flagrant as to alarm the most stedfast friends of Republicanism. I am persuaded I do not err in saying that the evils issuing from these sources contributed more to that uneasiness which produced the Convention, and prepared the public mind for a general reform, than those which accrued to our national character and interest from the inadequacy of the Confederation to its immediate objects." John P. Kaminski and Gaspare J. Saladino, ed., *Commentaries on the Constitution* (Vols. 13–17 of *The Documentary History of the Ratification of the Constitution*, Madison, Wis., 1976-), 1: 447.
[2]*Commentaries on the Constitution*, 1: 195–99.
[3]*Ibid.*, 238–40.
[4]*Ibid.*, 238.
[5]For Mason's objections and their circulation throughout America, see *ibid.*, 346–51.
[6]*Commentaries on the Constitution*, 2: 147–49.
[7]*Ibid.*, 364–66.
[8]October 5, *Commentaries on the Constitution*, 1: 323. "Brutus," New York's most important Antifederalist essayist, echoed Lee: "there are certain rights which mankind possess, over which government ought not to have any controul" (*New York Journal*, January 17, 1788, *Commentaries on the Constitution*, 3: 393).
[9]*Commentaries on the Constitution*, 1: 296.
[10]*Ibid.*, 329.
[11]"Brutus" II, *New York Journal*, November 1, 1787, *ibid.*, 525. Evidence indicates that "Brutus" might have been Melancton Smith.
[12]*Ibid.*, 339–40.
[13]Madison to Jefferson, October 17, 1788, Robert A. Rutland, ed., *The Papers of James Madison* (Charlottesville, Va., 1977), 11: 297.
[14]"Cincinnatus" I, *New York Journal*, November 1, 1787, *Commentaries on the Constitution*, 1: 529–33.
[15]Lee to Adams, October 27, 1787, *ibid.*, 484–85.
[16]Jefferson to Madison, December 20, Rutland, *Madison Papers*, 10:336.
[17]*Commentaries on the Constitution*, 2: 45–46.
[18]Merrill Jensen, John P. Kaminski, and Gaspare J. Saladino, ed., *Ratification of the Constitution by the States: Pennsylvania* (*The Documentary History of the Ratification of the Constitution*, Madison, Wis., 1976), 2: 388.
[19]*Commentaries on the Constitution*, 4: 60–69.
[20]Madison to Washington, February 15, 1788, Rutland, *Madison Papers*, 10: 510.
[21]Madison to Nicholas, Orange, April 8, 1788, Reuben T. Durrett Collection, University of Chicago Library.

[22]Patrick Henry Speech, June 9, 1788, *Debates and Other Proceedings of the Convention of Virginia* (3 vols., Petersburg, Va., 1788–89), 1: 160.

[23]Jefferson to Edward Carrington, May 27, 1788, Jefferson Papers, Library of Congress.

[24]Patrick Henry Speech, June 4, 1788, *Virginia Convention Debates*, 1: 36. All of the Virginia Convention debates will appear in the forthcoming *Ratification of the Constitution by the States: Virginia*, Volumes 2–3, ed. John P. Kaminski, Gaspare J. Saladino, Richard Leffler, and Charles D. Schoenleber (Volumes 9–10 of *The Documentary History of the Ratification of the Constitution*, Madison, Wis., 1990).

[25]Patrick Henry Speech, June 5, 1788, *Virginia Convention Debates*, 1: 56.

[26]Patrick Henry Speech, June 4, 1788, *ibid.*, 1: 37.

[27]Patrick Henry Speeches, June 4 and 9, 1788, *ibid.*, 1: 36, 159.

[28]Edmund Pendleton Speech, June 5, 1788, *ibid.*, 1: 49–50.

[29]Edmund Randolph Speech, June 6, 1788, *ibid.*, 1: 81.

[30]James Madison Speech, June 6, 1788, *ibid.*, 1: 96.

[31]Patrick Henry Speech, June 7, 1788, *ibid.*, 1: 141–42.

[32]James Monroe Speech, June 10, 1788, *ibid.*, 2: 28.

[33]James Monroe Speech, June 13, 1788, *ibid.*, 2: 130–31.

[34]James Monroe, *Some Observations on the Constitution* (n.p., 1788), 23–24.

[35]George Mason Speech, June 11, 1788, *Virginia Convention Debates*, 2: 67.

[36]George Mason Speech, June 16, 1788, *ibid.*, 3: 30–33.

[37]Patrick Henry Speech, June 16, 1788, *ibid.*, 3: 34–36.

[38]*Ibid.*

[39]Lamb to Clinton, June 17, 1788, Lamb Papers, The New-York Historical Society.

[40]Clinton to Lamb, June 21, 1788, *ibid.*

[41]Yates to George Mason, c. June 21, 1788, Emmet Collection, New York Public Library.

[42]Patrick Henry Speech, June 7, 1788, *Virginia Convention Debates*, 1: 142–43.

[43]Patrick Henry Speech, June 9, 1788, *ibid.*, 1: 175.

[44]*Ibid.*, 177.

[45]Edmund Randolph Speech, June 24, 1788, *ibid.*, 3: 170–71.

[46]James Madison Speech, June 24, 1788, *ibid.*, 3: 183.

[47]This letter was printed in the Albany *Federal Herald*, February 25, 1788 (*Commentaries on the Constitution*, 4: 200). It was reprinted four times in New York and once each in New Jersey, Pennsylvania, and Maryland.

[48]Thomas Tredwell Speech, July 2, 1788, *The Debates in the Several State Conventions on the Adoption of the Federal Constitution*, ed. Jonathan Elliot (2nd ed., rev., Philadelphia, 1836–1845), 2: 401.

[49]John P. Kaminski, "New York: The Reluctant Pillar," in *The Reluctant Pillar: New York and the Adoption of the Federal Constitution*, ed. Stephen L. Schechter (Troy, N.Y., 1985), 107–8.

[50]Abraham Bancker to Evert Bancker, July 12, Bancker Family Correspondence, The New-York Historical Society; DeWitt Clinton to Charles Tillinghast, July 12, DeWitt Clinton Papers, Columbia University Libraries.

[51]Kaminski, "The Reluctant Pillar," 108–9.

[52]Copy of a Letter from Poughkeepsie, dated Friday, July 25, 1788, New York *Independent Journal*, July 28 (supplement extraordinary).

[53]Samuel Osgood to Elbridge Gerry, February 13, 1789, Gerry Papers, Library of Congress.

[54]Merrill Jensen et al., ed., *The Documentary History of the First Federal Elections 1788–1790* (4 vols., Madison, Wis., 1976–1989), 1: 262.

[55]*Ibid.*, 263.

[56]"A Word to the Wise to the Electors of Pennsylvania," *Pennsylvania Mercury*, September 13, 1788, *ibid.*, 273.

[57]"Cassius," *Federal Gazette*, October 9, 1788, *ibid.*, 312.

[58]Madison to Thomas Jefferson, December 12, 1788, *ibid.*, 370.

[59]"Federalist," *Boston Gazette*, September 8, 1788, *ibid.*, 459–60.

[60]"A Federal Correspondent," Boston *Independent Chronicle*, September 11, 1788, *ibid.*, 461.

[61]"Honestus," Boston *Independent Chronicle*, October 30, 1788, *ibid.*, 473.

[62]Elbridge Gerry to Samuel Dexter, Cambridge, January 12, 1789, Manuscripts Department, Lilly Library, Indiana University.

[63]*First Federal Elections*, 1: 647.

[64]Gordon DenBoer and Lucy Trumbull Brown, ed., *The Documentary History of the First Federal Elections 1788-1790* (Madison, Wis., 1984), 2: 392.

[65]*Ibid.*, 276.

[66]Madison to George Eve, Orange, January 2, 1789, *ibid.*, 330–31.

[67]*Ibid.*, 346.

[68]DeWitt Clinton to Charles Clinton, New York, November 25, 1788, *First Federal Elections*, 3: 212.

[69]Lansing to Abraham Yates, Jr., August 3, 1788, *ibid.*, 202.

[70]*Ibid.*, 203.

[71]*Ibid.*, 207–8.

[72]"A Federal Republican," *New York Journal*, November 27, 1788, *ibid.*, 213.

[73]Smith to Livingston, January 1, 1788, *ibid.*, 260–61.

[74]Federal Republican Committee to County Committees of New York, November 4, 1788, *ibid.*, 207–8.

[75]"A Federal Republican" No. 2, *New York Journal*, December 11, 1788, *ibid.*, 214–15.

[76]Dorothy Twohig, ed., *Presidential Series*, in W.W. Abbot et al., ed., *The Papers of George Washington* (Charlottesville, Va., 1987), 2: 176.

[77]James Monroe to Thomas Jefferson, Fredericksburg, February 15, 1789, Jefferson Papers, Library of Congress.

[78]All of the congressional debate over the proposed amendments is found in Bernard Schwartz, ed., *The Roots of The Bill of Rights: An Illustrated Source Book of American Freedom* (5 vols., New York, 1971, 1980), volume 5.

[79]Mason to John Mason, July 31, 1789, Robert A. Rutland, ed., *The Papers of George Mason* (3 vols., Chapel Hill, N.C., 1970), 1164.

[80]Edmund Randolph to James Madison, Williamsburg, June 30, 1789, Rutland, *Madison*, 12: 273.

[81]Quoted in Kenneth R. Bowling, " 'A Tub to the Whale': The Founding Fathers and Adoption of the Federal Bill of Rights," *The Journal of the Early Republic* 8 (Fall 1989): 241.

[82]George Clymer to Tench Coxe, New York, June 28, 1789, Coxe Papers, Tench Coxe Section, Historical Society of Pennsylvania.

[83]Elbridge Gerry to Samuel R. Gerry, New York, June 30, 1790, Samuel Russel Gerry Papers, Massachusetts Historical Society.

[84]Washington to Madison, n.d., Rutland, *Madison*, 12: 191.

[85]James Madison Speech, August 13, 1789, Schwartz, *The Roots of The Bill of Rights*, 5: 1066–67.

[86]Roger Sherman Speech, August 13, 1789, *ibid.*, 1066.

[87]James Jackson Speech, August 13, 1789, *ibid.*, 1072.

[88]Misc. Legislative Papers, House Folder #3352, Massachusetts Archives.

[89]*Ibid.*, Senate File.

[90]Broadside (Evans #22655). The report was printed in the state's newspapers. See the supplement to the Boston *Independent Chronicle*, March 4, 1790.

[91]*Ibid.*

[92]*Ibid.*

[93]*Ibid.*

[94]Abigail Adams to Cotton Tufts, Tufts Papers, Ac. 13,324, Library of Congress.

[95]John Quincy Adams to John Adams, Newburyport, April 5, 1790, Worthington C. Ford, ed., *Writings of John Quincy Adams* (New York, 1931), 1: 51–52.

[96]Stephen Higginson to John Adams, Boston, March 24, 1790, "Letters of Stephen Higginson, 1783-1804," *Annual Report* of the American Historical Association for . . . 1896 (2 vols., Washington, D.C., 1897), 1: 776.

[97]Jefferson to William Short, Philadelphia, March 15, 1791, Short Papers, Library of Congress.

[98]Jefferson to Gore, Philadelphia, August 8, 1791, RG 59, Department of State, American Letters, National Archives. Jefferson had failed to consider the effect Vermont's admission to the Union on March 3, 1791, would have on the adoption of the proposed amendments—eleven states were now needed to obtain the necessary three-fourths approval.

[99]Gore to Jefferson, Boston, August 18, 1791, RG 59, Department of State, Miscellaneous Letters, National Archives.

[100]Lee and Grayson to Governor Randolph, New York, September 28, 1789, Virginia Miscellany, AC 2313, Library of Congress.

[101]*Ibid.*

[102]Grayson to Patrick Henry, New York, September 29, 1789, Patrick Henry Papers, Library of Congress.

[103]David Stuart to George Washington, December 3, 1789, Washington Papers, Library of Congress.

[104]Madison to George Washington, Orange, December 5, 1789, Rutland, *Madison*, 12: 458.

[105]Edward Carrington to James Madison, Richmond, December 20, 1789, *ibid.*, 463.

[106]James Madison to George Washington, Orange, November 20, 1789, *ibid.*, 453.

[107]Edmund Randolph to George Washington, Richmond, November 26, 1789, Washington Papers, Library of Congress.

[108]Hardin Burnley to James Madison, Richmond, November 28, 1789, Rutland, *Madison*, 12: 456. Madison quoted much of Burnley's letter in a letter to George Washington on December 5, *ibid.*, 12: 458-59.

[109]Carrington to Madison, Richmond, December 20, 1789, *ibid.*, 464. Hardin Burnley reported that "the ten first were agreed to with even less opposition than they experienced in the Committee [of the whole], & that wh. passed on the 11th & 12th. was rescinded by a majority of about twelve" (to James Madison, Richmond, December 5, 1789), *ibid.*, 460.

[110]The committee was composed of Ralph Wormeley, Edmund Randolph, Francis Corbin, Isaac Zane, Edward Carrington, Wilson Cary Nicholas, James Breckinridge, Henry Lee, Miles King, and Alexander Henderson.

[111]Hardin Burnley to James Madison, Richmond, December 5, 1789, Rutland, *Madison*, 12: 460.

[112]*Journal of the Senate of the Commonwealth of Virginia* (Richmond, 1790), 61-66.

[113]*Ibid.*, 66-67.

[114]John Dawson to James Madison, Richmond, December 17, 1789, Rutland, *Madison*, 12: 461.

[115]Edmund Randolph to George Washington, Richmond, December 15, 1789, Washington Papers, Library of Congress.

[116]James Madison to George Washington, Georgetown, January 4, 1790, Rutland, *Madison*, 12: 466-67.

[117]Richard Henry Lee to Patrick Henry, New York, June 10, 1790, James Curtis Ballagh, ed., *The Letters of Richard Henry Lee*, (2 vols., New York, 1914), 2: 522-25.

[118]Lee and Walker to the Speaker of the Virginia House of Delegates, New York, August 9, 1790, Executive Communications, Virginia State Library.

The Bill of Rights: A Bibliographic Essay

GASPARE J. SALADINO

University of Wisconsin-Madison

Most scholars of the United States Constitution agree that the document could not have been ratified if its supporters had not promised the American people in 1787 and 1788 that the first government under the Constitution would draft a bill of rights. Some believe that this promise was the principal reason for ratification, others that it was one of the major reasons; none deny its vital importance. Yet for about 150 years after its ratification in 1791 the Bill of Rights, as a concept, received scant attention from the courts and the public. Even scholars took little notice of it; not a single book devoted completely to the Bill of Rights was published, while only one (Nelson B. Lasson's 1937 study of the Fourth Amendment) appeared on an individual amendment. Between 1939 and 1941, stated Michael Kammen, the Bill of Rights was "discovered," as Americans celebrated that document's sesquicentennial, and many individuals and organizations had become worried that the rights of minorities were being threatened. After World War II, however, interest in the document waned. The Bill of Rights was "rediscovered" in 1955 and 1956, when a powerful reaction developed to the tyranny of McCarthyism and when black Americans, in increasing numbers, insisted upon equal rights.[1]

General Primary and Secondary Sources

The general works covered in this first section deal with all of the individual topics considered in subsequent sections; they will not be mentioned again unless they are deemed especially important to one of those topics. In this essay, the focus will be on the Bill of Rights—the first ten amendments—and not on the rights that are found in the body of the Constitution.

In 1950 Zechariah Chafee, Jr., developed a course at Harvard University entitled "Fundamental Human Rights" and in the next two years published three pamphlets of documents to accompany the course. Chafee was interested primarily in the human rights embodied in the Constitution, not the Bill of Rights. Nevertheless, these documents are critical to the study of the latter document. Most important, the pamphlets include the great documents of English constitutional history from Magna Carta (1215) to the Bill of Rights (1689); colonial charters; documents of the Continental and Confederation congresses (i.e., Declaration of Independence, Articles of Confederation, and Northwest Ordinance); and the state constitutions adopted before 1791. Although he did not demonstrate it, Chafee was convinced that the state constitutions and declarations of rights were the most important sources for the Bill of Rights. He printed this material because he believed that the documents of the debate over the ratification of the Constitution were not sufficiently informative about the intent of the Framers. Therefore, reasoned Chafee, the scholar has to determine the total knowledge and experience of the Framers in order to understand their intent. Chafee insisted that his documents were well known to the Framers. His approach was not unique, but no one had developed it so fully.[2]

In 1959, Richard L. Perry and John C. Cooper, following Chafee's pattern, published for the American Bar Foundation some thirty-two documents, with descriptive marginalia and succinct and informative headnotes and footnotes. Their purpose was "to present in a single usable volume the historic documents constituting the major legal sources of our individual liberties." "The liberties of the American citizen," stated Perry, "depend upon the existence of established and known rules of limiting the authority and discretion of men wielding the power of government." Virtually all of the documents that appear in this volume had already been printed by Chafee, although, like Chafee, the editors omitted the amendments that had been proposed by the state conventions that ratified the Constitution in 1787 and 1788.[3]

During the 1950s, two important monographs were published on the Bill of Rights by Robert A. Rutland and Edward Dumbauld. Rutland's book, *The Birth of the Bill of Rights, 1776–1791* (Chapel Hill, N.C., 1955), the first devoted solely to the Bill of Rights, discussed the English and colonial antecedents of that document; the pivotal role of the new revolutionary state constitutions and their declarations of rights (especially the Virginia Declaration of Rights written by George Mason); the role of the Constitutional Convention; the debate over the ratification of the Constitution (with particular emphasis on the ratifying conventions); the efforts to call a second constitutional convention; the debate in the first federal Congress that drafted the Bill of Rights; and the dynamic role of the central character in that congressional debate, James Madison, whose motives, according to Rutland, were primarily political. (Madison promised his constituents that he would fight for a bill of rights if they elected him to the first U.S. House of Representatives.) This outline of topics, though not unique to Rutland, firmly established a pattern that would be followed by most scholars of the Bill of Rights.

Rutland concluded that the Revolutionary generation insisted upon explicit statements of the personal rights that were theirs by common law and most particularly by the fundamental laws of nature. The Bill of Rights and the state declarations of rights represented "the sum total of American experience and experimentation with civil liberty up to their adoption"; the former "served notice to all the world that national independence, without personal liberty, was an empty prize." During the debate over the ratification of the Constitution, the issue of the Bill of Rights was, according to Rutland, the most "potent" weapon in the arsenal of the Antifederalists—"the chief stumbling block to ratification." It was a major issue in most of the states, especially in Pennsylvania, Massachusetts, Maryland, North and South Carolina, Virginia, and New York. In his appendices, Rutland reprinted the Virginia Declaration of Rights, followed by the twelve amendments that the first federal Congress submitted to the states in 1789.[4] No two documents concerning the Bill of Rights have been reprinted more often.

Edward Dumbauld, in *The Bill of Rights and What It Means Today* (Norman, Okla., 1957), stated that the Bill of Rights was the "vehicle whereby the political philosophy of the Declaration of Independence was incorporated into the Constitution." He traced the origin and significance of each of the first ten amendments. In both the text and a useful summary table, Dumbauld followed each amendment through its English antecedents, colonial practices, the state declarations of rights, and proposals made by the state ratifying conventions. He also followed through the first federal Congress the amendments that James Madison presented to that body. In appendices, Dumbauld published the proposals made by the state conventions or convention minorities and the principal documents recording the adoption of the passage of amendments by the first federal Congress. Dumbauld believed that the amendments proposed by the state conventions, especially those of the Virginia Convention, had the greatest influence upon James Madison. The state declarations of rights also influenced Madison, who created a bill of rights from several sources. Lastly, Dumbauld demonstrated that

Thomas Jefferson had a profound impact in getting Madison to support a bill of rights.[5]

In 1965, Irving Brant, Madison's principal biographer, published an unwieldy but learned volume on the Bill of Rights. Brant expanded the concept of the Bill of Rights to include the preamble to the Constitution (principles of government) and the libertarian provisions of the Constitution (*e.g.,* habeas corpus, bills of attainder, etc.). His work is best on the English and colonial antecedents of the Bill of Rights. Brant also maintained that Madison's motives were not primarily political.[6]

Six years later, Bernard Schwartz published a two-volume compendium on the first ten amendments, *The Bill of Rights: A Documentary History* (New York, 1971). This work is perhaps the single most useful source for the study of these amendments. Schwartz's plan of organization suggests his beliefs as to the nature of the key sources: its major sections are: (1) the English antecedents, 1215–1689; (2) the colonial charters and laws, 1606–1701; (3) the Revolutionary declarations and constitutions, 1761–1783; (4) examples of judicial review in the Confederation Period; (5) the U.S. Constitution (largely the ratification debates); (6) the state ratifying conventions; (7) the legislative history of the Bill of Rights; and (8) the ratification of the Bill of Rights. His compilation also includes a table of the sources of the Bill of Rights. Each section is preceded by a "commentary" or introduction, and occasionally a document is preceded by a "commentary," thereby forming a true documentary history. In 1977, Schwartz expanded his commentaries in a book entitled *The Great Rights of Mankind: A History of the American Bill of Rights* (New York). He argued that the "bill of rights concept is primarily American in origin" and that the Bill of Rights "represented a logical progression from what had gone before in both England and America." He showed that, during the American Revolution, the concept was fully developed; the Revolution linked colonial liberties and the Bill of Rights. Schwartz emphasized the concept of judicial review as "the sine qua non of an effective constitution or bill of rights." The ratification debate centered around George Mason's objections, the first of which complained about the lack of a declaration of rights; the ratifying conventions "gave voice to the public sentiment" for such a document. Schwartz stressed Madison's role and Thomas Jefferson's influence upon him. He included a detailed legislative history of the adoption of the Bill of Rights by the first federal Congress and a substantial account of that document's ratification by the states. Lastly, Schwartz provided several tables on the origins of the Bill of Rights.[7]

In 1987, to celebrate the Constitution's bicentennial, Philip B. Kurland and Ralph Lerner of the University of Chicago published, under the auspices of that university's press, a massive five-volume work called *The Founders' Constitution.* "Seeking to recover an 'original understanding' " of those who were involved in the debate over the Constitution, Kurland and Lerner collected numerous documents from well over 100 printed sources. The first volume (also published in paperback) prints "fundamental documents" that are concerned with seventeen major themes which the editors have keyed to the Preamble to the Constitution; each theme is preceded by a substantial introduction. Theme 14 is "Rights"; in their introduction to the fifty-six documents on rights (1639–1789), the editors stated that "From the beginning, it seems, the language of America has been the language of rights." The other volumes are organized by the clauses of the Constitution and by the clauses in the first twelve amendments to it. The fifth volume is devoted entirely to the concept of a bill of rights and the first twelve amendments; for the first ten amendments it presents documents that range from John Calvin's *Institutes of the Christian Religion* (1536) to the United States Senate's reception of abolition petitions (1836). At the end of the documents for each of the clauses are listed additional readings of documents. Because the volumes are organized by clauses, there is no subject index. There are, however, brief indices of constitutional provisions, authors, and documents, as well as a table of judicial cases.

In 1988, Leonard W. Levy published a fine article on the Bill of Rights. Levy viewed the Bill of Rights as a victory of individual liberty against the power of government; it demonstrated that "the citizen is the master of his government, not its subject." He argued that Antifederalists (some of whom were demagogues) overstated their case in order to get public support, but that the public's fears were genuine. Past experiences had shown Americans that declarations of rights were necessary. Federalist arguments denying the need for a bill of rights, he maintained, were "patently absurd"; Federalists made "a colossal error of judgment" by not including a bill of rights in the Constitution. Levy contended further that James Madison, who shepherded the Bill of Rights through the first federal Congress, should more properly be called the "father of the Bill of Rights," than of the Constitution. Madison was moved primarily by political expediency, Levy noted, but he also believed genuinely that the fears of the people had to be quieted and that the power of all branches of government had to be restricted. The ratification of the Bill of Rights had "a great healing effect," Levy suggested, as the opposition to the Constitution ended almost immediately.[8]

Students of the Bill of Rights should also consult the published papers of three of the major figures in the adoption of that document—James Madison, George Mason, and Thomas Jefferson. Volumes 10, 11, and 12 of *The Papers of James Madison*, edited and well annotated by Robert A. Rutland and Charles F. Hobson, are invaluable; they cover the ratification debate, the movement for a second constitutional convention, Madison's unsuccessful campaign for the first U.S. Senate, his successful campaign for the first U.S. House of Representatives, and the legislative history of the adoption of the Bill of Rights. Volume 12 includes a headnote analyzing the congressional sources for the study of the Bill of Rights. Rutland also edited a three-volume edition of *The Papers of George Mason* detailing Mason's lifelong interest in the protection of the rights and liberties of the people. Julian P. Boyd's comprehensive and heavily annotated edition of *The Papers of Thomas Jefferson* demonstrates that Jefferson had numerous correspondents on the Bill of Rights and that he impressed upon them its absolute necessity.[9]

Works by the two finest scholars of the Confederation Period provide the reader with the historical context in which to understand the adoption and ratification of the Constitution and the Bill of Rights. These are: Merrill Jensen, *The New Nation: A History of the United States During the Confederation, 1781-1789* (New York, 1950), and *The Making of the American Constitution* (Princeton, N.J., 1964); and Richard B. Morris, *The Forging of the Union, 1781-1789* (New York, 1987). Another useful secondary source is Forrest McDonald, *E Pluribus Unum: The Formation of the American Republic, 1776-1790* (1965; reprint ed., Indianapolis, 1979).

In the last two or three decades, many historians have contributed to our understanding of what Richard B. Morris called "the theoretical underpinnings of the Revolutionary generation"—and, by extension, of the Bill of Rights, one of that generation's most significant achievements. Listed below, by date of publication, are some of these works. Those for the years prior to and including 1980 are: *Fame and the Founding Fathers: Essays by Douglass Adair* [1944-1967], ed. Trevor Colbourn (New York, 1974); H. Trevor Colbourn, *The Lamp of Experience: Whig History and the Intellectual Origins of the American Revolution* (Chapel Hill, N.C., 1965); Bernard Bailyn, *The Ideological Origins of the American Revolution* (Cambridge, Mass., 1967); Gordon S. Wood, *The Creation of the American Republic, 1776-1787* (Chapel Hill, N.C., 1969); J.G.A. Pocock, *The Machiavellian Moment: Florentine Political Thought and the Atlantic Republican Tradition* (Princeton, N.J., 1975); Henry Steele Commager, *The Empire of Reason: How Europe Imag-*

ined and America Realized The Enlightenment (Garden City, N.Y., 1977); Lance Banning, *The Jeffersonian Persuasion: Evolution of a Party Ideology* (Ithaca, N.Y., 1978); Drew R. McCoy, *The Elusive Republic: Political Economy in Jeffersonian America* (Chapel Hill, N.C., 1980); and John M. Murrin, "The Great Inversion, or Court versus Country," in *Three British Revolutions, 1641, 1688, 1776*, ed. J.G.A. Pocock (Princeton, N.J., 1980).

Beginning in 1984, due perhaps in part to the coming bicentennial of the Constitution and the Bill of Rights, a veritable avalanche of books began to appear. These include: Joyce Appleby, *Capitalism and a New Social Order: The Republican Vision of the 1790s* (New York, 1984); John Patrick Diggins, *The Lost Soul of American Politics: Virtue, Self-Interest, and the Foundations of Liberalism* (New York, 1984); Forrest McDonald, *Novus Ordo Seclorum: The Intellectual Origins of the Constitution* (Lawrence, Kan., 1985); J.G.A. Pocock, *Virtue, Commerce, and History: Essays on Political Thought and History, Chiefly in the Eighteenth Century* (Cambridge, Eng., 1985); Jack P. Greene, *Peripheries and Center: Constitutional Development in the Extended Politics of the British Empire and the United States, 1607–1788* (Athens, Ga., 1986); John Phillip Reid, *The Constitutional History of the American Revolution: The Authority of Rights* (Madison, Wis., 1986); *Beyond Confederation: Origins of the Constitution and American National Identity*, ed. Richard Beeman, Stephen Botein, and Edward C. Carter II (Chapel Hill, N.C., 1987); Richard B. Bernstein with Kym S. Rice, *Are We To Be A Nation? The Making of the Constitution* (Cambridge, Mass., 1987); Ralph Lerner, *The Thinking Revolutionary: Principle and Practice in the New Republic* (Ithaca, N.Y., 1987); John Phillip Reid, *The Constitutional History of the American Revolution: The Authority to Tax* (Madison, Wis., 1987); *Conceptual Change and the Constitution*, ed. Terence Ball and J.G.A. Pocock (Lawrence, Kan., 1988); Anne M. Cohler, *Montesquieu's Comparative Politics and the Spirit of American Constitutionalism* (Lawrence, Kan., 1988); Michael Lienesch, *New Order of the Ages: Time, the Constitution, and the Making of Modern American Political Thought* (Princeton, N.J., 1988); Forrest McDonald and Ellen Shapiro McDonald, *Requiem: Variations on Eighteenth-Century Themes* (Lawrence, Kan., 1988); Edmund S. Morgan, *Inventing the People: The Rise of Popular Sovereignty in England and America* (New York and London, 1988); Thomas L. Pangle, *The Spirit of Modern Republicanism: The Moral Vision of the American Founders and the Philosophy of Locke* (Chicago, 1988); John Phillip Reid, *The Concept of Liberty in the Age of the American Revolution* (Chicago, 1988); Oscar and Lilian Handlin, *Liberty in Expansion,*

1760–1850 (New York, 1989); John Phillip Reid, *The Concept of Representation in the Age of the American Revolution* (Chicago, 1989); David A.J. Richards, *Foundations of American Constitutionalism* (New York, 1989); and Robert E. Shalhope, *The Roots of Democracy: American Thought and Culture, 1760–1800* (Boston, 1990). (The volume by the Handlins is the second of a projected four-volume series in which the Handlins will tell "the story of liberty in America.")

Useful historiographical articles on the question of republicanism are: Robert E. Shalhope, "Toward a Republican Synthesis: The Emergence of an Understanding of Republicanism in American Historiography," *William and Mary Quarterly*, 3rd ser., 29 (1972): 49–80, and "Republicanism and Early American Historiography," *ibid.* 39 (1982): 334–56; Isaac Kramnick, "Republican Revisionism Revisited," *American Historical Review* 87 (1982): 629–44; and Linda K. Kerber, "The Republican Ideology of the Revolutionary Generation," *American Quarterly* 37 (1985): 474–95. Also valuable is the bibliography in Shalhope's *The Roots of Democracy.*

Constitutional Convention: Primary and Secondary Sources

A bill of rights did not become an issue in the Constitutional Convention until its deliberations were almost over, at which time George Mason and Edmund Randolph of Virginia and Elbridge Gerry of Massachusetts demanded that one be added because the Constitution had created a powerful general government. Therefore, the amount of Convention material concerning a bill of rights is slight. Such is not the case, however, with the debates on the manner in which the Constitution was to be amended.

The basic source for the study of the Convention is Max Farrand's *The Records of the Federal Convention of 1787.* This work was first published in three volumes in 1911; it was reissued in 1923, 1927, and 1934, and expanded to four volumes in 1937, the sesquicentennial of the Constitution. *The Records* include the notes of debates of several members (especially James Madison), the journal of the Convention, and a large number of post-Convention documents written by members of that body. In 1987, James H. Hutson published a supplement to *The Records,* adding notes of debates, diaries, and letters of the members, among other things. The volumes are well-indexed.[10] For two works that rearrange the notes of the debates, by subject and article, respectively, the reader should consult *Drafting the Federal Constitution: A Rearrangement of Madison's Notes Giving Consecutive Developments of Provisions in the Constitution of the United States, Supplemented by*

Documents Pertaining to the Philadelphia Convention and to the Ratification Processes, and Including Insertions by the Compiler, comp. Arthur Taylor Prescott (University, La., 1941); and *1787: Drafting the U.S. Constitution,* ed. Wilbourn E. Benton, 2 vols. (College Station, Tex., 1986).

Three fine monographs on the Convention are Charles Warren's *The Making of the Constitution* (Boston, 1928), Clinton Rossiter's *1787, The Grand Convention* (New York and London, 1966), and Calvin C. Jillson, *Constitution Making: Conflict and Consensus in the Federal Convention of 1787* (New York, 1988). Rossiter's book, with a foreword by Richard B. Morris, was reissued in paperback by W.W. Norton and Company in 1987. Also useful is Ralph R. Martig's "Amending the Constitution, Article Five: The Keystone of the Arch," *Michigan Law Review* 35 (1937): 1253–85.[11] Another interesting article is René de Visme Williamson's "Political Process or Judicial Process: The Bill of Rights and the Framers of the Constitution," *Journal of Politics* 23 (1961): 199–211. Realizing that the Framers of the Constitution had said little about a bill of rights in the Convention, Williamson searched for their thoughts in statements that they made during the ratification debate. He concluded that the Framers wanted to protect the rights and liberties of the people through the political process, not the judicial one.

The Debate over the Ratification of the Constitution: Primary and Secondary Sources

Eleven states ratified the Constitution between December 7, 1787, and July 26, 1788; the other two, North Carolina and Rhode Island, ratified on November 21, 1789, and May 29, 1790, respectively. The addition of amendments, especially a bill of rights, was a critical issue in most of the states. The conventions of Massachusetts, South Carolina, New Hampshire, Virginia, and New York, in their forms of ratification, recommended amendments to the Constitution; the minorities of the Pennsylvania and Maryland conventions proposed amendments which did not become part of the records of those bodies. The first North Carolina convention, which adjourned on August 4, 1788, without ratifying the Constitution, drafted amendments that were sent to the Confederation Congress. Shortly after, the proposed amendments of these state conventions and the minority of the Maryland convention were published by printer Augustine Davis of Richmond, Virginia, under the title *The Ratifications of the New Foederal Constitution, Together with the Amendments, Proposed by the Several States* (reprinted elsewhere in this volume). Davis explained: "The Collection Was Made at the Instance of Several Gentlemen, Who Supposed, that It Would be Useful and Acceptable to the Public, to be Able to Compare at Once the Sentiments of the Different States Together." These "Several Gentlemen" probably wanted to use this pamphlet to encourage the calling of a second constitutional convention, or to influence the persons who would stand for election to the first federal Congress, or both. In May 1790, the Rhode Island convention became the last convention to propose amendments as part of its form of ratification. These Rhode Island amendments, along with the amendments that are part of the forms of ratification of the other state conventions, are in the second volume of the U.S. Department of State's *Documentary History of the Constitution of the United States of America, 1787–1790*, 5 vols. (Washington, D.C., 1894–1903).

Upon its completion in about fifteen years, *The Documentary History of the Ratification of the Constitution* will be the most extensive collection of documents ever published on that topic. This project has searched over 500 libraries and 150 newspapers for material written about the Constitution and the Bill of Rights between 1787 and 1791; these searches have yielded more than 50,000 items. Eight of twenty projected volumes have been printed; volume 20 will deal specifically with the Bill of Rights.[12] Much material on the Bill of Rights, however, can be found in six of this documentary history's eight published volumes: in the four volumes of *Commentaries on the Constitution: Public and Private*, in the volume on Pennsylvania and its accompanying microfiche supplement, and in the first of three projected volumes on Virginia. *Commentaries on the Constitution* is a series that presents the day-to-day regional and national debate on the Constitution, drawing together the most widely reprinted newspaper and magazine essays, the most widely circulated pamphlets and broadsides, and a host of private and public letters. The editors let the documents speak for themselves, although they provide information on the authorship, circulation, and impact of many items. In the Pennsylvania volume, the numerous newspaper items and the extensive debates of the Pennsylvania convention are especially useful on the issue of a bill of rights, while the first Virginia volume has many letters and newspaper items on amendments.[13] Volumes 2 and 3 of Virginia (scheduled for publication in 1990) will have many additional letters and newspapers, two lengthy pamphlets, and the voluminous debates of that state's convention.

Until *The Documentary History of the Ratification of the Constitution* is completed, the reader should turn to four enduring works that this edition will replace—*Debates in the Several State Conventions, on the Adoption of the Federal Constitution*, ed. Jonathan Elliot, 2nd ed.,

5 vols. (Philadelphia, 1836–1845); *Pamphlets on the Constitution of the United States Published During Its Discussion by the People, 1787–1788,* ed. Paul Leicester Ford (Brooklyn, N.Y., 1888); *Essays on the Constitution of the United States, Published During Its Discussion by the People, 1787–1788,* ed. Paul Leicester Ford (Brooklyn, 1892); and U.S. Department of State, *Documentary History of the Constitution of the United States of America, 1787–1790.* The fourth and fifth volumes of this last work are filled with correspondence of some of the principal participants in the ratification debate. (The "integrity" of Elliot's *Debates* is considered by James H. Hutson in his *Texas Law Review* article [see note 10].)

One of the most valuable collections of primary sources published in recent years is the late Herbert J. Storing's and Murray Dry's, *The Complete Anti-Federalist,* 7 vols. (Chicago, 1981).[14] The second volume includes the objections of the three delegates to the Constitutional Convention (Elbridge Gerry, George Mason, and Edmund Randolph) who refused to sign the Constitution and the major Antifederalist essays; the third through the sixth are organized by states; and the seventh is a comprehensive index. In his extensive and cogent commentaries and notes, Storing summarized the arguments of the major essays, identified quotations and references, speculated on the authorship of many essays, and provided numerous cross-references to similar arguments. The first volume, which is also printed separately, is an analysis of Antifederalist political thought; the last chapter before the conclusion is devoted to the Bill of Rights—the principal Antifederalist legacy. The Antifederalists, stated Storing, were pleased to get a bill of rights, but they also wanted structural amendments that would have weakened the general government even further. Storing argued that the emphasis placed upon the need for a bill of rights made the Constitution a very different document in 1788 from what it had been in 1787. The Constitution had been ratified, he concluded, with the belief that it would be amended immediately to include a bill of rights.[15]

Several one-volume collections of documents, which have substantial analytical introductions, are also valuable sources for a study of the Bill of Rights. Four of these collections were published in the mid-1960s at the height of the interest in the Constitution generated by the critiques and defenses of Charles A. Beard's influential *An Economic Interpretation of the Constitution of the United States* (New York, 1913). They are: *The States Rights Debate: Antifederalism and the Constitution,* ed. Alpheus Thomas Mason (Englewood Cliffs, N.J., 1964); *The Antifederalist Papers,* ed. Morton Borden (East Lansing, Mich., 1965); *The Antifederalists,* ed. Cecilia M. Kenyon (Indianapolis and New

York, 1966); and *Anti-Federalists versus Federalists: Selected Documents*, ed. John D. Lewis (San Francisco, 1967). Each of these historians recognized the central nature of the debate over the need for a bill of rights. Mason, for example, stated that the Bill of Rights was the "heart" of the Constitution; and that the Antifederalists "exploded with fury" once they realized the need for a bill of rights to counteract the consolidated government created by the Constitution. Borden declared that "almost to a man" the Antifederalists demanded a bill of rights, while Lewis placed the Antifederalist desire for a bill of rights alongside their fear of a national judiciary. (See below for Kenyon.)

In 1978, Walter Hartwell Bennett edited and published (with a lengthy commentary) *Letters from the Federal Farmer to the Republican* (University, Ala.). This slender volume includes the two pamphlets consisting of eighteen "letters" of the "Federal Farmer," one of the principal exponents of a bill of rights and perhaps the best of all the Antifederalist writers. (Many contemporaries believed that Richard Henry Lee of Virginia was the "Federal Farmer.") A selection of these "letters" is in *Empire and Nation: Letters from a Farmer in Pennsylvania, John Dickinson; Letters from the Federal Farmer, Richard Henry Lee*, ed. Forrest McDonald (Englewood Cliffs, N.J., 1962). (Richard Henry Lee's authorship of the "letters" has been seriously challenged by Gordon S. Wood, who concluded that the "Federal Farmer" was probably a New Yorker. He reached this conclusion in a well-researched and argued article entitled, "The Authorship of the *Letters from the Federal Farmer," William and Mary Quarterly*, 3rd ser., 31 [1974]: 299–308. For the assertion that this New Yorker was Antifederalist leader Melancton Smith, see Robert Webking, "Melancton Smith and the *Letters from the Federal Farmer," ibid.* 3rd ser. 44 [1987]: 510-28. Webking's assertion is reinforced by Joseph Kent McGaughy in "The Authorship of *The Letters from the Federal Farmer*, Revisited," *New York History* 70 [1989]: 153–70. And for a brief review of the question of authorship of the "Federal Farmer," see *The Documentary History of the Ratification of the Constitution*, ed. Kaminski and Saladino, 14: 15–16.)

The bicentennial of the Constitution has also produced several single-volume collections. These volumes, which lack the long analytical introductions of the above collections, are: *The Essential Antifederalist*, ed. W.B. Allen and Gordon Lloyd (Lanham, Md., 1985); *The Origins of the American Constitution: A Documentary History*, ed. Michael Kammen (New York, 1986); *The Anti-Federalist Papers and the Constitutional Convention Debates*, ed. Ralph Ketcham (New York and Scarborough, Ontario, 1986); *The American Constitution, For and Against: The Federalist and Anti-Federalist Papers*, ed. J.R. Pole (New York,

1987); and *Federalists and Antifederalists: The Debate Over the Ratification of the Constitution*, ed. John P. Kaminski and Richard Leffler (Madison, Wis., 1989). Allen and Lloyd insisted that, in order to understand the desire for a Bill of Rights, one must understand such basic Antifederalist complaints as the consolidated, despotic, and aristocratic nature of the government created by the Constitution. Kammen pointed to an important difference between the state bills of rights and the federal Bill of Rights. The former used the subjunctive voice; in other words, a person "ought" not to be required to do something. The latter employed the declarative or imperative voice; Congress "shall" or "shall not" do something. Kammen explained this shift in language by pointing out that the new Constitution had created a very powerful government whose powers had to be curbed. Pole and Ketcham also saw the demand for a bill of rights as a principal Antifederalist demand, while Kaminski and Leffler believed that it was the most important issue debated by Federalists and Antifederalists.[16]

Charles A. Beard's *An Economic Interpretation of the Constitution* has cast a long shadow over the general historiography of the Constitution and the Bill of Rights. Beard emphasized economic classes and geographical sections in explaining the ratification of the Constitution; he rarely mentioned the need for a bill of rights as a determining factor. His principal critics and defenders have essentially used his framework in subjecting his work to analysis; they seemed unwilling or unable to break his hold. For example, Robert E. Brown and Forrest McDonald, Beard's two most devastating critics, had little to say about the popular pressure for a bill of rights; Brown did not even have an index entry under the heading "bill of rights."[17]

Jackson Turner Main, a defender of Beard, was primarily interested in the socioeconomic reasons for the ratification of the Constitution, but he did not minimize the matter of a bill of rights. He argued that the vast majority of Antifederalists, whom he called democrats, insisted upon a bill of rights because the vast power concentrated in the general government endangered the rights and liberties of the people. Main examined thirty-eight major Antifederalist essays which made a relatively complete analysis of the Constitution, and found that thirty-one of them stressed the need for a bill of rights. "It would be safe to say," wrote Main, "that at least nine out of ten Antifederalists wanted a bill of rights." That said, Main proceeded to ignore the issue when analyzing the reasons for ratification in the individual states. Yet in explaining why the Federalists won, Main stated: "Finally there was the promise of amendments without which the Constitution could never have been ratified."[18]

In part, Gordon S. Wood also looked upon the ratification struggle in terms of democracy versus aristocracy. The Antifederalists, he suggested, were men of the Revolution, men of 1776, who wanted their rights and liberties made explicit and protected. They demanded a bill of rights as they became increasingly aware that the new government was a consolidated one. In Wood's view, the movement for a bill of rights grew until it became very powerful by the fall of 1788, as an overwhelming number of Americans began to fear for their rights and liberties. Wood concluded that James Madison eventually succumbed to this popular pressure and fought for a bill of rights in the first federal Congress.[19]

To Cecilia Kenyon, Antifederalists were not democrats; they were paranoid, "men of little faith." They greatly distrusted government and people in power; their fears for their rights and liberties were genuine, although often stated in "melodramatically picturesque terms." Hence, Antifederalists wanted more complex safeguards and limitations placed upon the general government. Even though their actions eventually led to the Bill of Rights, they distrusted majority rule in legislatures. Kenyon maintained that Antifederalists opposed a national democracy whereby Congress would have vast powers; they could not extend their democratic vision from the state to the national scene.[20]

Steven R. Boyd stressed the high degree of organization that Antifederalists developed in their drive to obtain amendments to the Constitution, including a bill of rights. He traced these efforts at organization and interstate cooperation back to October 1787. Boyd insisted that the Antifederalists did not want to reject the Constitution outright, but sought to work within the system, choosing not to be disruptive. The confidence that Antifederalists had in the calling of a second constitutional convention was misplaced, Boyd contended; there was little popular support for another convention. Having failed to get a second convention called, the Antifederalists turned to the first federal elections, hoping to get supporters of amendments elected to the first federal Congress.[21]

The literature on the ratification of the Constitution in the individual states is too vast to be discussed here. The reader should consult a recently published anthology: *The Constitution and the States: The Role of the Original Thirteen in the Framing and Adoption of the Federal Constitution*, ed. Patrick T. Conley and John P. Kaminski (Madison, Wis., 1988). This volume contains a general introduction and a chapter on each state. Several essays include material on the ratification of the Bill of Rights. The essays are not footnoted, but each has an annotated bibliography of secondary and primary sources. Conley's concluding chapter, a bibliographic essay on the creation of the Constitution, considers general interpretative accounts (Beard, McDonald, Main, etc.); the colonial charters and state constitutions; the Constitutional Convention (Framers and major issues); the political thought of Federalists and Antifederalists; anthologies of constitutional essays; and primary sources.[22] Another useful anthology on the ratification of the Constitution by the states is *Ratifying the Constitution*, ed. Michael Allen Gillespie and Michael Lienesch (Lawrence, Kan., 1989). The essays in this volume are footnoted.

The Second Convention Movement and the First Federal Elections: Primary and Secondary Sources

Three historians—Edward P. Smith, Robert A. Rutland, and Linda Grant DePauw—placed particular emphasis on the importance of the calling of a second constitutional convention in an effort to obtain amendments to the Constitution. All three traced the evolution of the idea of such a convention from the Constitutional Convention of 1787 to its eventual rejection late in 1788.[23]

Smith viewed the collapse of the movement as a good thing; there was no need for a second convention because Federalists, bowing to popular pressure, were willing to amend the Constitution. Smith characterized the supporters of a second convention as paper money men and other advocates of fraudulent schemes, men who wanted separate confederacies, and those who did not know the difference between a general government and a consolidated one.

Rutland believed that the second convention idea was an early Antifederalist tactic, which became "a firm antifederal tenet." Antifederalists "tenaciously . . . grasped the second convention straw as the *sine qua non* of their makeshift program." The movement was a "fiasco." The Antifederalists were not united: they had different ideas about what should go into a bill of rights; they were unable to get very many of their people elected to the new Congress; and they were outmaneuvered by the Federalists on the issue of a bill of rights. "Antifederalism collapsed in a wallow of confusion, sectional animosity, and downright insincerity. The federal Bill of Rights, instead of becoming a monument to the Antifederalists' devotion to principle, became the tombstone of their moribund party."

DePauw thought that the second convention movement failed because the American people believed in majority rule. The majority had accepted the Constitution. Rank and file Antifederalists had tired of hectic political activity, and the first federal elections took much of their energy. Most Americans were not interested in the sophisticated arguments put forth for structural amendments. Throughout the ratification debate, their common goal had been a bill of rights, and the Federalists had promised them one.

Much of the documentation for the second convention movement and the desire for amendments and a bill of rights in late 1788 and early 1789 may be found in *The Documentary History of the First Federal Elections, 1788–1790,* ed. Merrill Jensen, Robert A. Becker, Gordon DenBoer et al., 4 vols. (Madison, Wis., 1976–1989). Much of the material in these volumes has never been printed before. The volumes cover a period often ignored by historians who usually end their narratives with the ratification of the Constitution and pick them up again with the meeting of the first federal Congress. Since most Antifederalist leaders wanted structural amendments more than they wanted a bill of rights, the documents that are published are largely concerned with such amendments. Nevertheless, the reader should examine these volumes carefully because the plea for amendments was often meant to include a bill of rights.[24]

The First Federal Congress: Primary and Secondary Sources

On September 25, 1789, after debates that lasted intermittently for about two months, the two houses of the first federal Congress adopted twelve amendments to the Constitution for submission to the states for ratification by three-fourths of them. On October 2, President George Washington forwarded the amendments to the states, and by December 15, 1791, the requisite number of them had ratified ten of the amendments.

The principal primary sources for the congressional action on the amendments are the legislative journals of the House of Representatives and the Senate, and the debates of the House. The legislative journals have been published in volumes 1 and 3 of the *Documentary History of the First Federal Congress of the United States of America, March 4, 1789–March 3, 1791,* ed. Linda Grant DePauw, Charlene Bangs Bickford, Helen E. Veit et al. (Baltimore and London, 1972–). The editors produced an authoritative text of each journal by comparing various printed and manuscript versions of them. Their introductions include informative histories of the archival remains of both the Senate and House files. The fourth volume of this documentary history, the first of three called *Legislative Histories,* contains (in forty-eight pages) the legislative history of the twelve amendments sent to the states. Preceded by a detailed chronological calendar, this history assembles excerpts from the Senate and House journals, resolutions and motions, committee reports, and the amendments proposed by the conventions of Massachusetts, South Carolina, Virginia, and New York.[25] The fourth volume also has a bibliography of the imprints made for the first federal Congress, which is useful for locating the several imprints concerning the amendments.

The legislative history constructed by the *Documentary History of the First Federal Congress* does not include the debates on the amendments. The debates in the House, taken from newspapers and Thomas Lloyd's *The Congressional Register . . .*, are printed in *The Debates and Proceedings in the Congress of the United States . . .* [1789–1824], comp. Joseph Gales, Sr., 42 vols. (Washington, D.C., 1834–1856). The *Documentary History of the First Federal Congress* will eventually publish the authoritative version of the debates in volumes 10 and 11, but for now the reader must use the older version, usually called the *Annals of Congress*. In an appendix to his book on the establishment clause of the First Amendment (note 34), Leonard W. Levy indicated the deficiencies of the *Annals of Congress* and other sources for the amendments. Marion Tinling, who has translated Lloyd's shorthand notes, provided an analytical account of them in "Thomas Lloyd's Reports of the First Federal Congress," *William and Mary Quarterly*, 3rd ser., 18 (1961): 519–45.[26] Newspaper and shorthand reporters were not permitted to take notes of the Senate debates, but Senator William Maclay of Pennsylvania kept a voluminous diary, edited by Kenneth R. Bowling and Helen E. Veit, that the *Documentary History of the First Federal Congress* has published (in cloth and in paper) as its ninth volume. Unfortunately, Maclay was ill for most of the Senate debate on the amendments.

The best historical treatments of the legislative history of the Bill of Rights in the first federal Congress are in the general accounts by Rutland, Dumbauld, Brant, Schwartz, and Levy, and in David M. Matteson, *The Organization of the Government under the Constitution* (1941; reprint ed., New York, 1970). All agree that James Madison, against considerable odds and much apathy, took the lead in the House of Representatives, and that without his efforts there probably would have been no Bill of Rights. Madison's amendments, a distillation of those from the state conventions (especially Virginia's) were, for the most part, those that the House eventually adopted. The complex politics of the legislative fight for a bill of rights is considered in detail by Kenneth R. Bowling, " 'A Tub to the Whale': The Founding Fathers and Adoption of the Federal Bill of Rights," *Journal of the Early Republic* 8 (1988): 223–51. This article is an expansion of the work done by Bowling in his doctoral dissertation, completed at the University of Wisconsin–Madison in 1968.

Ratification of the Bill of Rights by the States

The primary sources for the ratification of the Bill of Rights by the states are minimal. The largest number of documents in one source is in Bernard Schwartz's documentary history. Many states ratified very quickly and without much debate. Moreover, the records of the heated debates that took place in a few of the state legislatures are non-existent. Newspapers had very little to say about a bill of rights; they did not have to convince the American public, who overwhelmingly supported such a document. The forms of ratification of the amendments are in volume 2 of the U.S. Department of State's *Documentary History of the Constitution of the United States of America, 1787–1790.*

The first comprehensive survey of the ratification of the amendments by the individual states was made by David M. Matteson; the other substantial account is in Schwartz's *The Great Rights of Mankind.* For most of the states, Matteson and Schwartz had only the actions of their legislatures as recorded tersely in their journals; such is not the case for Massachusetts and Virginia, where the debates were especially vigorous. Virginia ratified in December 1791, the last state to ratify in the eighteenth century; Massachusetts did not ratify at that time because its legislature refused to take final action on what it had done. The Virginia debate is discussed in Richard R. Beeman, *The Old Dominion and the New Nation, 1788–1801* (Lexington, Ky., 1972). The official records of the actions of the Massachusetts legislature, with commentary, are in Denys P. Myers, *Massachusetts and the First Ten Amendments to the Constitution* (Washington, D.C., 1936). Connecticut and Georgia also failed to ratify the Bill of Rights. Thomas LeDuc explains the reasons for Connecticut's refusal in *Connecticut and the First Ten Amendments to the Federal Constitution* (Washington, D.C., 1937). Massachusetts, Connecticut, and Georgia did not ratify the Bill of Rights until 1939, the sesquicentennial of the adoption of that document by the first federal Congress.

The First Ten Amendments: Secondary Sources

The articles and monographs discussed in this section on the individual amendments in the Bill of Rights were selected because each gives substantial space and consideration to the English and colonial antecedents, the public and private debate over the ratifica-

tion of the Constitution, the debate in the first federal Congress, and the legislative and public debate over ratification. The judicial history of the amendments, the importance of which cannot be minimized, is not within the scope of this bibliographic essay. The literature on the amendments is considerable, and only some of the best items have been selected for inclusion here. Wherever possible, the author has pointed the reader to other bibliographic sources, especially if they appear in an article or book under discussion. In the case of some amendments, there is considerable controversy, much of it over the "original intent" of the Framers. Another aspect of the controversy, to use Judge Thomas M. Cooley's terminology, was whether or not the amendments were "conservatory instruments" or "reformatory" ones. The reader is forewarned that many writers on the first ten amendments, especially the First, Second, Fifth, Eighth, and Ninth, are plainly advocates, the academic credentials of some notwithstanding. Each side of an issue has a political agenda that it is pursuing, and some advocates make no effort whatever to hide this fact.[27]

General

An excellent place to begin a study of any of the amendments is the *Encyclopedia of the American Constitution*, ed. Leonard W. Levy, Kenneth L. Karst, and Dennis J. Mahoney, 4 vols. (New York and London, 1986). This scholarly reference work, commemorating the bicentennial of the Constitution, goes beyond judicial decisions and combines the disciplines of history, law, and political science. Each of the first ten amendments and its component parts is discussed by a well-known expert, some of whom have already published significant studies on their topics. Major topics, such as the First Amendment, are covered in articles of about 6,000 words; the component parts of this amendment— freedom of the press, freedom of speech, freedom of assembly and association, freedom of petition, establishment of religion, religious liberty, and separation of church and state—are also treated separately. Each essay is followed by a brief, selected bibliography, in which the entries are arranged alphabetically with the date of publication prominently displayed.

Another general source, also commemorative, is *The Bill of Rights: A Lively Heritage*, ed. Jon Kukla (Richmond, 1987). This collection of essays on the individual amendments, designed to describe their "major elements . . . in terms that ordinary citizens (including the editor) can understand and appreciate," first appeared serially in the *Virginia*

Cavalcade between 1982 and 1986. Most of the articles are well foot-noted; some discuss the conflicting scholarly opinions on the origins and meanings of the amendments; some are concerned largely with the English and colonial antecedents of the amendments; and others consider the judicial decisions concerning the amendments. In short, the articles do not fall into a uniform pattern, but they are well-done and useful.

Two more general sources are also valuable. One is a series of twenty volumes published by Garland Publishing and edited by Kermit L. Hall under the title "United States Constitutional and Legal History" (1987). This series reprints more than 450 scholarly articles. Two particularly useful volumes are those entitled *Civil Liberties in the United States*, in which appear a number of articles that are discussed below. (See the footnotes for citations to these volumes.) In the late fall of 1989, Garland Publishing announced that it would soon publish, under the editorship of Paul L. Murphy, another twenty-volume series, "The Bill of Rights and American Legal History," that would include reprints of over 300 scholarly articles. The prospectus issued by Garland Publishing, giving the contents of each volume, reveals that this series will include some of the articles that are considered below. Especially useful will be the volume entitled *The Historic Background of the Bill of Rights*. Both Hall and Murphy provide editorial introductions for each of the volumes.

First Amendment

Two component parts of the First Amendment, those dealing with the freedom of the press and speech and the establishment clause, have probably generated the most historical controversy. Zechariah Chafee, Jr., in his seminal *Free Speech in the United States* (Cambridge, Mass., 1941), stated that the Framers, with their deep knowledge of English and colonial history, sought "to wipe out" the common law principle of seditious libel, making government prosecutions for criticism "forever impossible." This view was supported by most scholars and judges. (Chafee's volume is a revision of his *Freedom of Speech* which first appeared in 1920. For his role as an advocate of the doctrine of the First Amendment, see note 2.)

In 1960 Leonard W. Levy, after a lengthy analysis of English and colonial antecedents and the debate over the ratification of the Constitution, concluded that freedom of the press meant only the absence of prior restraints and that the First Amendment was not intended to override the common law of seditious libel. In politics, freedom of speech was not broadly conceived until the passage of the Sedition Act in 1798.[28] Many reviewers attacked Levy's conclusions, and several major articles and books tried to swing the pendulum back to Chafee. For example, George Anastaplo insisted that the First Amendment was an absolute prohibition on congressional interference with the freedom of the press and speech. David A. Anderson declared that prior restraint was a non-issue; the issue was seditious libel. Philip B. Kurland agreed that the focus of the press clause was on seditious libel; the clause sought to protect political speech against majorities and government officials. William T. Mayton stated that the First Amendment was an affirmation of such structural guarantees in the Constitution as the treason clause. Since this clause limited the government's power only to treasonable conduct involving "overt acts," the government could not punish dissident political speech.[29]

Reacting to this criticism, Levy published a revised and enlarged version of his earlier book. The new book is entitled *Emergence of a Free Press* (New York, 1985). Levy's preface reviewed his debate with a host of absolutists who believed that the government has no power whatever over the expression of ideas. He refused to retreat from his basic premise, although he expressed regret about his narrow definition of the freedom of the press. That concept, he conceded, also meant that under criminal law people could be held responsible for abusing this freedom and that the press was expected to be "a watchdog" in a republic. The law of seditious libel existed, but the press acted as if it did not and, for the most part, got away with it. Levy concluded by noting that there is not enough evidence to demonstrate the original intent of the Framers when they drafted the amendment.

Since original intent was central to much of what he had written on the Constitution and the Bill of Rights, Levy focused upon it in his massive, recently published *Original Intent and The Framers' Constitution* (New York, 1988). Writing "in the context of the contemporary controversy over original intent," Levy criticized conservative proponents of original intent who employ it in order to pursue a political agenda. Nevertheless, he did not dismiss the concept as irrelevant; "when clearly discernible," it should be followed; "it is always entitled to the utmost respect and consideration as an interpretative guide." Original intent, however, should not always be pursued. Levy noted that even the Framers refused to rely on their original intent—nor did they even agree on what it was. Some constitutional provisions were left deliberately vague and ambiguous, while others were given broad principles and purposes. The Framers expected that judges, on a case-by-case basis, would employ a number of techniques to interpret the Constitution. Moreover,

Levy maintained that inadequate sources often make it difficult or impossible to discern original intent.[30]

Chapter 10 of his *Original Intent and the Framers' Constitution* summarized *Emergence of a Free Press*, but in this latest version Levy did not answer two major critics of that work—David M. Rabban and Jeffrey A. Smith. In a review essay, Rabban argued that Levy would have had a better understanding of the original intent of the Framers about the press clause if he had not so narrowly focused on the law of seditious libel. Levy, declared Rabban, ignored recent scholarship on the popular and democratic movements of the period and the growth of libertarian thought that was incorporated into the Constitution and the Bill of Rights. Republican political theory, accepted by the Framers, had pushed the concept of freedom of expression well beyond the bounds of English common law. In short, Rabban averred, the amendment could only be understood in the context of R.R. Palmer's "age of the democratic revolution." Smith, in articles published in 1986 and 1987 and a book printed in 1988, also stated that there is much evidence from which to discern the original intent of the Framers. Smith, an historian of journalism, used this evidence to support the absolutist position, maintaining firmly that the First Amendment prohibits any governmental restraint on the expression of ideas. The republicanism of the Framers was "strongly antiauthoritarian," Smith argued, and the First Amendment reflected this thinking. The amendment was intended to preserve the victory won in the Zenger case (1735), after which printers did not have to worry about seditious libel. When James Madison introduced the First Amendment in Congress in 1789, he said that the freedom of the press and liberty of conscience were the "choicest privileges of the people." Prior restraint, declared Smith, was not an issue in the debate over the Constitution; it had long since been "interred."[31]

Robert C. Palmer, conversant with the debate between Levy and his critics, decided to take a different approach from either of these groups. Palmer believed that they have "treated the first amendment as embodying an ideology, as being a principle." By contrast, Palmer sought "to find the meaning" of the press clause "by direct reference to the structure" of the Bill of Rights itself and "the function of the provision within that document." He found that the Bill of Rights was necessary because the Constitution had created a powerful government with "minority-favoring" and "anti-popular elements" that endangered the liberties of the people and the rights of the states. Consequently, the liberties in the Bill of Rights were made extraordinarily broad. Freedom of speech and the press included protection against prior restraints and subsequent punishments; it was "very much in accord with what one might mean with the designation of freedom of movement." Freedom of the press was "so broad as to be occasionally dangerous and certainly never determined by considerations of 'reasonability.' "[32]

The establishment clause of the First Amendment has generated much heat since 1947 when the Supreme Court declared in *Everson v. Board of Education* (330 U.S. 1) that the First Amendment provided for the complete separation of church and state and that the government could not support one or all religions, or pass laws respecting the establishment of religion. The "nonpreferentionalists" have opposed the Court's decision, while the "separationists" have praised it.

Among the principal "nonpreferentionalists" are Edward S. Corwin, James M. O'Neill, Chester James Antieau (and associates), Walter Berns, and Rodney K. Smith. Writing soon after the *Everson* case, Corwin and O'Neill insisted that all that James Madison, the author of the amendment, and the two houses of Congress intended by the establishment clause was to prevent Congress from giving preferred status to any religious faith, sect, or denomination. In the eighteenth century, "an establishment of religion" meant only that; a congressional act favoring religion in general did not come within the meaning of that phrase. O'Neill, in particular, emphasized that the amendment does not prohibit Congress from using public funds to aid religion in general; nor does it prohibit religion in public education. Madison, he argued, would have agreed on both counts. Antieau and his associates believed that the amendment was a reaction to the support that some states had given to individual religions; it sought to make certain that the federal government not prefer one religion over another. Berns argued that the amendment only prohibits Congress from establishing a single religion. Congressional debates on the amendment, he contended, reveal, that the federal government was not prevented from giving aid to religion in general, providing it did not discriminate. Smith focused on James Madison whose views on religion and the separation of church and state he analyzed in depth for the decade of the 1780s. Madison believed in religious liberty and was absolutely opposed to the establishment of any church. He thought, however, that government could aid all religions provided it did so equally and nonpreferentially. His views were held by most Americans.[33]

Arrayed on the side of the Supreme Court are Leo Pfeffer, Leonard W. Levy, Thomas J. Curry, and Anson Phelps Stokes. Pfeffer, a lawyer involved in many court cases on this amendment, believed that the amendment was absolute; it called for the complete separation of church and state. Congress was prohibited from passing any laws on religion; Pfeffer even believed the amendment extended to the executive and judicial branches of government. The American people had insisted upon this amendment.[34] In an article on "The Original Meaning of the Establishment Clause," Levy concluded that neither the federal nor state governments could establish a church or pass laws aiding one or all religions. Between 1787 and 1789, most Americans, except those in New England, agreed with this view. James Madison, a sincere advocate of religious freedom, did not think the amendment was necessary (Levy agreed), but that it would quiet the Antifederalists and the people.[35] Once again, Levy noted that the Framers "were vague if not careless draftsmen"; to determine the meaning of the words in the establishment clause, historians must study the preceding years.[36] No one did this better for the establishment clause than one of Levy's students, Thomas J. Curry, who comprehensively reviewed the meaning of religious liberty and the establishment of religion from earliest colonial times to 1789. Curry, a Roman Catholic priest, drew the same conclusions as his mentor, and he reminded his readers that the concepts of religious freedom and establishment can only be understood in the context of Protestant Christianity. He also concluded that the First Amendment meant: "that each citizen had the right to the free exercise of his or her religion as long as it did not 'break out into overt acts against peace and order.' " The free exercise of one's religious beliefs, then, was not absolute.[37]

Most scholars place Anson Phelps Stokes among the strict "separationists," but some of his views caused Levy, a strict "separationist," to label him "a moderate preferentialist." In his "classic, monumental, [and] comprehensive" three-volume study on church and state in America, Stokes, a canon of the Episcopal Church, rejoiced in the collapse of his church's establishments in eighteenth-century America, and he celebrated the triumph of religious freedom and liberty in America. The separation of church and state and religious freedom were both democratic principles. Stokes, however, also delighted in the manner in which the Continental, Confederation, and United States congresses found ways of "encouraging the religious spirit in the new nation, while at the same time avoiding favoritism to any denomination." Democracy could not exist without the force of religion; this romantic notion made possible a more accommodating relationship between government and religion.[38]

The role of James Madison and his thoughts on religion and religious freedom were treated by about two dozen scholars in *James Madison on Religious Liberty*, ed. Robert S. Alley (New York, 1985). Some of the essays are original to this volume, others are reprints from scholarly journals. Freedom of religion was "a burning issue" for

Madison for almost his entire public life, and his commitment to it can be best understood in the context of his commitment to republicanism.[39]

Robert A. Rutland came to essentially the same conclusion about George Mason, whose Virginia Declaration of Rights is the "grandfather" of *"all"* bills of rights. Mason believed that the First Amendment was the best means of preserving republican government.[40] With his "Objections" to the Constitution, printed in the fall of 1787, Mason led the clamor for a bill of rights.

On the rights of assembly and association, two more component parts of the First Amendment, see Glenn Abernathy, *The Right of Assembly and Association*, 2nd ed. (Columbia, S.C., 1981); Charles E. Rice, *Freedom of Association* ([New York], 1962); and David Fellman, *The Constitutional Right of Association* (Chicago, 1963). On the right of petition, see Don L. Smith, "The Right of Petition for Redress of Grievances: Constitutional Development and Interpretations" (Ph.D. diss., Texas Tech University, 1971); Raymond C. Bailey, *Popular Influence upon Public Policy: Petitioning in Eighteenth-Century Virginia* (Westport, Conn., and London, 1979); and Stephen A. Higginson, "A Short History of the Right to Petition Government for the Redress of Grievances," *Yale Law Journal* 96 (1986): 142–66.

Second Amendment

The historical controversy over the Second Amendment has led to the development of two principal schools of thought: the "individualist" and the "collectivist" (or states' rights school). The "individualist" school argues that the amendment guaranteed individuals the right to possess arms for a variety of reasons: (1) personal or self-defense (i.e., crime prevention); (2) hunting and fowling; (3) national defense; and (4) protection of personal liberty and popular institutions against domestic despotism (right of revolution) or domestic insurrection. The amendment blended the personal right to bear arms and the need for a militia; the right to possess arms was a personal right and a collective duty. Some of the proponents of this school, such as Stephen P. Halbrook and Joyce Malcolm, trace the philosophical origins of the amendment back to the Greek and Roman classics and seventeenth-century England.

In order of their date of publication, some of the principal works representing the "individualist" school are: Stuart R. Hays, "The Right to Bear Arms, A Study in Judicial Misinterpretation," *William and Mary Law Review* 2 (1960): 381–406; Stephen P. Halbrook, "The Jurisprudence of the Second and Fourteenth Amendments," *George Mason*

University Law Review 4 (1981): 1–69; Robert E. Shalhope, "The Ideological Origins of the Second Amendment," *Journal of American History* 69 (1982–83): 599–614; Don B. Kates, Jr., "Handgun Prohibition and the Original Meaning of the Second Amendment," *Michigan Law Review* 82 (1983): 204–73; Joyce Malcolm, "The Right of the People to Keep and Bear Arms: The Common Law Tradition," *Hastings Constitutional Law Quarterly* 10 (1983): 285–314; Halbrook, *That Every Man Be Armed: The Evolution of a Constitutional Right* (Albuquerque, N.M., 1984); Halbrook, "What the Framers Intended: A Linguistic Analysis of the Right to 'Bear Arms,' " *Law and Contemporary Problems* 49 (1986): 151–62; Robert E. Shalhope, "The Armed Citizen in the Early Republic," *ibid.*, 125–41; David T. Hardy, "Armed Citizens, Citizen Armies: Toward a Jurisprudence of the Second Amendment," *Harvard Journal of Law & Public Policy* 9 (1986): 559–638; Hardy, "The Second Amendment and the Historiography of the Bill of Rights," *Journal of Law and Politics* 4 (1987): 1–62; and Halbrook, *A Right to Bear Arms: State and Federal Bills of Rights and Constitutional Guarantees* (New York, Westport, Conn. and London, 1989). The articles by Kates and Hardy are also useful for the literature on this controversy.

The "collectivist" or states' rights school argues that the Second Amendment is a limitation upon the general government. The states sought protection against the general government's usurpation of their power over their militias. The amendment also reflects the almost paralyzing Anglo-American fear of standing armies. The right to keep and bear arms meant the collective right of the people to maintain and serve in an effective militia. The most recent exponent of this school, Lawrence Delbert Cress, places the study of the Second Amendment within the concept of republicanism. A well-regulated militia was the best way to protect republican liberty; an armed and trained citizenry was collectively responsible for the defense of the republic against foreign invasion and domestic insurrection.

In the order of their date of publication, some of the principal works of the "collectivist" school are: Peter Buck Feller and Karl L. Gotting, "The Second Amendment: A Second Look," *Northwestern University Law Review* 61 (1966–67): 46–70; John Levin, "The Right to Bear Arms: The Development of the American Experience," *Chicago-Kent Law Review* 47 (1970): 148–67; Roy G. Weatherup, "Standing Armies and Armed Citizens: An Historical Analysis of the Second Amendment," *Hastings Constitutional Law Quarterly* 2 (1975): 961–1001; Lawrence Delbert Cress, *Citizens in Arms: The Army and the Militia in American Society to the War of 1812* (Chapel Hill, N.C., 1982); Cress, "An Armed Community: The Origins and Meaning of the Right to Bear

Arms," *Journal of American History* 71 (1984): 22–41; and Cress, "A Well-Regulated Militia: The Origins and Meaning of the Second Amendment," in *The Bill of Rights: A Lively Heritage*, ed. Kukla, 55–65. Cress's works are useful for the historiography of this controversy.

For an exchange between an exponent of each school, see Robert E. Shalhope and Lawrence Delbert Cress, "The Second Amendment and the Right to Bear Arms: An Exchange," *Journal of American History* 71 (1984): 587–93; and for an article that does not take sides but which surveys (with tables) what the states have done with respect to the right to bear arms, see Robert J. Taylor, "American Constitutions and the Right to Bear Arms," *Proceedings of the Massachusetts Historical Society* 95 (1983): 52–66.

Third and Fourth Amendments

The Third and Fourth amendments have attracted considerably less attention and controversy. In fact, no case, states B. Carmon Hardy, has ever been tried in the United States Supreme Court concerning the Third Amendment. Nevertheless, the amendment was crucial to the Revolutionary generation because the quartering of troops had been a major problem in the colonies. The amendment demonstrated a concern for the sanctity of the home, the protection of private property, and the subordination of the civilian to the military.[41]

The first book written on a specific amendment was Nelson B. Lasson's work on the Fourth Amendment, published in 1937. Lasson argued that this amendment, a reaction to the abuse of executive power in the colonies, sought to prevent the general government from issuing warrants without probable cause. Joseph J. Stengel agreed, although he also emphasized the great fear of a strong general government. William Cuddihy and B. Carmon Hardy, after an exhaustive search of legislative and court records, concluded that the amendment was an effort of the states to deprive the general government of a right that they exercised themselves. In 1789, all states employed general searches.[42]

Fifth Amendment

In 1955, Erwin N. Griswold, Dean of the Harvard Law School, delivered three lectures on the Fifth Amendment that paid particular attention to the due process clause and the clause against self-incrimination. One of the lectures stressed the popular (but erroneous) seventeenth- and eighteenth-century belief that the due process clause protected every individual against an arbitrary government's assault on his liberties. The

Framers accepted this belief and incorporated it into the Fifth Amendment. The clause's intent, then, was to protect individual liberty. Stephen F. Williams rejected this interpretation, claiming that life, liberty, and property referred only to criminal trials; the Fifth Amendment sought to protect those interests that might be jeopardized in such a trial. Keith Jurow, focusing entirely on English history, agreed that due process had nothing to do with protecting an individual against an arbitrary government.[43]

Griswold's lectures, in part a reaction to McCarthyism, were largely concerned with the privilege against self-incrimination. He believed that the clause became part of the Bill of Rights because it was well-established as part of the English common law and it was universally accepted in America. The "privilege against self-incrimination is one of the great landmarks in man's struggle to make himself civilized." Griswold probably drew some of his conclusions from studies on this privilege made by R. Carter Pittman in 1935 and Edmund M. Morgan in 1949.[44]

It remained, however, for Leonard W. Levy to write the definitive study on the privilege against self-incrimination. Most of his monumental study is concerned with the triumph in the common law of England of the accusatory system of justice over the inquisitorial system. Under the former, the burden of proof is on the accuser; under the latter, it is on the accused. Levy demonstrated that by the seventeenth century the right against self-incrimination—linked to the freedom of speech and religion—had been attained in both criminal and civil cases. Although the right had to be won in each of the American colonies, it was widely accepted by 1776. It became part of the Fifth Amendment because the Framers wanted to protect this basic individual right against the power of government. The burden of proof was on the government, but only in criminal cases.[45]

Another component of the Fifth Amendment—double jeopardy—was considered by Jay A. Sigler, who described the right as an ancient one. The language of the amendment lacks precision and its meaning is unclear because the boundaries of criminal law had not been established. The Framers, however, believed that no one should suffer twice for the same act. Double jeopardy is a concept that each generation must define through its courts and legislatures. The history of the just compensation or eminent domain clause of the Fifth Amendment was reviewed by William Michael Treanor whose 1985 article also has a good discussion of the secondary literature on the subject. Treanor saw the clause as a national commitment to the preservation of property.[46]

Sixth and Seventh Amendments

Francis H. Heller's study of the Sixth Amendment was one of the first books devoted to an individual amendment. The American colonists accepted the English concept of trial by jury in criminal cases, although they adapted certain jury procedures. Heller paid close attention to Virginia, whose court records are very good. State constitutions included this right, and it was heatedly debated during the struggle for the ratification of the Constitution. Heller found that James Madison, to answer Antifederalist criticisms, drew up a comprehensive amendment, closely following the Virginia Convention's recommendation, which, in turn, had been influenced by George Mason's Declaration of Rights. John M. Murrin and A.G. Roeber studied Virginia's county court system in considerably more depth than Heller and concluded that by the end of the colonial period the petit jury system in civil and criminal cases had become the bulwark of liberty. In his Declaration of Rights, Mason sought to defend and protect this right, which became part of the federal Bill of Rights.[47]

In 1966, Edith Guild Henderson wrote that the Seventh Amendment concerning jury trials in civil cases was a principal Antifederalist demand. There was, however, no consensus on the extent of the civil jury's power, and state practices were too diverse for the right to be hammered out precisely. Nevertheless, she noted, the amendment accepted the concept of the common-law trial by jury and the jury's right to reach important decisions. Charles W. Wolfram, after a detailed investigation of the debate over the ratification of the Constitution, concluded that the Seventh Amendment was a reaction to the powerful government established by the Constitution. Antifederalists, who were sincere about this right, sought to protect debtors, overturn vice admiralty court practices, and protect litigants from oppressive judges. Most important, they wanted the benefits of a jury trial where juries could reach verdicts that judges could not or would not reach.[48]

Because the common law of the Seventh Amendment was the English common law, Patrick Devlin launched a study of the English court system in 1789 to determine the amendment's meaning. He stated that the right to a jury trial in a civil case was not absolute in England because the chancellor had the power to prevent a suit if it was too complex. After studying equity jurisdiction in both England and America, Morris S. Arnold rejected Devlin's assertion that particularly complex civil suits were withheld from juries in either place. Americans so revered trial by jury that they insisted it be used regularly in chancery courts. Consequently, he concluded, the Seventh Amendment should not be interpreted to allow complex cases to be withheld from juries. James S. Campbell and Nicholas Le Poidevin defended Devlin's position against Arnold's criticisms and asserted that the Framers incorporated into the Seventh Amendment the English distinction between common law suits and equity proceedings described by Devlin. Even Antifederalists, whose fears led to the adoption of the amendment, never insisted that juries be employed in all civil cases. In reply, Arnold restated his position about America's love affair with trial by jury and maintained that his critics failed to cite a single case where equity courts dispensed with juries in complex cases.[49]

Eighth Amendment

William F. Duker viewed the right to bail in the Eighth Amendment as part of the concept of individual liberty, although the right was not absolute. By 1789, bail was granted in those cases where the legislature said it could be granted. It was not a constitutional guarantee. Richard H. Williamson traced the evolution of the concept of excessive bail through English history up to the American Bill of Rights and showed that it became increasingly stronger to the point where the amendment uses the phrase "shall not." The amendment, however, does not guarantee bail in all criminal cases.[50]

Anthony F. Granucci insisted the clause on cruel and unusual punishments was intended only to mean that certain barbaric punishments were prohibited. Since Americans did not resort to barbaric punishments, the clause has rarely been invoked. Granucci also believed that the Eighth Amendment has embedded in it the principle of proportionality, namely, that the punishment should fit the crime. In 1972, Granucci's article was cited by United States Supreme Court Justices William O. Douglas and Thurgood Marshall in concurring opinions in *Furman v. Georgia* (408 U.S. 238); in that case, the Court ruled that the sovereign power of the states to levy the death penalty was restricted by the cruel and unusual punishments clause.[51]

Raoul Berger, in a book on the death penalty, decried the justices' use of Granucci's article. Berger rejected Granucci's idea concerning proportionality which the Court used. He insisted that the Framers did not believe that capital punishment was cruel and unusual punishment. As proof, he showed that the Fifth Amendment accepted the death penalty and that a law passed in 1790 provided for the death penalty for certain federal offenses. He attacked the Supreme Court for trying to rewrite the Constitution and for twisting the meaning of the common law as it was precisely understood by the Framers. Nor, he asserted, should the Bill of Rights have been applied to the states. Lastly, Berger dismissed the concept that "the Court is empowered to revise the Constitution, discreetly expressed as 'adaptation' to changing conditions."[52]

Opponents of the death penalty, outraged by Berger's book, rallied to the defense of the Supreme Court. Most of the critics, such as Hugo Adam Bedau, Stephen Gillers, Peter J. Kalis, David A.J. Richards, G. Edward White, and Timothy Foley, generally agreed that Berger was not interested in the question of the death penalty, but only in pursuing his beliefs that judges must act with restraint. Berger, they argued, used his book as a forum to strike at some old foes of his constitutional philosophy. They accused him of being bloodthirsty and criticized him for not expressing his views about the death penalty. Berger's critics generally accepted the idea that the Constitution is a living, progressive document that must be adapted to changing conditions, values, and beliefs. They asserted that there is much more to constitutional interpretation than mere original intent. The Constitution is rooted not only in history, they proclaimed, but in "nature and culture, and that . . . those grounds simultaneously at work, affect what everything is, does, and means." They also insisted that the question of human dignity has a central place in the Eighth Amendment and that the amendment not only affirms human dignity but attacks tyranny and one of its favorite tools—the death penalty. One critic (David A.J. Richards) demonstrated that even in the eighteenth century certain segments of society were repelled by the barbarity of the death penalty. Another (Timothy Foley) defended federal judges against the charge that they are trying to remake society in accordance with their own biases. "Rather," federal judges, "are members of a civilized society attempting to interpret and apply the rights and protections that make up the foundation of a community striving (perhaps too weakly) for justice."[53]

Berger answered some of these critics. He chided Bedau and Gillers for having had to admit that the Fifth Amendment and the law of 1790 provided for the death penalty. He advised Bedau to stick to philosophy and to stop being so self-righteous. He reminded Gillers that the dignity of man was not a basic concept of the Framers and that ignominy and disgrace were part of the American legal system in the late eighteenth century. Finally, Berger told White that judicial activism, not judicial restraint, is "singularly eccentric."[54]

Ninth Amendment

About thirty-five years ago, Bennett B. Patterson published a book entitled *The Forgotten Ninth Amendment* (Indianapolis, 1955) in which he stated that the amendment, the "cornerstone" of the Constitution, was "intended as a general declaration of human rights." It was a declaration of the sovereignty and dignity of the individual, and it protected the individual's personal rights and liberties. Patterson also printed the complete congressional debates on amendments. In 1965, ten years after this book appeared, Justice Arthur Goldberg invoked the Ninth Amendment in his concurring opinion in *Griswold v. Connecticut* (381 U.S. 479), in which the United States Supreme Court struck down a Connecticut anti-birth-control law. From about that time until 1980, in the estimate of Raoul Berger, the amendment was invoked in some 1,200 court cases.

Historians have also been attracted to the amendment in large numbers. Leslie W. Dunbar said that the amendment was James Madison's answer to the Antifederalist charge that any enumeration of rights would be imperfect. Not a restriction on the power of government, the amendment was directed primarily to the courts who were to protect all rights, including those not created by law. David K. Sutelan wrote that the amendment directed the courts back to the "due process" clause of the Fifth Amendment; they were being asked to use that clause which was intended to protect basic, unenumerated rights. Terence J. Moore and Mark N. Goodman believed that the amendment reflected the Framers' firm belief in natural and inviolable rights, and that the amendment protected rights that could be reduced to language. Moore also saw the amendment as a barrier against government encroachment. Raoul Berger agreed. The Ninth and Tenth amendments demonstrated the great Antifederalist distrust of a powerful central government. One protected the rights retained by the people, the other the rights reserved to the states or the people. Russell L. Caplan rejected the notion of the Ninth Amendment as "a cornucopia of undefined federal rights," and insisted that it is limited to "the maintenance of rights guaranteed by the laws of the states." These state rights were derived from natural law theory and the hereditary rights of Englishmen. James Madison drafted this amendment in answer to the charge that a federal bill of rights would supplant the state bills of rights. All of the rights in the first eight amendments were derived from state laws; the Ninth Amendment, then, protected those state rights that had not been singled out. Lawrence E. Mitchell supported Caplan's belief that the Ninth Amendment applies to the states, but insisted that it also protects the rights not enumerated in the Bill of Rights. Furthermore, the broad language of the amendment demonstrates that the Framers wanted the Constitution to be adapted to changes in society. Any interpretation of the Constitution had to go beyond the mere words; the amendment rejects the notion of original intent. And Calvin R. Massey declared that the Ninth Amendment protects "positive rights" that had their source in the common, constitutional, and statutory law of the states and the "natural rights" that were based upon ideas of man's inalienable rights. The Ninth Amendment reflects the Framers' concern for state sovereignty and individual liberty.[55]

Leonard W. Levy, surveying both the primary sources and the historical literature on the Ninth Amendment in his recent *Original Intent and The Framers' Constitution*, concluded that the amendment protected the unenumerated rights of the people. The Ninth Amendment was one of the most significant innovations of James Madison, the "father" of the Bill of Rights. Levy declared that the unenumerated rights were "natural rights," including the pursuit of happiness, the protection of property, and the equality of treatment before law. They also consisted of "positive rights," those rights based upon the social compact with the general government. The Ninth Amendment, he asserted, "might [even] have had the purpose of providing the basis for the rights then unknown, which time alone might disclose." The Framers wanted the amendment to have a "vitality" that would secure the rights of the people.

Tenth Amendment

Historians of the Tenth Amendment agree that it was an outgrowth of the Antifederalist belief that the Constitution had created a consolidated government; but they part company over the meaning of the amendment. For example, Charles A. Lofgren believed that the amendment reaffirmed the consolidating tendency of the new government. The removal of the word "expressly" from the phrase "expressly delegated" made the clause meaningless. Federalists wanted no part of the term because it reminded them of Article II of the Articles of Confederation. That sweeping article had placed the locus of sovereignty in the states, not the central government. The word "expressly" would have amounted to a bill of rights for the states. By adding "or to the people," the Federalists cemented their position. The amendment says nothing about state sovereignty. Raoul Berger disagreed. The amendment has great meaning even without the word "expressly"; it was intended to protect the states against the great powers of the central government and to preserve the powers of the states. The amendment was "a political bargain" that recognized that the states would remain the primary legislative agents in their own affairs. Charles F. Hobson declared that the amendment established a "new federalism," the type found in "our civics textbooks." The people became the new element. The advocates of states' rights did not suffer a total loss because they forced nationalists to deny the idea of consolidation and to move toward the "new federalism." Both the states and the central government were now subordinate to the people. When the Bill of Rights was finally ratified in 1791, the Constitution began and ended with the "people."[56]

Conclusion

The Bill of Rights is a powerful presence in contemporary American life, but it has only been thirty-five years since scholars turned a microscope on it. They had become concerned that the principles embodied in that extraordinary document were being eroded by the actions of governments, organizations, institutions, and individuals. Their writings on the subject are voluminous. In recent years, the investigation of the Bill of Rights has been the particular province of lawyers and political scientists and most of their work is in law journals. Political and constitutional historians—with the singular exceptions of Leonard W. Levy (the dean of the historians of the Bill of Rights) and his students— have not played as substantial a role as they had in the early years. In the historical profession, their place has been taken, for the most part, by the highly competent practitioners in the "booming" field of legal history. Also prominent are the historians of journalism who have contributed much to our understanding of the press clause of the First Amendment.

The search to discover the meaning of the first ten amendments has taken scholars back to ancient, medieval, and early modern history, particularly to the constitutional and legal history of England and the British American colonies. They have even ventured into the more ethereal discipline of philosophy, as they constantly broaden their research to gain understanding, or to validate an opinion. For instance, David A.J. Richards, an opponent of the death penalty, in order to support his position, used a study on the growing revulsion to that practice in late eigtheenth-century France. In some instances, the erudition displayed is most impressive, as in the cases of Leonard W. Levy's and Monsignor Thomas J. Curry's work on the First Amendment, Levy's study on the Fifth Amendment, and Canon Anson Phelps Stokes's magnum opus on the separation of church and state.

In the last decade, students of the Bill of Rights have battled with the meaning of the "original intent" of the Framers, a struggle made difficult by the meager notes of the congressional debates on the drafting of that document. Some have minutely examined and reexamined the congressional debates. Others have found this exercise limiting and have turned to the prolific public and private debate over the ratification of the Constitution, as more records of that debate become available. Consequently, each side of the debate over the meaning of "original intent" has gathered considerable ammunition to argue its viewpoint persuasively, so much so that the unprejudiced reader has difficulty determining who is winning. The proponents of "original intent," whether on the left or on the right, often have a political agenda that drives their interpretation of the historical evidence. On the other hand, some opponents of "original intent" go so far as to insist that judges ignore the origins of the Constitution and interpret it to meet changing conditions, values, and beliefs.

Most of the writers on the first ten amendments are fierce advocates. They feel so deeply about such issues as the freedom of the press and speech, the separation of church and state, the right to bear arms, the right to trial by jury, the death penalty, and the right of privacy that many of them cannot hide their prejudices. Some are not even inclined to be objective. This is not to suggest that they are dishonest, only that their intense feelings and beliefs have clearly conditioned their conclusions. Too often, the debaters accuse one another of dishonesty, inadequate research, or a failure to understand the sources. These charges are met with countercharges and the debate often becomes vituperative and personal. The reader, then, is warned to proceed with extreme caution.

NOTES:

*This essay does not consider articles published in law journals (and most historical journals) for 1989. The avalanche of articles that will be published to celebrate the bicentennial of the Bill of Rights (1989–1991) deserves an essay of its own. The author wishes to thank Richard B. Bernstein, whose close readings of this article improved it. Stephen L. Schechter, Shirley A. Rice, Wendell Tripp, and Richard Leffler also made helpful suggestions with respect to both style and content. Lastly, the author is indebted to computer programmer and operator Charles D. Hagermann and to the circulation, reference, acquisition, and cataloguing departments of the Law Library of the University of Wisconsin-Madison and the library of the State Historical Society of Wisconsin, Madison.

¹*A Machine That Would Go of Itself: The Constitution in American Culture* (New York, 1986), 336–56. Kammen's entitled his chapter: "Our Bill of Rights Is Under Subtle and Pervasive Attack." One of the more interesting manifestations of the "discovery" of the Bill of Rights was the establishment in 1938 of the Bill of Rights Committee of the American Bar Association. Between the summer of 1940 and the summer of 1942,

the committee published a quarterly journal entitled *The Bill of Rights Review* because the legal profession and informed laymen wanted "to *learn more* concerning the history and nature of our fundamental rights." Through the quarterly publication, the committee sought "to disseminate information generally concerning our constitutional liberties to the end that violations thereof may be the better recognized and proper steps taken to prevent or correct them." In addition to containing articles on a wide variety of subjects, each issue of the *Review* included "Notes and Cases," in which were reviewed "the more important situations and decisions in the field of civil liberties." Each issue also contained the text of the Bill of Rights. For the Lasson book, see note 42 below and the accompanying text.

²These pamphlets were later reprinted, with a long preface, as *Documents on Fundamental Human Rights: The Anglo-American Tradition, Compiled, Edited, and With a Preface, How Human Rights Got into the Constitution*, 2nd ed., 2 vols. (New York, 1963). The preface consists of the Gaspar G. Bacon lectures that Chafee delivered at Boston University in November 1951 and which that university's press published the next year. See also Chafee, *Three Human Rights in the Constitution of 1787* (1956; reprint ed., Lawrence, Kan., and London, 1968). This reprint edition of Chafee's book has a foreword on his career by Arthur E. Sutherland, his colleague at the Harvard Law School.

For a full-scale biography of Chafee, see Donald L. Smith, *Zechariah Chafee, Jr.: Defender of Liberty and Law* (Cambridge, Mass., 1986). See also two articles by David M. Rabban that discuss, in part, Chafee's role as an advocate of the doctrine of the First Amendment: "The First Amendment in the Forgotten Years," *Yale Law Journal* [YLJ] 90 (1981): 514–95; and "The Emergence of Modern First Amendment Doctrine," *University of Chicago Law Review* 50 (1983): 1205–1355. Also useful is Alexis J. Anderson, "The Formative Period of First Amendment Theory, 1870-1915," *American Journal of Legal History* [AJLH] 24 (1980): 56–75. The Rabban and Anderson articles are reprinted in *Civil Liberties in American History*, ed. Kermit L. Hall, 2 vols. (New York and London, 1987), 1: 1–20; 2: 193–421.

For the extent of knowledge and the reading of the Framers to which Chafee alludes, see Jack P. Greene, *The Intellectual Heritage of the Constitutional Era: The Delegates' Library* (Philadelphia, 1986); and Robert A. Rutland, *"Well Acquainted with Books": The Founding Framers of 1787: With James Madison's List of Books for Congress* (Washington, D.C., 1987). Both pamphlets also have select bibliographies of secondary works that include scholarly studies of many of the political thinkers read by the Founding Fathers.

³*Sources of Our Liberties: Documentary Origins of Individual Liberties in the United States Constitution and Bill of Rights* (Chicago, 1959). In 1972 the New York University Press issued this volume in paperback.

⁴In 1983, *The Birth of the Bill of Rights* was reprinted by the Northeastern University Press, with the last chapter (entitled "Since 1791") revised by Rutland. See also Rutland's "Framing and Ratifying the First Ten Amendments," in *The Framing and Ratification of the Constitution*, ed. Leonard W. Levy and Dennis J. Mahoney (New York and London, 1987), 305–16, and note 23 for a book that he published on the Antifederalists and the ratification of the Constitution.

For a brief analysis of some of the historical literature examining James Madison's motives in supporting the adoption of a bill of rights, see James H. Hutson, "The Birth of the Bill of Rights: The State of Current Scholarship," *Prologue: The Journal of the National Archives* [PJNA] 20 (1988): 153–54.

⁵See also Dumbauld's "Thomas Jefferson and American Constitutional Law," *Journal of Public Law* 2 (1953): 370–89, and "State Precedents for the Bill of Rights," *ibid.* 7 (1958): 323–44. In the latter article, Dumbauld tested the validity of Zechariah Chafee, Jr.'s, statement that the state declarations of rights were the most important sources for the Bill of Rights. For general studies of state constitutions that also consider the matter of bills of rights, see Elisha P. Douglass, *Rebels and Democrats: The Struggle for Equal Political Rights and Majority Rule During the American Revolution* (Chapel Hill, N.C., 1955); Willi Paul Adams, *The First American Constitutions: Republican Ideology and*

the Making of State Constitutions in the Revolutionary Era (Chapel Hill, N.C., 1980); and Donald S. Lutz, *Popular Consent and Popular Control: Whig Political Theory in the Early State Constitutions* (Baton Rouge, La., and London, 1980). (See also Lutz, *The Origins of American Constitutionalism* [Baton Rouge, La., and London, 1988].) Adams's work, first printed in German in 1973, has a useful bibliography. For a good state study that appeared after Adams's book was written, see Ronald M. Peters, Jr., *The Massachusetts Constitution of 1780: A Social Compact* (Amherst, Mass., 1978).

For the texts of the state constitutions and declarations of rights, see *The Federal and State Constitutions, Colonial Charters, and Other Organic Laws*, ed. Francis Newton Thorpe, 7 vols. (Washington, D.C., 1909); and *Sources and Documents of United States Constitutions*, ed. William F. Swindler, 10 vols. (Dobbs Ferry, N.Y., 1973–79). The reader is forewarned that the compilation by Thorpe omits the Delaware Declaration of Rights of 1776.

[6] *The Bill of Rights: Its Origins and Meaning* (Indianapolis, Kansas City, and New York, 1965). See also Brant's *James Madison: Father of the Constitution, 1787–1800* (Indianapolis and New York, 1950); and "The Madison Heritage," in *The Great Rights*, ed. Edmond Cahn (New York and London, 1963), 15–39; and note 39 below.

[7] In 1980, Schwartz's documentary history was reprinted, in five volumes and with 144 illustrations, by the same publisher as *The Roots of The Bill of Rights: An Illustrated Source Book of American Freedom*.

[8] "The Bill of Rights," in *The American Founding: Essays on the Formation of the Constitution*, ed. J. Jackson Barlow, Leonard W. Levy, and Ken Masugi (New York, Westport, Conn., and London, 1988), 295–327. This revised article, without the footnotes and with an additional section on English and colonial antecedents, had appeared earlier in the *Encyclopedia of American Political History: Studies of the Principal Movements and Ideas*, ed. Jack P. Greene, 3 vols. (New York, 1984), 1: 104–25; and in Levy, *Constitutional Opinions: Aspects of the Bill of Rights* (New York, 1986), 105–34. See also chapter 8, "Why We Have the Bill of Rights," in Levy's *Original Intent and The Framers' Constitution* (New York, 1988).

[9] *The Papers of James Madison*, ed. William T. Hutchinson, William M.E. Rachal, Robert A. Rutland et al. (Chicago and Charlottesville, Va., 1962-); *The Papers of George Mason, 1745–1792*, ed. Robert A. Rutland, 3 vols. (Chapel Hill, N.C., 1970); and *The Papers of Thomas Jefferson*, ed. Julian P. Boyd, Charles T. Cullen et al. (Princeton, N.J., 1952-). Also useful on George Mason is Robert P. Davidow's "George Mason and the Tension Between Majority Rule and Minority Rights," *George Mason University Law Review* 10 (1987): 1–105. About seventy-five pages of this item consist of an appendix of ninety-two documents (1773–91) supporting Davidow's thesis that Mason opposed unchecked majority rule and that his support for a bill of rights was one means of establishing limits on such rule. Davidow is also the editor of a collection of essays on Mason entitled, *Natural Rights and Natural Law: The Legacy of George Mason* (Fairfax, Va., 1986).

Biographies of these three men are also helpful. For Madison, see those by Irving Brant, Ralph L. Ketcham, and Robert A. Rutland; on Mason, those by Rutland and Helen Hill Miller; and for Jefferson, those by Dumas Malone, Merrill Peterson, and Noble E. Cunningham, Jr. For a detailed consideration of one of the principal documents in the American tradition of separation of church and state—Jefferson's Virginia statute for religious freedom (1786)—see *The Virginia Statute for Religious Freedom: Its Evolution and Consequences in American History*, ed. Merrill D. Peterson and Robert C. Vaughan (New York, 1987).

[10] *The Records of the Federal Convention of 1787*, ed. Max Farrand, 3 vols. (New Haven, 1987); and *Supplement to Max Farrand's The Records of the Federal Convention of 1787*, ed. James H. Hutson (New Haven, 1987). In his introduction, Hutson discussed the integrity of the sources for the Convention, although he had a more detailed analysis of them in his article, "The Creation of the Constitution: The Integrity of the Documentary Record," *Texas Law Review* [TLR] 65 (1986): 1–39. For Hutson's discussion of the historical literature on the Convention since the mid-1960s, see "Riddles of the Federal

Constitutional Convention,'' *William and Mary Quarterly* [WMQ], 3rd ser., 44 (1987): 411-23.

[11]For a good bibliography on the methods of amending the Constitution, see chapter 9 of Earlean M. McCarrick, *U.S. Constitution: A Guide to Information Sources* (Detroit, 1980), and for the most recent study on the convention method of amending the Constitution, see Russell L. Caplan, *Constitutional Brinkmanship: Amending the Constitution by National Convention* (New York and Oxford, Eng., 1988).

For a review of recent studies on the Constitutional Convention, most of them geared to a general audience, see Richard B. Bernstein, "Charting the Bicentennial," *Columbia Law Review* [CLR] 87 (1987): 1610-11, 1614-18.

[12]*The Documentary History of the Ratification of the Constitution*, ed. Merrill Jensen, John P. Kaminski, Gaspare J. Saladino et al. (Madison, Wis., 1976-).

[13]On Pennsylvania, the reader should also consult *Pennsylvania and the Federal Constitution, 1787-1788*, ed. John Bach McMaster and Frederick D. Stone (1888; reprint ed., New York, 1970).

[14]In 1985 the same press published Murray Dry's one-volume abridgement entitled *The Anti-Federalist*. For a lengthy review of the Storing-Dry volumes, see John P. Kaminski, "Antifederalism and the Perils of Homogenized History: A Review Essay," *Rhode Island History* 42 (1983): 30-37.

[15]See Storing, *What the Antifederalists Were For: The Political Thought of the Opponents of the Constitution* (Chicago, 1981). See also Storing, "The Constitution and the Bill of Rights," in *Essays on the Constitution of the United States*, ed. M. Judd Harmon (Port Washington, N.Y., 1978), 32-48; in *Taking the Constitution Seriously: Essays on the Constitution and Constitutional Law*, ed. Gary L. McDowell (Dubuque, Ia., 1981), 266-81; and in *The American Founding: Politics, Statesmanship, and the Constitution*, ed. Ralph A. Rossum and Gary L. McDowell (Port Washington, N.Y., 1981), 29-45.

For an historiographic essay that focuses on the Antifederalists and their attitudes toward a bill of rights, see James H. Hutson, "The Birth of the Bill of Rights: The State of Current Scholarship," PJNA 20 (1988): 144-51.

[16]See also Ketcham, "The Dilemma of Bills of Rights in Democratic Government," in *The Legacy of George Mason*, ed. Josephine F. Pacheco (Fairfax, Va., London, and Toronto, 1983), 29-59.

[17]Brown, *Charles Beard and the Constitution: A Critical Analysis of "An Economic Interpretation of the Constitution"* (Princeton, N.J., 1956); and McDonald, *We the People: The Economic Origins of the Constitution* (Chicago and London, 1958).

[18]*The Anti-Federalists: Critics of the Constitution, 1781-1788* (Chapel Hill, N.C., 1961).

[19]*The Creation of the American Republic, 1776-1787* (Chapel Hill, N.C., 1969). In celebration of the bicentennial of the Constitution, the editors of the *William and Mary Quarterly* invited scholars to comment on Wood's seminal book. The commentaries of twelve prominent historians and Wood's response are in "FORUM, *The Creation of the American Republic, 1776-1787:* A Symposium of Views and Reviews," WMQ, 3rd ser., 44 (1987): 539-640.

[20]"Men of Little Faith: The Anti-Federalist on the Nature of Representative Government," WMQ, 3rd ser., 12 (1955): 3-43. The essay appears in expanded form as the introduction to Kenyon's reader, *The Antifederalists*. In 1983, the Northeastern University Press reprinted Kenyon's reader with a foreword by Gordon S. Wood. "Men of Little Faith" is reprinted in *The Formation and Ratification of the Constitution*, ed. Kermit L. Hall (New York and London, 1987), 348-88.

[21]*The Politics of Opposition: Antifederalists and the Acceptance of the Constitution* (Millwood, N.Y., 1979); and "Antifederalists and the Acceptance of the Constitution: Pennsylvania, 1787-1792," *Publius: The Journal of Federalism* 9 (1979): 123-37. Boyd's article is reprinted in *The Formation and Ratification of the Constitution*, ed. Hall, 78-92.

[22]For useful state studies that have appeared after the publication of the Conley-Kaminski anthology, see Edward C. Papenfuse, "An Afterword: With What Dose of Liberty? Maryland's Role in the Movement for a Bill of Rights," *Maryland Historical*

Magazine 83 (1988): 58–68; Gregory A. Stiverson, "Maryland's Antifederalists and the Perfection of the U.S. Constitution," *ibid.*, 18–35; Jon Kukla, "A Spectrum of Sentiments: Virginia's Federalists, Antifederalists, and 'Federalists Who Are for Amendments,' 1787–1788," *Virginia Magazine of History and Biography* 96 (1988): 277–96; Roger C. Henderson, "John Smilie, Antifederalism, and the 'Dissent of the Minority,' 1787–1788," *Western Pennsylvania Historical Magazine* 71 (1988): 235–61; David E. Narrett, "A Zeal for Liberty: The Anti-Federalist Case against the Constitution in New York," in *Essays on Liberty and Federalism: The Shaping of the U.S. Constitution*, ed. David E. Narrett and Joyce S. Goldberg (College Station, Tex., 1988), 49–87; and Robert Ernst, "The Long Island Delegates and the New York Ratifying Convention," *New York History* 70 (1989): 55–78. A shorter version of Narrett's article is printed in *New York History* 69 (1988): 285–317.

Other useful historiographic or bibliographic essays and reference works are, in chronological order by date of publication: Jack P. Greene, "Revolution, Confederation, and Constitution, 1763–1787," in *The Reinterpretation of American History and Culture*, ed. William H. Cartwright and Richard L. Watson, Jr. (Washington, D.C., 1973), 259–95; *Confederation, Constitution, and Early National Period, 1781–1815*, comp. E. James Ferguson (Northbrook, Ill., 1975); *Era of the American Revolution: A Bibliography*, ed. Dwight L. Smith and Terry A. Simmerman (Santa Barbara, Calif., 1975); *A Selected Bibliography of American Constitutional History*, ed. Stephen M. Millett (Santa Barbara, Calif., 1975); James H. Hutson, "Country, Court, and Constitution: Antifederalism and the Historians," WMQ, 3rd ser., 38 (1981): 337–68; Hutson, "The Creation of the Constitution: Scholarship at a Standstill," *Reviews in American History* [RAH] 12 (1984): 463–77; *Revolutionary America, 1763–1789: A Bibliography*, comp. Ronald M. Gephart, 2 vols. (Washington, D.C., 1984); Jack P. Greene, *A Bicentennial Bookshelf: Historians Analyze the Constitutional Era* (Philadelphia, 1986); Richard Beeman, "Introduction" in *Beyond Confederation: Origins of the Constitution and American National Identity*, ed. Richard Beeman, Stephen Botein, and Edward C. Carter II (Chapel Hill, N.C., and London, 1987), 3–19; Richard B. Bernstein, "Charting the Bicentennial," CLR 87 (1987): 1565–1624; James H. Hutson, "The Birth of the Bill of Rights: The State of Current Scholarship," PJNA 20 (1988): 142–61; Peter S. Onuf, "Introduction: Historians and the Founding," in *Essays on Liberty and Federalism*, ed. Narrett and Goldberg, 3–19; and Onuf, "FORUM, Reflections on the Founding: Constitutional Historiography in Bicentennial Perspective," WMQ, 3rd ser., 46 (1989): 341–75.

For historiographic and bibliographic articles on a single state, see Gaspare J. Saladino, "A Guide to Sources for Studying the Ratification of the Constitution by New York State," *The Reluctant Pillar: New York and the Adoption of the Federal Constitution*, ed. Stephen L. Schechter (Troy, 1985), 118–47, and "A Supplement to 'A Guide to Sources for Studying the Ratification of the Constitution by New York State,' " *New York and the Union: Contributions to the American Constitutional Experience*, ed. Schechter and Richard B. Bernstein (Albany, 1990), forthcoming.

[23]Smith, "The Movement for a Second Constitutional Convention in 1788," in *Essays in the Constitutional History of the United States in the Formative Period, 1775–1789*, ed. J. Franklin Jameson (1889; reprint ed., New York, 1970), 46–115; Rutland, *The Ordeal of the Constitution: The Antifederalists and the Ratification Struggle of 1787–1788* (Norman, Okla., 1966), 279–300; and DePauw, "The Anticlimax of Antifederalism: The Abortive Second Convention Movement, 1788–89," PJNA 2 (1970): 98–114. In 1983, Rutland's book was reprinted by the Northeastern University Press.

[24]These volumes also have useful maps and bibliographies of secondary works and primary sources that provide background for the first federal elections. Each volume has its own index.

[25]For a source that combines only the proceedings of the Senate and House journals on the amendments (and was used by Bernard Schwartz in his documentary history on the Bill of Rights), see *History of Congress; Exhibiting A Classification of The Proceedings of the Senate, and the House of Representatives, from March 4, 1789, to March 3, 1793; Embracing the First Term of the Administration of General Washington* (Philadelphia, 1843).

[26]For other criticisms of the *Annals of Congress*, see Dumbauld, *The Bill of Rights*, ix; and Hutson's article in the *Texas Law Review*, note 10 above.

[27]Useful bibliographies for the study of individual amendments are, in chronological order by date of publication: *Freedom of the Press; An Annotated Bibliography*, ed. Ralph E. McCoy (Carbondale, Ill., 1968), and *Freedom of the Press: A Bibliocyclopedia Ten-Year Supplement (1967-1977)* (Carbondale and Edwardsville, Ill., 1979); *American Constitutional Development*, comp. Alpheus Thomas Mason and D. Grier Stephenson, Jr. (Arlington Heights, Ill., 1977); *A Comprehensive Bibliography of American Constitutional and Legal History, 1896-1979*, ed. Kermit L. Hall, 5 vols. (Millwood, N.Y., 1984); *U.S. Constitution: A Guide to Information Sources*, ed. Earlean M. McCarrick (Detroit, 1980); William E. Nelson and John Phillip Reid, *The Literature of American Legal History* (New York, London, and Rome, 1985); *Church and State in America: A Bibliographical Guide*, ed. John F. Wilson, 2 vols. (Westport, Conn., 1986); *Sources and Documents of United States Constitutions. Second Series. Bibliography Chronology*, ed. and comp. William F. Swindler, Bernard D. Reams, Jr., Stuart D. Yoak, and Irving J. Sloan (London, Rome, and New York, 1987); and *Bibliography of Original Meaning of the United States Constitution*, ed. Bernard H. Siegan (n.p., 1988). The bibliography (without the chronology) compiled by Swindler and others was also printed as *The Constitution of the United States: A Guide and Bibliography to Current Scholarly Research*, ed. Bernard D. Reams, Jr., and Stuart D. Yoak (Dobbs Ferry, N.Y., 1987).

Paul Finkelman assessed some of these bibliographies and guides in "The Coming of Age of American Legal History: A Review Essay," *Maryland Historian* 16 (Fall/Winter 1985): 1-11. The work by William E. Nelson and John Phillip Reid, a volume in the New York University School of Law's "Linden Studies in Legal History," consists of seventeen chapters that trace the evolution of the literature of American legal history. Chapter 1 discusses the literature before the 1960s; while chapters 2-16 survey annually, for the most part, the literature from 1962 to 1984. The concluding chapter treats the manner in which legal historians apply critical standards to one another's work. Volume 1 of John F. Wilson's guide on church and state has an essay by Elizabeth B. Clark, entitled "Church–State Relations in the Constitution-Making Period."

[28]*Legacy of Suppression: Freedom of Speech and Press in Early American History* (Cambridge, Mass., 1960). See also a volume edited by Levy that has documents supporting his thesis: *Freedom of the Press from Zenger to Jefferson: Early American Libertarian Theories* (Indianapolis, New York, and Kansas City, 1966). For an article which, like Levy's *Legacy of Suppression*, has much to say about the impact of English history on the adoption of the press and speech clauses, see David S. Bogen, "The Origins of Freedom of Speech and Press," *Maryland Law Review* 42 (1983): 429–65.

[29]Anastaplo, *The Constitutionalist: Notes on the First Amendment* (Dallas, Tex., 1971); Anderson, "The Origins of the Press Clause," *UCLA Law Review* [UCLALR] 30 (1983): 455–541; Kurland, "The Original Understanding of the Freedom of the Press Provision of the First Amendment," *Mississippi Law Review* 55 (1985): 225–58; and Mayton, "Seditious Libel and the Lost Guarantee of a Freedom of Expression," CLR 84 (1984): 91–142.

For Levy's reply to Anderson, see "On the Origins of the Free Press Clause," UCLALR 32 (1984): 177-218, and for his response to Mayton, see "The *Legacy* Reexamined," *Stanford Law Review* [SLR] 37 (1985): 767–93. For Mayton's rejoinder, see "From a Legacy of Suppression to the 'Metaphor of the Fourth Estate,' " *ibid.* 39 (1986): 139–60. Anderson waited until the publication of the *Emergence of a Free Press* (see text following note 29) to answer Levy which he did in a book review entitled "Levy Vs. Levy," *Michigan Law Review* [McLR] 84 (1986): 777–86. For a review of *Emergence of a Free Press* that cogently discusses the issues involved in this debate, see Dwight L. Teeter, Jr., "From Revisionism to Orthodoxy," RAH 13 (1985): 518–25. See also Teeter, "Decent Animadversions: Notes Toward a History of Free Press Theory," in *Newsletters to Newspapers: Eighteenth-Century Journalism*, ed. Donovan H. Bond and W. Reynolds McLeod (Morgantown, W. Va., 1977), 237–45.

[30]Levy's volume has full analytical notes and an extensive bibliography. For some valuable articles on question of original intent, see H. Jefferson Powell, "The Original Understanding of Original Intent," *Harvard Law Review* [HLR] 98 (1985): 889–948; Raoul Berger, " 'Original Intention' in Historical Perspective," *The George Washington Law Review* 54 (1986): 296–337; and Charles A. Lofgren, "The Original Understanding of Original Intent," *Constitutional Commentary* 5 (1988): 77–113. Richard B. Bernstein compiled a representative list of articles on the "original intent grist mill" from law journals printed between 1983 and 1987 in his review essay, "Charting the Bicentennial," CLR 87 (1987): 1599n. Also useful is a lengthy listing of citations from original and secondary sources concerning original intent, gathered under the editorship of Bernard H. Siegan, that was published in January 1988 by the Federal Justice Research Program, Office of Legal Policy, U.S. Department of Justice, with the title—*Bibliography of Original Meaning of the United States Constitution*.

[31]Rabban, "The Ahistorical Historian: Leonard Levy on Freedom of Expression in Early American History," SLR 37 (1985): 795–856; and Smith, "Legal Historians and the Press Clause," *Communications and the Law* 8 (August 1986): 69–80, "Prior Restraint: Original Intentions and Modern Interpretations," *William and Mary Law Review* [WMLR] 28 (1987): 439–72, "Public Opinion and the Press Clause," *Journalism History* [JH] 14 (1987): 8–17, and *Printers and Press Freedom: The Ideology of Early American Journalism* (New York, 1988). Rabban's article and Smith's book are also useful because they reviewed the historical literature of the debate; the latter's work is especially good on the literature for the colonial period. For a criticism of Smith's book and a defense of Levy, see Norman L. Rosenberg, "Another World: Freedom of the Press in the Eighteenth Century," RAH 16 (1988): 554–59.

For a recent criticism of Levy by another historian of journalism, see Carol Sue Humphrey, " 'That Bulwark of Our Liberties': Massachusetts Printers and the Issue of a Free Press, 1783–1788," JH 14 (1987): 34–38. Humphrey argued that the tradition of a free press was developing in practice, even though it did not yet exist in law. Levy's preface to his book lists many historians of journalism who have criticized him over the years.

A valuable historiographical article that discusses both Levy and his critics, including some historians of journalism, is: Wm. David Sloan and Thomas A. Schwartz, "Freedom of the Press, 1690–1801: Libertarian or Limited?" *American Journalism* 5 (1988): 159–77. Sloan and Schwartz considered the historical literature dating back to 1810 and divided it into different schools of thought. They placed Levy's recent critics in the "Neo-Libertarian School (1963-present)," stating that, although they forced Levy to modify his position, they have not triumphed over him. "It is doubtful," Sloan and Schwartz concluded, that Levy's critics "can return historical explanation to the pre-Levy libertarianism." Also useful on the historical literature is Sloan's *American Journalism History: An Annotated Bibliography* (New York, Westport, Conn., and London, 1989).

[32]Palmer, "Liberties as Constitutional Provisions, 1776–1791," in William E. Nelson and Palmer, *Liberty and Community: Constitution and Rights in the Early American Republic* (New York, London, and Rome, 1987), 55–148. This is a volume in the New York University School of Law's "Linden Studies in Legal History."

[33]Corwin, "The Supreme Court as a National School Board," *Law and Contemporary Problems* 14 (Winter 1949), 3–22; O'Neill, *Religion and Education Under the Constitution* (New York, 1949); Antieau, Arthur T. Downey, Edward C. Roberts et al., *Freedom From Federal Establishment: Formation and Early History of the First Amendment Religion Clauses* (St. Paul, Minn., 1964); Berns, *The First Amendment and the Future of American Democracy* (New York, 1970); and Smith, "Getting Off on the Wrong Foot and Back on Again: A Reexamination of the History and Framing of the Religion Clauses of the First Amendment and a Critique of the *Reynolds* and *Everson* Decisions," *Wake Forest Law Review* 20 (1984): 569–643.

The issue of *Law and Contemporary Problems* in which Corwin's article appeared is devoted entirely to religion and the state. His essay is reprinted in *American Constitutional History: Essays by Edward S. Corwin*, ed. Alpheus T. Mason and Gerald Garvey

(New York, Evanston, Ill., and London, 1964), 197–215, and in Richard Loss's compilation, *Corwin on the Constitution*, 3 vols. (Ithaca, N.Y., 1981–1988), 3: 130–49. In 1985 Berns's book was reprinted in paperback by Regnery Gateway.

Two recent "nonpreferentialist" works that also deserve mention, although most reviewers found them disappointing, are Michael J. Malbin, *Religion and Politics: The Intentions of the Authors of the First Amendment* (Washington, D.C., 1978); and Robert L. Cord, *Separation of Church and State: Historical Fact and Current Fiction* (New York, 1982). The latter work has a foreword by political commentator and columnist, William F. Buckley, Jr.

³⁴*Church, State, and Freedom*, rev. ed. (Boston, 1967). For Pfeffer's autobiographical sketch and a list of his voluminous writings, see *Religion and the State: Essays in Honor of Leo Pfeffer*, ed. James E. Wood, Jr. (Waco, Tex., 1985), 487–568.

³⁵Levy's article is in Levy, *Constitutional Opinions*, 135–61. Done with the assistance of Thomas J. Curry, this revision of an earlier essay is also published in *Religion and the State: Essays in Honor of Leo Pfeffer*, ed. Wood, 43–83. The earlier version—"No Establishment of Religion: The Original Understanding"—appeared in Levy's *Judgments: Essays on American Constitutional History* (Chicago, 1972), 169–224. See also Levy, "The Establishment Clause," in *How Does the Constitution Protect Religious Freedom?*, ed. Robert A. Goldwin and Art Kaufman (Washington, D.C., 1987), 69–98.

For a superlative study on the growth of religious freedom in New England, see William G. McLoughlin, *New England Dissent, 1630–1833: The Baptists and Separation of Church and State*, 2 vols. (Cambridge, Mass., 1971).

³⁶*The Establishment Clause: Religion and the First Amendment* (New York and London, 1986). Note 1 to page 208 lists the major "nonpreferentialists," and pages 221–22 present an annotated selective bibliography of the major "separationists" and "nonpreferentialists." A summary of *The Establishment Clause* appears in chapter 9 of Levy's *Original Intent and The Framers' Constitution*

³⁷*The First Freedoms: Church and State in America to the Passage of the First Amendment* (New York, 1986). This volume is a revision of Curry's doctoral dissertation which runs to almost 900 pages. Also good on the adoption of the establishment clause is Philip B. Kurland, "The Origins of the Religion Clauses of the Constitution," WMLR 27 (1986): 839–61; and Douglas Laycock, " 'Nonpreferential' Aid to Religion: A False Claim about Original Intent," *ibid.*, 875–923. Laycock is especially useful for his comments on the writings of "separationists" Levy and Curry and those of "nonpreferentialists" Cord, Malbin, and Smith.

Two books that focus on religion in American life rather than the constitutional and legal aspects of the adoption of the First Amendment, but which are valuable for understanding the principles behind that amendment are William Lee Miller, *The First Liberty: Religion and the American Republic* (New York, 1986), and Edwin S. Gaustad, *Faith of Our Fathers: Religion and the New Nation* (San Francisco, 1987). Gaustad's volume also has two valuable appendices—"Major Documents Pertinent to Religion, 1785–1789," and "Selected State Declarations of Rights and Constitutions with Respect to Religion, 1776–1799." Also useful is Gaustad's "A Disestablished Society: Origins of the First Amendment," *Journal of Church and State* 11 (1969): 409–25. The attitudes of both Federalists and Antifederalists toward religion were discussed by Morton Borden in "Federalists, Antifederalists, and Religious Freedom," *ibid.* 21 (1979): 469–82.

For the battle to extend the protections of the First Amendment beyond the bounds of Protestant Christianity, especially among Jews, see Morton Borden, *Jews, Turks, and Infidels* (Chapel Hill, N.C., and London, 1984).

³⁸*Church and State in the United States*, 3 vols. (New York, 1950). The romantic view of the relationship of government and religion held by Stokes was popularized, according to Elizabeth B. Clark (note 27 above), by Philip Schaff's *Church and State in the United States, or The American Idea of Religious Liberty and Its Practical Effect, With Official Documents* (1888; reprint ed., New York, 1972). Schaff described "the distinctive character of American Christianity in its organized social aspect and in its rela-

tion to the national life" in this manner: "It is a FREE CHURCH IN A FREE STATE, or a SELF-SUPPORTING AND SELF-GOVERNING CHRISTIANITY IN INDEPEN-DENT BUT FRIENDLY RELATION TO THE CIVIL GOVERNMENT." In 1964 Leo Pfeffer, upon the request of the estate of Canon Stokes and publisher Harper & Row, published a one-volume abridgement of Stokes's work. Pfeffer also brought the text and the bibliography up-to-date and added a chapter on the decisions of the Supreme Court in the area of church-state relations.

³⁹The articles by Marvin K. Singleton, Ralph L. Ketcham, and Donald L. Drakeman, all reprints, are especially valuable. For other useful studies of Madison, see Brant, "Madison: On the Separation of Church and State," WMQ, 3rd ser., 8 (1951): 3–24, and in *Civil Liberties*, ed. Hall, 1: 264–85; Paul J. Weber, "James Madison and Religious Equality: The Perfect Separation," *Review of Politics*, 44 (1982): 163–86; and Robert J. Morgan, *James Madison on the Constitution and the Bill of Rights* (New York, Westport, Conn., and London, 1988).

⁴⁰"George Mason and the Origins of the First Amendment," in *The First Amendment: The Legacy of George Mason*, ed. T. Daniel Shumate (Fairfax, Va., London, and Toronto, 1985), 81–104.

⁴¹"A Free People's Intolerable Grievance: The Quartering of Troops and the Third Amendment," in *The Bill of Rights: A Lively Heritage*, ed. Kukla, 67–82.

⁴²Lasson, *The History and Development of the Fourth Amendment to the United States Constitution* (Baltimore, 1937); Stengel, "Background of the Fourth Amendment to the Constitution of the United States," *University of Richmond Law Review* 3 (1968–69): 278–98, 4 (1969–70): 60–75; and Cuddihy and Hardy, "A Man's House Was Not His Castle: Origins of the Fourth Amendment to the Constitution," WMQ, 3rd ser., 37 (1980): 371–400; and Cuddihy, "From General to Specific Warrants: The Origins of the Fourth Amendment," in *The Bill of Rights: A Lively Heritage*, ed. Kukla, 85–98. At present, Cuddihy is completing a doctoral dissertation on the Fourth Amendment under Leonard W. Levy's direction at the Claremont Graduate School. Levy praised and incorporated some of Cuddihy's findings in his chapter on the Fourth Amendment in his *Original Intent and The Framers' Constitution*.

⁴³Griswold, *The Fifth Amendment Today* (Cambridge, Mass., 1955); Williams, " 'Liberty' in the Due Process Clauses of the Fifth and Fourteenth Amendments: The Framers' Intentions," *University of Colorado Law Review* 53 (1981): 117–36; and Jurow, "Untimely Thoughts: A Reconsideration of the Origins of Due Process of Law," AJLH 19 (1975): 265–79. For more on the history of "due process," see A.E. Dick Howard, *The Road from Runnymede: Magna Carta and Constitutionalism in America* (Charlottesville, Va., 1968).

⁴⁴Pittman, "The Colonial and Constitutional History of the Privilege against Self-Incrimination in America," *Virginia Law Review* [VLR], 21 (1935): 763–89; and Morgan, "The Privilege against Self-Incrimination," *Minnesota Law Review* [MnLR], 34 (1949): 1–45.

⁴⁵*Origins of the Fifth Amendment: The Right Against Self-Incrimination* (New York, 1968). In 1986 this book was reissued with a second preface in which Levy defended the Supreme Court's 1966 decision in *Miranda v. Arizona* (384 U.S. 436). A summary of the *Origins of the Fifth Amendment* is in chapter 12 of Levy's *Original Intent and The Framers' Constitution*. See also Levy's "History and Judicial History: The Case of the Fifth Amendment," in his *Constitutional Opinions*, 193–209. This is a revision of an article that appeared under title "The Right Against Self-Incrimination: History and Judicial History," in the *Political Science Quarterly* 84 (1969): 1–29. This last version is reprinted in *Civil Liberties*, ed. Hall, 1: 609–37.

⁴⁶Sigler, "A History of Double Jeopardy," AJLH 7 (1963): 283–309, and *Double Jeopardy: The Development of a Legal and Social Policy* (Ithaca, N.Y., 1969); and Treanor, "The Origins and Original Significance of the Just Compensation Clause of the Fifth Amendment," YLJ 94 (1985): 694–716. Also useful on the right of eminent domain is William B. Stoebuck, "A General Theory of Eminent Domain," *Washington Law Review* 47 (1972): 553–608.

[47] Heller, *The Sixth Amendment to the Constitution of the United States* (Lawrence, Kan., 1951); and Murrin and Roeber, "Trial by Jury: The Virginia Paradox," in *The Bill of Rights: A Lively Heritage*, ed. Kukla, 109–29.

[48] Henderson, "The Background of the Seventh Amendment," HLR 80 (1966): 289–337; and Wolfram, "The Constitutional History of the Seventh Amendment," MnLR 57 (1973): 639–747.

[49] Devlin, "Jury Trials of Complex Cases: English Practice at the Time of the Seventh Amendment," CLR 80 (1980): 43–107; Arnold, "A Historical Inquiry Into the Right to Trial by Jury in Complex Civil Litigation," *University of Pennsylvania Law Review* 128 (April 1980): 829–48; Campbell and Le Poidevin, "Complex Cases and Jury Trials: A Reply to Professor Arnold," *ibid.*, 965–85; and Arnold, "A Modest Replication to a Lengthy Discourse," *ibid.*, 986–88.

[50] Duker, "The Right to Bail: An Historical Inquiry," *Albany Law Review* 42 (1977): 33–120; and Williamson, "Bail, Fines, and Punishment: The Eighth Amendment's Safeguards," in *The Bill of Rights: A Lively Heritage*, ed. Kukla, 131–39. Williamson's article is good on the literature of the amendment.

[51] "'Nor Cruel and Unusual Punishments': The Original Meaning," *California Law Review* [CaLR] 57 (1969): 839–65.

[52] *Death Penalties: The Supreme Court's Obstacle Course* (Cambridge, Mass., 1982).

[53] Bedau, "Berger's Defense of the Death Penalty: How Not to Read the Constitution," McLR 81 (1983): 1152–65; Gillers, "Berger Redux," YLJ 92 (1983): 731–48; Kalis, "Sense and Censure," *University of Pittsburgh Law Review* 44 (1983): 635–46; Richards, "Constitutional Interpretation, History, and the Death Penalty," CaLR 71 (1983): 1372–98; White, "Judicial Activism and the Identity of the Legal Profession," *Judicature* 67 (1983): 246–55; and Foley, "The Ongoing Debate: The Constitutionality of Death," *Harvard Civil Rights—Civil Liberties Law Review* 19 (1984): 245–60.

Raoul Berger's philosophy of judicial restraint, alluded to by his critics, is central to his writings, but one should examine one of his works in particular—*Government by Judiciary: The Transformation of the Fourteenth Amendment* (Cambridge, Mass., 1977). Berger himself estimated that by October 1984 he had answered the critics of his philosophy of judicial restraint in about twenty-four responses, totaling some 800 pages (Berger, "G. Edward White's Apology for Judicial Activism," TLR 63 [1984]: 384).

When David A.J. Richards referred to the growing revulsion to the death penalty in the eighteenth century, he used a study on France by John McManners entitled *Death and the Enlightenment: Changing Attitudes to Death among Christians and Unbelievers in Eighteenth-century France* (Oxford, Eng., and New York, 1981). For a recent study on the death penalty in America, see Louis P. Masur, *Rites of Execution: Capital Punishment and the Transformation of American Culture, 1776–1865* (New York and Oxford, Eng., 1989).

[54] "Death Penalties and Hugo Bedau: A Crusading Philosopher Goes Overboard," *Ohio State Law Journal* 45 (1984): 863–81; "G. Edward White's Apology for Judicial Activism," TLR 63 (1984): 367–85; and "Death Penalties: A Response to Stephen Gillers," *Willamette Law Review* 24 (Winter 1988): 1–34.

[55] Dunbar, "James Madison and the Ninth Amendment," VLR 42 (1956): 627–43; Sutelan, "The Ninth Amendment: Guidepost to Fundamental Rights," WMLR 8 (1966): 101–20; Moore, "The Ninth Amendment—Its Origins and Meaning," *New England Law Review* 7 (1972): 216–309; Goodman, *The Ninth Amendment: History, Interpretation, and Meaning* (Smithtown, N.Y., 1981); Berger, "The Ninth Amendment," *Cornell Law Review* 66 (1980): 1–26; Caplan, "The History and Meaning of the Ninth Amendment," VLR 69 (1983): 223–68; Mitchell, "The Ninth Amendment and the Jurisprudence of Original Intention," *Georgetown Law Journal* 74 (1986): 1719–42; and Massey, "Federalism and Fundamental Rights: The Ninth Amendment," *Hastings Law Journal* 38 (1987): 305–44. The Goodman book and the Berger and Mitchell articles are also valuable for the literature on this amendment.

Other valuable articles on the Ninth Amendment are John P. Kaminski, "Restoring the Declaration of Independence: Natural Rights and the Ninth Amendment," in *The*

Bill of Rights: A Lively Heritage, ed. Kukla, 141–50; Norman Redlich, "Are There 'Certain Rights' . . . Retained by the People," *New York University Law Review* 37 (1962): 787–812; and Lawrence G. Sager, "You Can Raise the First, Hide Behind the Fourth, and Plead the Fifth. But What on Earth Can You Do with the Ninth Amendment?," *Chicago-Kent Law Review* 64 (1988): 239–64. Another article of interest, probably the first written solely on the Ninth Amendment, is Knowlton H. Kelsey, "The Ninth Amendment of the Federal Constitution," *Indiana Law Journal* 11 (1936): 309–23. Another useful work for the study of the Ninth Amendment is David A.J. Richards, *Foundations of American Constitutionalism* (New York and Oxford, Eng., 1989).

Excerpts from Patterson's book and the complete articles by Berger, Caplan, Kelsey, Massey, and Redlich are among the writings on the Ninth Amendment reprinted in *The Rights Retained by the People: The History and Meaning of the Ninth Amendment*, ed. Randy E. Barnett (Fairfax, Va., 1989). The reader should also consult Barnett's historical and analytical introduction, "James Madison's Ninth Amendment"; his bibliography and case index; and his appendices which include the amendments to the Constitution proposed by the state ratifying conventions and Justice Goldberg's concurring opinion in *Griswold v. Connecticut*.

[56]Lofgren, "The Origins of the Tenth Amendment, History, Sovereignty, and the Problems of Constitutional Intention," in *Constitutional Government in America*, ed. Ronald K.L. Collins (Durham, N.C., 1980), 331–57, and *"Government from Reflection and Choice": Constitutional Essays on War, Foreign Relations, and Federalism*, ed. Lofgren (New York and Oxford, Eng., 1986), 70–115; Berger, *Federalism: The Founders' Design* (Norman, Okla., and London, 1987); and Hobson, "The Tenth Amendment and the New Federalism of 1789," in *The Bill of Rights: A Lively Heritage*, ed. Kukla, 153–63. Berger's book also discusses the literature of the amendment. Another useful essay is Walter Berns, "The Meaning of the Tenth Amendment," in *A Nation of States: Essays on the American Federal System*, ed. Robert A. Goldwin (Chicago, 1963), 126–48, and in *Taking the Constitution Seriously*, ed. McDowell, 162–77.

APPENDIX

Augustine Davis
(d. 1825)

THOMAS E. BURKE
New York State Bicentennial Commission

The early identity of Augustine Davis is difficult to establish. The first United States census (1790) lists an Augustine Davis as living at the city of Williamsburg, Virginia. Davis' household included four persons, three white and one black. In 1784, however, an Augustus Davis was counted as residing in Hampshire County, Virginia, where seven persons lived in a single dwelling.

Apparently, by 1786, Augustine Davis the printer was living in Richmond, where on July 26, 1786, he published the first issue of *The Virginia Independent Chronicle*. A year's subscription cost 15 shillings. His printing office was in the basement of a house at the corner of Main and Eleventh streets. During this period, Davis also petitioned for and received printing assignments from the State of Virginia. In March 1787, for example, Davis was authorized to complete 2,000 copies of the Articles of War. Subsequent assignments included the printing of six copies of a blank general return of the militia, and the laws of the session of the General Assembly of Virginia.

It is also possible that Davis was acting as postmaster of Richmond during this period. In 1787, he submitted an account for postage of public dispatches from November 26, 1786, to March 20, 1787.

Davis was a Federalist and served as the printer for the 1788 Virginia ratifying convention. He celebrated the adoption of the federal Constitution in the *Independent Chronicle:*

> What Virginian's breast glows not with expectation of this boon,
> when he considers that its first shoot sprung from this State; . . .
> that it is The Tree of Life, whose fruit will enthrone this western
> empire high among the nations, and raise the firmest and fairest
> temple to liberty that has every yet dignified this globe!

Shortly thereafter, Davis printed *The Ratifications of the New Foederal Constitution Together with the Amendments Proposed by the Several States.* The pamphlet omitted the ratifications of states such as Connecticut and New Jersey that did not propose amendments. It is possible that Davis produced the pamphlet at the urging of Edmund Randolph. In correspondence to James Madison dated September 12, 1788, at Richmond, Randolph wrote: "I desired Davis to make a collection, of which the inclosed is a copy."

Subsequently, on October 17, 1788, Madison wrote to Thomas Jefferson, enclosing a "little pamphlet" which would provide "a collective view of the alterations which have been proposed for the new Constitution." Although neither Randolph nor Madison specifically mentioned *The Ratifications of the New Foederal Constitution,* there is a copy in the Madison collection of pamphlets at the Library of Congress and, as late as 1961, another copy, with Madison's signature and marginal notations, was in the possession of Charles M. Storey of Boston, Massachusetts.

Davis remained a resident of Richmond throughout the 1790s. He continued as the local postmaster, a position which he received as a reward for his loyalty to the Federalist party. On at least one instance, he was the recipient of correspondence from Alexander Hamilton.

As late as 1800, Davis was still living at Richmond where he printed *The Virginia Gazette and Richmond Advertiser.* Davis operated the post office in the same building as the newspaper. Davis was a known foe of President Thomas Jefferson, however, who fired him as postmaster.

THE

RATIFICATIONS

OF THE

New Foederal Constitution,

TOGETHER WITH THE

AMENDMENTS,

PROPOSED BY THE

SEVERAL STATES.

This Collection was made at the instance of several Gentlemen, who supposed, that it would be useful and acceptable to the Public, to be able to compare at once the sentiments of the different States together.

RICHMOND:

PRINTED BY AUG. DAVIS.

M,DCC,LXXXVIII.

Provisional Note.

*_*The Ratification of Connecticut, New–Jersey, Delaware, Pennsylvania, and Georgia, being unconditional, and not even proposing an amendment, we omit them.

RATIFICATION of the CONSTITUTION
by the CONVENTION of the State of New-York.

We the delegates of the people of the state of New-York, duly elected and met in convention, having maturely considered the Constitution for the United States of America, agreed to on the seventeenth day of September, in the year one thousand seven hundred and eighty-seven, by the Convention then assembled at Philadelphia, in the Commonwealth of Pennsylvania (a copy whereof precedes these presents) and having also seriously and deliberately considered the present situation of the United States, DO declare and make known,

That all power is originally vested in and consequently derived from the people, and that government is instituted by them for their common interest, protection and security.

That the enjoyment of life, liberty, and the pursuit of happiness are essential rights which every government ought to respect and preserve.

That the powers of government may be reassumed by the people, whensoever it shall become necessary to their happiness; that every power, jurisdiction and right, which is not by the said Constitution clearly delegated to the Congress of the United States, or the departments of the government thereof, remains to the people of the several states, or to their respective state governments, to whom they may have granted the same; and that those clauses in the said constitution, which declare that Congress shall not have or exercise certain powers, do not imply that Congress is entitled to any powers not given by the said Constitution; but such clauses are to be construed either as exceptions to certain specified powers, or as inserted merely for greater caution.

That the people have an equal, natural and unalienable right, freely and peaceably to exercise their religion according to the dictates of conscience; and that no religious sect or society ought to be favored or established by law in preference of others.

That the people have a right to keep and bear arms; that a well regulated militia, including the body of the people *capable of bearing arms*, is the proper, natural, and safe defence of a free state.

That the militia should not be subject to martial law except in time of war, rebellion or insurrection.

That standing armies in time of peace are dangerous to liberty, and ought not to be kept up, except in cases of necessity, and that at all times the military should be under strict subordination to the civil power.

That in the time of peace no soldier ought to be quartered in any house without the consent of the owner; and in time of war only by the civil magistrate, in such manner as the Laws may direct.

That no person ought to be put twice in jeopardy of life or limb for one and the same offence, nor, unless in case of impeachment, be punished more than once for the same offence.

That no person ought to be put twice in jeopardy of life or limb for one in same offence, nor, unless in case of impeachment, be punished more than once for the same offence.

That every person restrained of his liberty is entitled to an enquiry into the lawfulness of such restraint, and to a removal thereof if unlawful, and that such enquiry and removal ought not to be denied or delayed, except when, on account of public danger, the Congress shall suspend the privilege of the writ of habeas corpus.

That excessive bail ought not to be required, nor excessive fines imposed; nor cruel or unusual punishments inflicted.

That (except in the government of the land and naval forces, and of the militia when in actual service, and in cases of impeachment) a presentment or indictment by a grand jury ought to be observed as a necessary preliminary to the trial of all crimes cognizable by the judiciary of the United States; and such trial should be speedy, public, and by an impartial jury of the county where the crime was committed; and that no person can be found guilty without the unanimous consent of such jury. But in cases of crimes not committed within any county of any of the United States, and in cases of crimes committed within any county in which a general insurrection may prevail, or which may be in the possession of a foreign enemy, the enquiry and trial may be in such county as the Congress shall by law direct; which county in the two cases last mentioned, should be as near as conveniently may be to that county in which the crime may have been committed. And that in all criminal prosecutions, the accused ought to be informed of the cause and nature of his accusation, to be confronted with his accusers and the witnesses against him, to have the means of producing his witnesses, and the assistance of council for his defence, and should not be compelled to give evidence against himself.

That the trial by jury in the extent that it obtains by the common law of England is one of the greatest securities to the rights of a free people, and ought to remain inviolate.

That every freeman has a right to be secure from all unreasonable searches and seizures of his person, his papers or his property: and therefore, that all warrants to search suspected places, or seize any freeman, his papers or property, without information upon oath or affirmation of sufficient cause, are grievous and oppressive; and that all general warrants (or such in which the place or person suspected are not particularly designated) are dangerous and ought not to be granted.

That the people have a right peaceably to assemble together to consult for their common good, or to instruct their representatives, and that every person has a right to petition or apply to the legislature for redress of grievances.

That the freedom of the press ought not to be violated or restrained.

That there should be once in four years, an election of the President and Vice-President, so that no officer who may be appointed by the Congress to act as President, in case of the removal, death, resignation or inability of the President and Vice-President, can in any case continue to act beyond the termination of the period for which the last President and Vice-President were elected.

That nothing contained in the said Constitution, is to be construed to prevent the legislature of any state from passing laws at its discretion, from time to time, to divide such state into convenient districts, and to apportion its representatives to, and among such districts.

That the prohibition contained in the said Constitution, against *ex post facto* laws, extends only to laws concerning crimes.

That all appeals in causes, determinable according to the course of the common law, ought to be by writ of error, and not otherwise.

That the judicial power of the United States, in cases in which a State may be a party, does not extend to criminal prosecutions, or to authorise any suit, by any person against a State.

That the judicial power of the United States, as to controversies between citizens of the same State, claiming lands under grants of different States, is not to be construed to extend to any other controversies between them, except those which relate to such lands, so claimed, under grants of different States.

That the jurisdiction of the Supreme Court of the United States, or of any other Court to be instituted by the Congress, is not in any case to be encreased, enlarged, or extended, by any action, collusion, or mere suggestion; and that no treaty is to be construed, so to operate, as to alter the Constitution of any State.

UNDER these impressions, and declaring that the rights aforesaid cannot be abridged or violated, and that the explanations aforesaid are consistent with the said Constitution, and in confidence that the amendments which shall have been proposed to the said Constitution will receive an early and mature consideration: WE, the said delegates, in the name and in behalf of the People of the State of New-York, DO, by these presents, assent to and RATIFY the said Constitution. In full confidence, nevertheless, that until a Convention shall be called and convened for proposing amendments to the said Constitution, the militia of this State will not be continued in service out of this State for a longer term than six weeks, without the consent of the legislature thereof; that the Congress will not make or alter any regulation in this State, respecting the times, places, and manner of holding elections for senators or representatives, unless the legislature of this State shall neglect or refuse to make laws or regulations for the purpose, or from any circumstance be incapable of making the same; and that in those cases such power will only be exercised until the legislature of this State shall make provision in the premises; that no excise will be imposed on any article of the growth, production or manufacture of the United States, or any of them, within this State, ardent spirits excepted; and that the Congress will not lay direct taxes within this state, but when the monies arising from the impost and excise shall be insufficient for the public exigencies, nor until Congress shall first have made a requisition upon this State to assess, levy and pay the amount of such requisition made agreeably to the census fixed in the said Constitution, in such way and manner as the legislature of this State shall judge best; but that in such case, if the State shall neglect or refuse to pay its proportion, pursuant to such requisition, then the Congress may assess and levy this State's proportion, together with interest at the rate of six per centum per annum, from the time at which the same was required to be paid.

> DONE in Convention at Poughkeepsie, in the county of Dutchess, in the State of New-York, the 26th day of July, in the year of our Lord one thousand seven hundred and eighty-eight.
> By order of the Convention,
>   GEO. CLINTON, President.
>   John McKesson,
> Attested,   } Secretaries.
>   Abm. B. Bancker,

AND the Convention do, in the name and behalf of the people of the State of New-York enjoin it upon their representatives in the Congress, to exert all their influence and use all reasonable means to obtain a ratification of the following amendments to the said Constitution in the manner prescribed therein; and in all laws to be passed by the Congress in the mean time, to conform to the Spirit of the said amendments as far as the Constitution will admit.

That there shall be one representative for every thirty thousand inhabitants, according to the enumeration or census mentioned in the Constitution, until the whole number of representatives amounts to two hundred; after which that number shall be continued or encreased, but not diminished, as Congress shall direct, and according to such ratio as the Congress shall fix, in conformity to the rule prescribed for the apportionment of representatives and direct taxes.

That the Congress do not impose any excise on any article (except ardent spirits) of the growth, production or manufacture of the United States, or any of them.

That Congress do not lay direct taxes, but when the monies arising from the impost and excise, shall be insufficient for the public exigencies, [nor then], until Congress shall first have made a requisition upon the States, to assess, levy and pay their respective proportion of such requisition, agreeably to the census fixed in the said Constitution, in such way and manner, as the Legislature of the respective States shall judge best; and in such case, if any State shall neglect or refuse to pay its proportion, pursuant to such requisition, then Congress may assess and levy such State's proportion, together with interest, at the rate of six percentum, per annum, from the time of payment, prescribed in such requisition.

That the Congress shall not make or alter any regulation, in any state, respecting the times, places and manner of holding elections for senators or representatives, unless the legislature of such state shall neglect or refuse to make laws or regulations for the purpose, or from any circumstance, be incapable of making the same, and then only until the legislature of such state shall, make provision in the premises provided that Congress may prescribe the time for the election of representatives.

That no persons, except natural born citizens, or such as were citizens on or before the fourth day of July, 1776, or such as held commissions under the United States during the war, and have at any time, since the 4th of July, 1776, become citizens of one or other of the United States, and who shall be freeholders, shall be eligible to the places of President, Vice-President, or members of either house of the Congress of the United States.

That the Congress do not grant monopolies, or erect any company with exclusive advantages of commerce.

That no standing army or regular troops shall be raised, or kept up in time of peace, without the consent of two-thirds of the senators and representatives present in each house.

That no money be borrowed on the credit of the United States without the assent of two-thirds of the Senators and representatives present in each house.

That the Congress shall not declare war without the concurrence of two-thirds of the Senators and representatives present in each house.

That the privilege of the *Habeas Corpus* shall not by any law be suspended for a longer term than six months, or until twenty days after the meeting of the Congress next following the passing of the act for such suspension.

That the right of the Congress to exercise exclusive legislation over such district, not exceeding ten miles square, as may by cession of a particular state, and the acceptance of Congress, become the seat of the government of the United States, shall not be so exercised as to exempt the inhabitants of such district from paying the like taxes, imposts, duties and excises, as shall be imposed on the other inhabitants of the state in which such district may be; and that no person shall be privileged within the said district from arrest for crimes committed, or debts contracted out of the said district.

That the right of exclusive legislation with respect to such places as may be purchased for the erection of forts, magazines, arsenals, dock yards, and other needful buildings, shall not authorise the Congress to make any law to prevent the laws of the states respectively in which they may be, from extending to such places in all civil and criminal matters, except as to such persons as shall be in the service of the United States; nor to them with respect to crimes committed without such places.

That the compensation for the senators and representatives be ascertained by standing laws; and that no alteration of the existing rate of compensation shall operate for the benefit of the representatives, until after a subsequent election shall have been had.

That the journals of the Congress shall be published at least once a year, with the exception of such parts relating to treaties of military operations, as in the judgment of either house shall require secrecy: and that both houses of Congress shall always keep their doors open during their session, unless the business may in their opinion require secrecy. That the yeas and nays shall be entered on the journals whenever two members in either house may require it.

That no capitation tax shall ever be laid by the Congress.

That no persons be eligible for a senator for more than six years in any term of twelve years; and that the legislatures of the respective states may recall their senators or either of them, and elect others in their stead, to serve the remainder of the time for which the senators so recalled were appointed.

That no senator or representative shall, during the time for which he was elected, be appointed to any office under the authority of the United States.

That the authority given to the executives of the states to fill the vacancies of senators be abolished, and that such vacancies be filled by the respective legislatures.

That the power of Congress to pass uniform laws concerning bankruptcy, shall only extend to merchants and other traders; and that the states respectively may pass laws for the relief of other insolvent debtors.

That no person shall be eligible to the office of president of the United States, a third time.

That the executive shall not grant pardons for treason, unless with the consent of the Congress; but may, at his discretion, grant reprieves to persons convicted of treason, until their causes can be laid before the Congress.

That the president or person exercising his powers for the time being, shall not command an army in the field in person, without the previous desire of the Congress.

That all letters patent, commissions, pardons, writs and process of the United States, shall run in the name of *the People of the United States*, and be tested in the name of the President of the United States, or the person exercising his powers for the time being, or the first judge of the court out of which the same shall issue, as the case may be.

That the Congress shall not constitute, ordain, or establish any tribunals or inferior courts, with any other than appellate jurisdiction, except such as may be necessary for the trial of causes of admiralty, and maritime jurisdiction, and for the trial of piracies and felonies committed on the high seas; and in all other cases to which the judicial power of the United States extends, and in which the supreme court of the United States has not original jurisdiction, the causes shall be heard, tried, and determined, in some one of the state courts, with the right of appeal to the supreme court of the United States, or other proper tribunal to be established for that purpose, by the Congress, with such exceptions, and under such regulations as the Congress shall make.

That the court for the trial of impeachments shall consist of the senate, the judges of the supreme court of the United States, and the first or senior judge, for the time being, of the highest court of general and ordinary common law jurisdiction, in each state; that the Congress shall, by standing laws, designate the courts in the respective states answering this description, and in the states having no courts exactly answering this description, shall designate some other court, preferring such, if any there be, whose judge or judges may hold their places during good behaviour: provided that no more than one judge, other than judges of the supreme court of the United States, shall come from one state. That the Congress be authorised to pass laws for compensating the said judges for such services, and for compelling their attendance; and that a majority at least of the said judges shall be requisite to constitute the said court. That no persons impeached shall sit as a member thereof—that each member shall, previous to the entering upon any trial, take an oath or affirmation, honestly and impartially to hear and determine the cause; and that a majority of the members present shall be necessary to a conviction.

That persons aggrieved by any judgment, sentence or decree of the supreme court of the United States, in any cause in which that court has original jurisdiction, with such exceptions and under such regulations as the Congress shall make concerning the same, shall, upon application have a commission to be issued by the President of the United States to such men learned in the law as he shall nominate, and by and with the advice and consent of the senate appoint not less than seven, authorising such commissioners or any seven or more of them, to correct the errors in such judgment, or to review such sentence, and decree as the case may be, and to do justice to the parties in the premises.

That no judge of the supreme court of the United States shall hold any other office under the United States, or any of them.

That the judicial power of the United States shall extend to no controversies respecting land, unless it relate to claims of territory or jurisdiction between states, or to claims of land between individuals, or between states and individuals under the grants of different states.

That the militia of any state shall not be compelled to serve without the limits of the state for a longer term than six weeks, without the consent of the legislature thereof.

That the words *without the consent of the Congress*, in the seventh clause of the ninth section of the first article of the constitution be expunged.

That the senators and representatives, and all executive and judicial officers of the United States, shall be bound by oath or affirmation not to infringe or violate the constitutions or rights of the respective states.

That the legislatures of the respective states may make provision by law, that the electors of the election districts, to be by them appointed, shall choose a citizen of the United States, who shall have been an inhabitant of such district for the term of one year immediately preceding the time of his election, for one of the representatives of such state.

DONE in Convention, at Poughkeepsie, in the county of
Dutchess, in the State of New-York, the 26th day of July,
in the year of our Lord one thousand seven hundred and
eighty-eight.
By order of the Convention,

GEO. CLINTON, President.

John McKesson,
Attested,   } Secretaries.
Abm. B. Bancker,

****

In Convention at Poughkeepsie, state of New-York, July 26, 1788.

(C I R C U L A R)

SIR,

WE the members of the Convention of this state have deliberately
and maturely considered the Constitution proposed for the United
States. Several articles in it appears so exceptionable to a majority of
us, that nothing but the fullest confidence of obtaining a revision of
them by a General Convention, and an invincible reluctance to separating
from our sister states, could have prevailed upon a sufficient number
to ratify it, without stipulating for previous amendments. We all unite
in opinion that such a revision will be necessary to recommend it to
the approbation and support of a numerous body of our constituents.
We observe that amendments have been proposed, and are anxiously
desired by several of the states as well as by this; and we think it of great
importance that effectual measures be immediately taken for calling a
Convention to meet at a period not far remote; for we are convinced,
that the apprehensions and discontents which those articles occasion
cannot be removed or allayed unless an act to provide for it, be among
the first that shall be passed by the new Congress. As it is essential that
an application for the purpose should be made to them by two-thirds
of the states, we earnestly exhort and request the legislature of your state
to take the earliest opportunity of making it. We are persuaded that
a similar one will be made by our legislature at their next session, and
we ardently wish and desire, that the other states may concur in adopting and promoting the measure. It cannot be necessary to observe that
no government however construed can operate well unless it possesses
the confidence and good will of the great body of the people; and as
we desire nothing more than that the amendments proposed by this or

other states be submitted to the consideration and decision of a General Convention, we flatter ourselves that motives of mutual affection and conciliation will conspire with the obvious dictates of sound policy to induce even such of the states as may be content with every article in the Constitution, to gratify the reasonable desires of that numerous class of American citizens, who are anxious to obtain amendments of some of them.

Our amendments will manifest that none of them originated in local views as they are such as, if acceded to, must equally affect every state in the Union. Our attachment to our sister states and the confidence we repose in them cannot be more forcibly demonstrated, than by acceding to a government, which many of us think very imperfect, and devolving the power of determining whether that government shall be rendered perpetual in its present form, or altered agreeable to our wishes, on a minority of the states with whom we unite.

We request the favor of your Excellency to lay this letter before the legislature of your state, and we are persuaded that your regard for our national harmony and good government will induce you to promote a measure which we are unanimous in thinking very conducive to those interesting objects.

We have the honor to be, With the highest respect, Your Excellency's most obedient servants, By the unanimous order of the Convention.

GEO. CLINTON, President.

His Excellency the Governor of Virginia.

Ratification of the Foederal Constitution of the Commonwealth of Massachusetts,

In CONVENTION of the Delegates of the People of the Commonwealth of MASSACHUSETTS, Feb. 6, 1788.

The Convention, having impartially discussed and fully considered the Constitution for the United States of America, reported to Congress by the Convention of Delegates from the United States of America; and submitted to us by a resolution of the General Court of the said Commonwealth, passed the 25th day of October last past; and acknowledging with grateful hearts the goodness of the supreme ruler of the universe, in affording the people of the United States, in the course of his providence, an opportunity, deliberately and peaceably, without fraud or surprise, of entering into an explicit and solemn compact with each other, by assenting to and ratifying a new Constitution, in order to form a more perfect union, establish justice, insure domestic tranquility, provide for the common defence, promote the general welfare, and secure the blessings of liberty to themselves and their posterity; do, in the name and in behalf of the people of the commonwealth of Massachusetts, *assent to* and *ratify* the said *Constitution for the United States of America.*

And as it is the opinion of this Convention, that certain amendments and alterations in the said Constitution would remove the fears and quiet the apprehensions of many of the good people of this commonwealth, and more effectually guard against an undue administration of the Foederal Government; the Convention do therefore recommend that the following alterations and provisions be introduced into the said Constitution:

First, That it be explicitly declared, that all powers not expressly delegated by the aforesaid Constitution, are reserved to the several states; to be by them exercised.

Secondly, That there shall be one representative to every thirty thousand persons, according to the census mentioned in the Constitution, until the whole number of representatives amount to 200.

Thirdly, That Congress do not exercise the powers vested in them by the 4th sect. of 1st art. but in cases when a state neglect or refuse to make regulations therein mentioned, or shall make regulations subversive of the rights of the people, to a free and equal representation in Congress, agreeable to the Constitution.

Fourthly, That Congress do not lay direct taxes but when the monies arising from the import and excise are insufficient for the public exigencies; nor then, until Congress shall have first made a requisition upon the States, to assess, levy, and pay their respective proportions of such requisition, agreeably to the census fixed in the said Constitution, in such way and manner as the legislature of the state shall think best— and in such case, if any state shall neglect or refuse to pay its proportion, pursuant to such requisition, then Congress may assess and levy such state's proportion, together with interest thereon, at the rate of six per cent, per annum, from the time of payment prescribed in such requisition.

Fifthly, That Congress erect no company of merchants, with exclusive advantages of commerce.

Sixthly, That no person shall be tried for any crime by which he may incur an infamous punishment, or loss of life, until he be first indicted by a grand jury, except in such cases as may arise in the government and regulation of the land and naval forces.

Seventhly, The Supreme Judicial Foederal Court shall have no jurisdiction of causes between citizens of different states, unless the matter in dispute, whether it concerns reality or personality, be of the value of 3000 dollars at the least; nor shall the foederal judicial powers extend to any actions between citizens of different states, where the matter in dispute, whether it concerns the reality or personality, is not of the value of 1500 dollars at the least.

Eighthly, In civil actions, between citizens of different states, every issue of fact arising in actions at common law shall be tried by a jury, if the parties, or either of them, request it.

Ninthly, Congress shall, at no time, consent, that any person, holding an office of trust or profit, under the United States, shall accept of a title of nobility, or any other title or office, from any king, prince, or foreign state.

AND the Convention do, in the name and in Behalf of the people of this commonwealth, enjoin it upon their representatives in Congress, at all times, until the alterations and provisions aforesaid have been considered, agreeably to the fifth article of the said Constitution, to exert all their influence, and use all reasonable and legal methods to obtain a ratification of the said alterations and provisions, in such manner as is provided in said article.

And that the United States in Congress assembled, may have due notice of the assent and ratification of said Constitution by this Convention;

It is RESOLVED, That the assent and ratification aforesaid be engrossed on parchment, together with the recommendation and injunction aforesaid, and with this resolution, and that his Excellency JOHN HANCOCK, Esq; President, and the Honorable WILLIAM CUSHING, Esq; Vice-President of this Convention, transmit the same, countersigned by the Secretary of the Convention, under their hands and seals, to the United States in Congress assembled.

(Signed)   JOHN HANCOCK, President.
          W. CUSHING, Vice-President.
(Countersigned)
GEO. RICHD. MINOT, Secretary.

IN CONVENTION of the Delegates of the People of the State of New-Hampshire, June the Twenty-first, 1788.

THE CONVENTION having impartially discussed and fully considered the Constitution for the United States of America, reported to the Congress by the Convention of Delegates from the United States of America, and submitted to us by a resolution of the General Court of said State, passed the fourteenth day of December last past, and acknowledging with grateful hearts the goodness of the Supreme Ruler of the Universe, in affording the people of the United States in the course of his Providence, an opportunity, deliberately and peaceably, without fraud or surprise, of entering into an explicit and solemn compact with each other, by assenting to and ratifying a new Constitution, in order to form a more perfect Union, establish justice, ensure domestic tranquility, provide for the common defence, promote the general welfare, and secure the blessings of liberty to themselves and their posterity—DO, in the name and behalf of the people of the State of New Hampshire, assent to and ratify the said Constitution for the United States of America. And as it is the opinion of this Convention that certain amendments and alterations in the said Constitution would remove the fears and quiet the apprehensions of many of the good people of this state, and more effectually guard against an undue administration of the Foederal Government, the Convention do therefore recommend that the following alterations and provisions be introduced into the said Constitution:

1st. That it be explicitly declared, that all powers not expressly and particularly delegated by the aforesaid constitution, are reserved to the several states, to be by them exercised.

2d. That there shall be one representative to every 30,000 persons, according to the census mentioned in the constitution, until the whole number of the representatives amount to 200.

3d. That Congress do not exercise the powers vested in them by the 4th section of the 1st article but in cases when a state shall neglect or refuse to make the regulations therein mentioned, or shall make regulations contrary to a free and equal representation.

4th. That Congress do not lay direct taxes, but when the money arising from the impost, excise, and their other resources are insufficient for the public exigencies; nor then, until Congress shall have first made a requisition upon the states to assess, levy and pay their respective proportions of such requisition, agreeably to the census fixed in the said constitution, in such way and manner as the legislature of the state shall think best; and in such case if any state shall neglect or refuse to pay its proportion, pursuant to such requisition, then Congress may assess and levy such state's proportion—together with the interest thereon at the rate of 6 per cent, per annum, from the time of payment prescribed in such requisition.

5th. That Congress erect no company of merchants with exclusive advantages of commerce.

6th. That no person shall be tried for any crime by which he may incur an infamous punishment, or loss of life, until he be first indicted by a grand jury; except in such cases as may arise in the government and regulation of the land and naval forces.

7th. All common law causes between citizens of different states shall be commenced in the common law courts of the respective states—and no appeal shall be allowed to the foederal court in such cases, unless the sum or value of the thing in controversy amount to 3000 dollars.

8th. In civil actions between citizens of different states, every issue of fact arising in actions at common law, shall be tried by a jury, if the parties or either of them request it.

9th. Congress shall at no time consent that any person holding an office of trust or profit under the United States, shall accept of a title of nobility, of any other title or office from any king, prince, or foreign state.

10th. That no standing army shall be kept up in time of peace, unless with the consent of three-quarters of the members of each branch of Congress—nor shall soldiers in time of peace be quartered upon private houses, without the consent of the owners.

11th. Congress shall make no laws touching religion, or to infringe the rights of conscience.

12th. Congress shall never disarm any citizen, unless such as are or have been in actual rebellion.

AND THE CONVENTION DO, in the name and behalf of the people of this State, enjoin it upon the Representatives in Congress, at all times until the alterations and provisions aforesaid have been considered agreeably to the fifth article of the said constitution, to exert all their influence, and use all reasonable and legal methods to obtain a ratification of the said alterations and provisions, in such manner as is provided in the said article. And, that the United States in Congress assembled may have due notice of the assent and ratification of the said Constitution by this Convention—It is resolved that the assent and ratification aforesaid, be engrossed on parchment, together with the recommendation and injunction aforesaid, and with this resolution: and that John Sullivan, Esquire, President of Convention, and John Langdon, Esquire, President of the State, transmit the same, countersigned by the Secretary of Convention and the Secretary of the State, under their hands and seals, to the United States in Congress assembled.

JOHN SULLIVAN, President of the Convention. L.S.
JOHN LANGDON, President of the State. L.S.
By Order, JOHN CALFE, Secretary of Convention.
JOSEPH PEARSON, Secretary of State.

In Convention of the Delegates of the People of the State of Maryland, April 28, 1788.

We, the Delegates of the People of the state of Maryland; having fully considered the Constitution of the United States of America, reported by Congress, by the Convention of deputies from the United States of America, held in Philadelphia, on the 17th September, 1787, and submitted to us by a resolution of the General Assembly of Maryland, in November session, 1787, do, for ourselves, and in the name and on the behalf of the people of this State, assent to and ratify the said Constitution. In witness whereof we have hereunto subscribed our names,

Tuesday, April 29, 1788

RESOLVED, that the proceedings of this Convention to the vote for assenting to and ratifying the proposed plan of foederal government for the United States, and the yeas and nays be fairly engrossed, signed by the President, and attested by the clerk and assistant clerk: And that the President request the Governor and Council, to transmit the same proceedings, together with the ratification of the same foederal government, subscribed by the members of this Convention, to the United States in Congress assembled.

The Committee were now called upon to report, when the house was informed that, although the Committee had acceded to several of the propositions referred to them, nevertheless they could come to no agreement to make any report.

Upon this a vote of thanks was moved to the President and carried.

It was then moved "that this Convention adjourn without day." The yeas and nays appear as follow:—YEAS 47 —NAYS 27.

PROPOSED AMENDMENTS.

THAT it be declared that all persons entrusted with the legislative or executive powers of government, are the trustees and servants of the public, and as such accountable for their conduct:

WHEREFORE, whenever the ends of government are perverted, and public liberty manifestly endangered, and all other means of redress are ineffectual, the people may, and of right ought, to object to, reform the old, or establish a new government—That the doctrine of non-resistance against arbitrary power and oppression is absurd, slavish, and destructive of the good and happiness of mankind—That it be declared, that every man hath a right to petition the legislature, for the redress of grievances, in a peaceable and orderly manner—That in all criminal prosecutions every man hath a right to be informed of the accusation against him, to have a copy of the indictment or charge in due time (if required) to prepare for his defence, to be allowed council, to be confronted with the witnesses against him, to have process for his witnesses, to examine the witnesses for and against him, on oath, and to a speedy trial, by an impartial jury.

That no freeman ought to be taken, or imprisoned, or deprived of his freehold, liberties or privileges, or outlawed or exiled, or in any manner destroyed, or deprived of his life, liberty or property, but by the lawful judgment of his Peers, or by the law of the land.

That no power of suspending laws, or the execution of laws, unless derived from the legislature, ought to be exercised or allowed.

That all warrants, without oath, or affirmation of a person conscientiously scrupulous of taking an oath, to search suspected places, or to seize any person, or his property, are grievous and oppressive; and all general warrants, to search suspected places, or to apprehend any person suspected, without naming or describing the place or person in special, are dangerous and ought not to be granted.

That there be no appeal to the Supreme Court of Congress in a criminal case.

Congress shall have no power to alter or change the regulations respecting the times, places, or manner of holding elections for senators or representatives.

All imposts and duties laid by Congress, shall be placed to the credit of the state in which the same be collected, and shall be deducted out of such state's quota of the common or general expences of government.

No member of Congress shall be eligible to any office of trust, or profit, under Congress, during the time for which he shall be chosen.

That there be no national religion established by law; but that all persons be equally entitled to protection in their religious liberty.

That Congress shall not lay direct taxes on land, or other property, without a previous requisition of the respective quotas of the states, and a failing, within a limited time, to comply therewith.

In all cases of trespasses, torts, abuses of power, personal wrongs, and injuries done on land, or within the body of a county, the party injured shall be entitled to trial by jury, in the state where the offence shall be committed; and the state courts, in such cases, shall have concurrent jurisdiction with the Foederal Courts; and there shall be no appeal, excepting on matters of law.

That the Supreme Foederal Court shall not admit of fictions, to extend its jurisdiction; nor shall citizens of the same state, having controversies with each other, be suffered to make collective assignments of their rights, to citizens of another state, for the purpose of defeating the jurisdiction of the state courts; nor shall any matter, or question, already determined in the state courts, be revived or agitated in the Foederal Courts; that there be no appeal from law, or fact, to the Supreme Court, where the claim, or demand, does not exceed three hundred pounds sterling.

That no standing army shall be kept up in time of peace, unless with the consent of three-fourths of the members of each branch of Congress: Nor shall soldiers, in time of peace, be quartered upon private houses, without the consent of the owners.

No law of Congress, or treaties, shall be effectual to repeal or abrogate the constitutions, or bill of rights, of the states, or any of them, or any part of the said constitutions, or bills of rights.

Militia not to be subject to the rules of Congress, nor marched out of the state, without consent of the legislature of such state.

That Congress have no power to lay a poll tax.

That the people have a right to freedom of speech, of writing and publishing their sentiments, and therefore that the freedom of the press ought not to be restrained, and the printing presses ought to be free to examine the proceedings of government, and the conduct of its officers.

That Congress shall exercise no power by what is expressly delegated by the Constitution.

That the President shall not command the army, in person, without the consent of Congress.

> True extract from the minutes of the Convention, of the
> State of Maryland.
>   WILLIAM HARWOOD, Clk.
>   Con.

Done in Convention, April 26, 1788.

****

RATIFICATION of the CONSTITUTION, by the State of South-Carolina, May 23, 1788.

YESTERDAY the Convention determined that a Committee should be appointed to consider if any and what amendments ought to be made in the new Constitution, previous to putting the grand question.

The members of the Committee were Mr. E. Rutledge, Mr. Bee, Mr. Pringle, Judge Pendleton, Rev. Mr. Cummings, Mr. Hunter, Col. Huges, Col. Hill, and Mr. William Wilson.

The Committee reported in nearly the following words:

As the obtaining the following amendments *would tend to remove the apprehensions of some of the good people of this state,* and confirm the blessings intended by the said Constitution, We do declare, that as the right to regulate elections to the Foederal Legislature, and to direct the manner, times, and places of holding the same is, and ought to remain to all posterity, a fundamental right,

Resolved, That in the opinion of this Convention the general government of the United States ought not to interfere therein, but in cases where the legislatures shall refuse or neglect to execute that branch of their duty to the Constitution.

Resolved, That in the opinion of this Convention, the 3d section of article 6th, should be amended, by inserting the word "other" between the words *no* and *religious.*

Resolved, That the general government of the United States ought never to impose direct taxes but where the monies arising from the duties, imposts and excise are insufficient for the public exigencies; nor then, until Congress shall have made a requisition upon the states to assess, levy, and pay their respective proportions of such requisitions, and in case such state shall neglect or refuse to pay its proportion, pursuant to such requisition, then Congress may assess and levy such state's proportion, together with interest thereon, after the rate of six per cent, per annum, from the time of payment prescribed by such requisitions.

Resolved, That the states respectively, do retain every power not expressly delegated by this Constitution to the general government of the Union.

Resolved, That it be a standing instruction to such delegates as may hereafter be elected, to represent this state in the general government, to use every possible and necessary exertion to obtain an alteration of the Constitution, conformable to the aforegoing resolutions.

May 24. Yesterday the Convention went through the new Constitution, and also the proposed amendments published yesterday, after which it was moved, That this Convention do assent to and ratify the Constitution agreed to on the 17th of September last, by the Convention of the United States of America held at Philadelphia.

The yeas and nays being called for, there appeared to be, for the ratification 149. Against it, 73.

****

Form of Ratification, which was read and agreed to by the Convention of Virginia.

WE the Delegates of the people of Virginia, duly elected in pursuance of a recommendation from the General Assembly, and now met in Convention, having fully and freely investigated and discussed the proceedings of the Foederal Convention, and being prepared as well as the most mature deliberation hath enabled us, to decide thereon, DO in the name and in behalf of the people of Virginia, declare and make known that the powers granted under the Constitution, being derived from the people of the United States may be resumed by them whensoever the same shall be perverted to their injury or oppression, and that every power not granted thereby remains with them and at their will: that therefore no right of any denomination, can be cancelled, abridged, restrained or modified, by the Congress, by the senate or house of representatives acting in any capacity, by the President or any department or officer of the United States, except in those instances in which power is given by the Constitution for those purposes: and that among other essential rights, the liberty of conscience and of the press cannot be cancelled, abridged, restrained or modified by any authority of the United States.

With these impressions, with a solemn appeal to the searcher of hearts for the purity of our intentions, and under the conviction, that, whatsoever imperfections may exist in the Constitution, ought rather to be examined in the mode prescribed therein, than to bring the Union into danger by a delay, with a hope of obtaining amendments, previous to the ratification:

We the said Delegates, in the name and in behalf of the People of Virginia, do by these presents assent to, and ratify the Constitution recommended on the seventeenth day of September, one thousand seven hundred and eighty-seven, by the Foederal Convention for the Government of the United States; hereby announcing to all those whom it may concern, that the said Constitution is binding upon the said People, according to an authentic copy hereto annexed, in the words following:

[*Here followed the Constitution.*]

Mr. Wythe reported, from the Committee appointed, such amendments to the proposed Constitution of Government for the United States, as were by them deemed necessary to be recommended to the consideration of the Congress which shall first assemble under the said Constitution, to be acted upon according to the mode prescribed in the fifth article thereof; and he read the same in his place, and afterwards delivered them in at the clerk's table, where the same were again read, and are as followeth;

That there be a Declaration or Bill of Rights asserting and securing from encroachment the essential and unalienable rights of the people in some such manner as the following:

1st. That there are certain natural rights of which men, when they form a social compact, cannot deprive or divest their posterity, among which are the enjoyment of life, and liberty, with the means of acquiring, possessing and protecting property, and pursuing and obtaining happiness and safety.

2d. That all power is naturally vested in, and consequently derived from, the people; that magistrates therefore are their trustees, and agents, and at all times amenable to them.

3d. That government ought to be instituted for the common benefit, protection and security of the people; and that the doctrine of nonresistance against arbitrary power and oppression, is absurd, slavish, and destructive to the good and happiness of mankind.

4th. That no man or set of men are entitled to exclusive or separate public emoluments or privileges from the community, but in consideration of public services; which not being descendible, neither ought the offices of magistrate, legislator or judge, or any other public office to be hereditary.

5th. That the legislative, executive and judiciary powers of government should be separate and distinct, and that the members of the two first may be restrained from oppression by feeling and participating the public burthens, they should at fixed periods be reduced to a private station, return into the mass of the people; and the vacancies be supplied by certain and regular elections; in which all or any part of the former members to be eligible or ineligible, as the rules of the Constitution of Government, and the laws shall direct.

6th. That elections of representatives in the legislature ought to be free and frequent, and all men having sufficient evidence of permanent common interest with, and attachment to the community, ought to have the right of suffrage: and no aid, charge, tax or fee can be set, rated, or levied upon the people without their own consent, or that of their representatives, so elected, nor can they be bound by any law, to which they have not in like manner assented for the public good.

7th. That all power of suspending laws, or the execution of laws by any authority without the consent of the representatives, of the people in the legislature, is injurious to their rights, and ought not to be exercised.

8th. That in all criminal and capital prosecutions, a man hath a right to demand the cause and nature of his accusation, to be confronted with the accusers and witnesses, to call for evidence and be allowed counsel in his favor, and to a fair and speedy trial by an impartial jury of his vicinage, without whose unanimous consent he cannot be found guilty (except in the government of the land and naval forces) nor can he be compelled to give evidence against himself.

9th. That no freeman ought to be taken, imprisoned, or disseized of his freehold, liberties, privileges or franchises, or outlawed, or exiled, or in any manner destroyed or deprived of his life, liberty or property, but by the law of the land.

10th. That every freeman restrained of his liberty is entitled to a remedy to enquire into the lawfulness thereof, and to remove the same, if unlawful, and that such remedy ought not to be denied nor delayed.

11th. That in controversies respecting property, and in suits between man and man, the ancient trial by jury, is one of the greatest securities to the rights of the people, and ought to remain sacred and inviolable.

12th. That every freeman ought to find a certain remedy by recourse to the laws for all injuries and wrongs he may receive in his person, property, or character. He ought to obtain right and justice freely without fale, completely and without denial, promptly and without delay, and that all establishments, or regulations contravening these rights, are oppressive and unjust.

13th. That excessive bail ought not to be required, nor excessive fines imposed, nor cruel and unusual punishments inflicted.

14th. That every freeman has a right to be secure from all unreasonable searches, and seizures of his person, his papers, and property; all warrants therefore to search suspected places, or seize any freeman, his papers or property, without information upon oath (or affirmation of a person religiously scrupulous of taking an oath) of legal and sufficient cause, are grievous and oppressive, and all general warrants to search suspected places, or to apprehend any suspected person without specially naming or describing the place or person, are dangerous and ought not to be granted.

15th. That the people have a right peaceably to assemble together to consult for the common good, or to instruct their representatives; and that every freeman has a right to petition or apply to the Legislature for redress of grievances.

16th. That the people have a right to freedom of speech, and of writing and publishing their sentiments; that the freedom of the press is one of the greatest bulwarks of liberty, and ought not to be violated.

17th. That the people have a right to keep and bear arms, that a well regulated militia composed of the body of the people trained to arms, is the proper, natural and safe defence of a free state. That standing armies in time of peace are dangerous to liberty, and therefore ought to be avoided, as far as the circumstances and protection of the community will admit; and that in all cases, the military should be under strict subordination to and governed by the civil power.

18th. That no soldier in time of peace ought to be quartered in any house without the consent of the owner, and in time of war in such manner only as the laws direct.

19th. That any person religiously scrupulous of bearing arms ought to be exempted upon payment of an equivalent to employ another to bear arms in his stead.

20th. That religion, or the duty which we owe to our Creator, and the manner of discharging it, can be directed only by reason and conviction, not by force or violence, and therefore all men have an equal, natural and unalienable right to the free exercise of religion according to the dictates of conscience, and that no particular religious sect or society ought to be favored or established by law in preferrence to others.

AMENDMENTS to the CONSTITUTION

1st. That each state in the Union shall respectively retain every power, jurisdiction and right, which is not by this Constitution delegated to the Congress of the United States, or to the departments of the Foederal Government.

2d. That there shall be one representative for every thirty thousand, according to the enumeration or census mentioned in the Constitution, until the whole number of representatives amounts to two hundred; after which that number shall be encreased as Congress shall direct, upon the principles fixed in the Constitution, by apportioning the representatives of each state to some greater number of people from time to time as population encreases.

3d. When the Congress shall lay direct taxes or excises, they shall immediately inform the Execute power of each State, of the quota of such state according to the census herein directed, which is proposed to be thereby raised; and if the Legislature of any State shall pass a law which shall be effectual for raising such quota at the time required by Congress, the taxes and excises laid by Congress, shall not be collected in such State.

4th. That the members of the Senate and House of Representatives shall be ineligible to, and incapable of holding any civil office under the authority of the United States, during the time for which they shall respectively be elected.

5th. That the journals of the proceedings of the Senate and House of Representatives shall be published at least once in every year, except such parts thereof relating to treaties, alliances, or military operations, as in their judgment require secrecy.

6th. That a regular statement and account of the receipts and expenditures of all public money, shall be published at least once in every year.

7th. That no commercial treaty shall be ratified without the concurrence of two-thirds of the whole number of the members of the Senate; and no treaty, ceding, contracting, restraining or suspending the territorial rights or claims of the United States, or any of them, or their, or any of their rights or claims to fishing in the American seas, or navigating the American rivers, shall be made, but in cases of the most urgent and extreme necessity, nor shall any such treaty be ratified without the concurrence of three-fourths of the whole number of the members of both houses respectively.

8th. That no navigation law or law regulating commerce shall be passed without the consent of two-thirds of the members present, in both houses.

9th. That no standing army or regular troops shall be raised, or kept up in time of peace, without the consent of two-thirds of the members present, in both houses.

10th. That no soldier shall be inlisted for any longer term than four years, except in time of war, and then for no longer term than the continuance of the war.

11th. That each state respectively shall have the power to provide for organizing, arming, and disciplining its own militia, whensoever Congress shall omit or neglect to provide for the same. That the militia shall not be subject to martial law, except when in actual service in time of war, invasion or rebellion, and when not in the actual service of the United States, shall be subject only to such fines, penalties and punishments as shall be directed or inflicted by the laws of its own state.

12th. That the exclusive power of legislation given to Congress over the Foederal Town and it adjacent district, and other places, purchased or to be purchased by Congress of any of the states, shall extend only to such regulations as respect the police and good government thereof.

13th. That no person shall be capable of being President of the United States for more than eight years in any term of sixteen years.

14th. That the judicial power of the United States shall be vested in one Supreme Court, and in such Courts of Admiralty as Congress may from time to time ordain and establish in any of the different states: The judicial power shall extend to all cases on law and equity arising under treaties made, or which shall be made under the authority of the United States; to all cases affecting ambassadors, other foreign ministers and consuls; to all cases of admiralty and maritime jurisdiction, to controversies to which the United States shall be a party; to controversies between two or more states, and between parties claiming land under the grants of different states. In all cases affecting ambassadors, other foreign ministers and consuls, and those in which a state shall be a party, the Supreme Court shall have original jurisdiction; in all other cases before mentioned, the Supreme Court shall have appellate jurisdiction, as to matters of law only: except in cases of equity, and of admiralty and maritime jurisdiction, in which the Supreme Court shall have appellate jurisdiction both as to law and fact, with such exceptions and under such regulations as the Congress shall make: But the judicial power of the United States shall extend to no case where the cause of action shall have originated before the ratification of this Constitution; except in disputes between states about their territory; disputes between persons claiming lands under the grants of different states, and suits for debts due to the United States.

15th. That in criminal prosecutions, no man shall be restrained in the exercise of the usual and accustomed right of challenging or excepting to the jury.

16th. That Congress shall not alter, modify, or interfere in the times, places, or manner of holding elections for Senators and Representatives, or either of them, except when the Legislature of any state shall neglect, refuse, or be disabled by invasion or rebellion to prescribe the same.

17th. That those clauses which declare that Congress shall not exercise certain powers, be not interpreted in any manner whatsoever, to extend the powers of Congress; but that they be construed either as making exceptions to the specified powers where this shall be the case, or otherwise, as inserted merely for greater caution.

18th. That the laws ascertaining the compensation of senators and representatives for their services, be postponed in their operation, until after the election of representatives immediately succeeding the passing thereof; that excepted, which shall first be passed on the subject.

19th. That some tribunal other than the senate be provided for trying impeachments of senators.

20th. That the salary of a judge shall not be encreased or diminished during his continuance in office otherwise than by general regulations of salary, which may take place on a revision of the subject at stated periods of not less than seven years, to commence from the time such salaries shall be first ascertained by Congress.

AND the Convention do, in the name and behalf of the people of this commonwealth, enjoin it upon their representatives in Congress to exert all their influence and use all reasonable and legal methods to obtain a RATIFICATION of the foregoing alterations and provisions in the manner provided by the fifth article of the said Constitution; and in all congressional laws to be passed in the meantime, to conform to the spirit of these amendments as far as the said Constitution will admit.

And so much of the said amendments as is contained in the first twenty articles, constituting the Bill of Rights, being again read;

Resolved, That this Convention doth concur therein.

The other amendments to the said proposed Constitution contained in twenty-one articles, being then again read, a motion was made, and the question being put, to amend the same by striking out the third article, containing these words;

"When the Congress shall lay direct taxes or excises, they shall immediately inform the Executive power of such state, of the quota of each state according to the census herein directed, which is proposed to be thereby raised; and if the Legislature of any state shall pass a law which shall be effectual for raising such quota at the time required by Congress, the taxes and excises laid by Congress shall not be collected in such state."

It passed in the negative,

AYES 65
NOES 85

STATE of NORTH-CAROLINA
In Convention, August 2, 1788.

RESOLVED, That a Declaration of Rights, asserting and securing from encroachment the great Principles of civil and religious Liberty, and the unalienable Rights of the People, together with amendments to the most ambiguous and exceptionable parts of the said Constitution of Government, ought to be laid before Congress, or the Convention of the States that shall or may be called for the purpose of amending the said Constitution, for their consideration, previous to the Ratification of the Constitution aforesaid, on the part of the State of North-Carolina.

Declaration of Rights.

1st. THAT there are certain natural rights of which men, when they form a social compact, cannot deprive or divest their posterity, among which are the enjoyment of life, and liberty, with the means of acquiring, possessing and protecting property, and pursuing and obtaining happiness and safety.

2d. That all power is naturally vested in, and consequently derived from the people; that magistrates therefore are their trustees, and agents, and at all times amenable to them.

3d. That Government ought to be instituted for the common benefit, protection and security of the people; and that the doctrine of non resistance against arbitrary power and oppression is absurd, slavish, and destructive to the good and happiness of mankind.

4th. That no man or set of men are entitled to exclusive or separate public emoluments or privileges from the community, but in consideration of public services; which not being descendible, neither ought the offices of Magistrate, Legislator or Judge, or any other public office, to be hereditary.

5th. That the Legislative, Executive and Judiciary powers of Government should be separate and distinct, and that the members of the two first may be restrained from oppression by feeling and participating the public burthens, they should at fixed periods be reduced to a private station, return into the mass of the people; and the vacancies be supplied by certain and regular elections; in which all or any part of the former members to be eligible or ineligible, as the rules of the Constitution of Government, and the laws shall direct.

6th. That elections of representatives in the legislature ought to be free and frequent, and all men having sufficient evidence of permanent common interest with, and attachment to the community, ought to have the right of suffrage: and no aid, charge, tax or fee can be set, rated, or levied upon the people without their own consent, or that of their representatives, so elected, nor can they be bound by any law, to which they have not in like manner assented for the public good.

7th. That all power of suspending laws, or the execution of laws by any authority without the consent of the representatives, of the people in the legislature, is injurious to their rights, and ought not to be exercised.

8th. That in all capital and criminal prosecutions, a man hath a right to demand the cause and nature of his accusation, to be confronted with the accusers and witnesses, to call for evidence and be allowed counsel in his favor, and to a fair and speedy trial by an impartial jury of his vicinage, without whose unanimous consent he cannot be found guilty (except in the government of the land and naval forces) nor can he be compelled to give evidence against himself.

9th. That no freeman ought to be taken, imprisoned, or disseized of his freehold, liberties, privileges or franchises, or outlawed, or exiled, or in any manner destroyed or deprived of his life, liberty, or property, but by the law of the land.

10th. That every freeman restrained of his liberty is entitled to a remedy to enquire into the lawfulness thereof; and to remove the same, if unlawful, and that such remedy ought not to be denied nor delayed.

11th. That in controversies respecting property, and in suits between man and man, the ancient trial by jury; is one of the greatest securities to the rights of the peopie, and ought to remain sacred and inviolable.

12th. That every freeman ought to find a certain remedy by recourse to the laws for all injuries and wrongs he may receive in his person, property, or character. He ought to obtain right and justice freely without fale, completely and without denial, promptly and without delay, and that all establishments, or regulations contravening these are oppressive and unjust.

13th. That excessive bail ought not to be required, nor excessive fines imposed, nor cruel and unusual punishments inflicted.

14th. That every freeman has a right to be secure from all unreasonable searches, and seizures of his person, his papers, and property; all warrants therefore to search suspected places, or seize any freeman, his papers or property, without information upon oath (or affirmation of a person religiously scrupulous of taking an oath) of legal and sufficient cause, are grievous and oppressive, and all general warrants to search suspected places, or to apprehend any suspected person without specially naming or describing the place or person, are dangerous and ought not to be granted.

15th. That the people have a right peaceably to assemble together to consult for the common good, or to instruct their representatives; and that every freeman has a right to petition or apply to the Legislature for redress of grievances.

16th. That the people have a right to freedom of speech, and of writing and publishing their sentiments; that the freedom of the press is one of the greatest bulwarks of liberty, and ought not to be violated.

17th. That the people have a right to keep and bear arms: that a well regulated militia composed of the body of the people trained to arms, is the proper, natural and safe defence of a free state. That standing armies in time of peace are dangerous to liberty, and therefore ought to be avoided, as far as the circumstances and protection of the community will admit; and that in all cases, the military should be under strict subordination to and governed by the civil power.

18th. That no soldier in time of peace ought to be quartered in any house without the consent of the owner, and in time of war in such manner only as the laws direct.

19th. That any person religiously scrupulous of bearing arms ought to be exempted upon payment of an equivalent to employ another to bear arms in his stead.

20th. That religion, or the duty which we owe to our Creator, and the manner of discharging it, can be directed only by reason and conviction, not by force or violence, and therefore all men have an equal, natural and unalienable right to the free exercise of religion according to the dictates of conscience, and that no particular religious sect or society ought to be favored or established by law in preference to others.

AMENDMENTS to the CONSTITUTION.

1st. That each state in the Union shall respectively retain every power, jurisdiction and right, which is not by this Constitution delegated to the Congress of the United States, or to the departments of the Foederal Government.

2d. That there shall be one representative for every thirty thousand, according to the enumeration or census mentioned in the Constitution, until the whole number of representatives amounts to two hundred; after which that number shall be continued or encreased as Congress shall direct, upon the principles fixed in the Constitution, by apportioning the representatives of each state to some greater number of people from time to time as population encreases.

3d. When Congress shall lay direct taxes or excises, they shall immediately inform the Executive power of each State, of the quota of such state according to the census herein directed; which is proposed to be thereby raised; and if the Legislature of any State shall pass a law which shall be effectual for raising such quota at the time required by Congress, the taxes and excises laid by Congress, shall not be collected in such State.

4th. That the members of the Senate and House of Representatives shall be ineligible to, and incapable of holding any civil office under the authority of the United States, during the time for which they shall respectively be elected.

5th. That the journals of the proceedings of the Senate and House of Representatives shall be published at least once in every year, except such parts thereof relating to treaties, alliances, or military operations, as in their judgment require secrecy.

6th. That a regular statement and account of the receipts and expenditures of the public money, shall be published at least once in every year.

7th. That no commercial treaty shall be ratified without the concurrence of two-thirds of the whole number of the members of the

Senate; and no treaty, ceding, contracting, or restraining or suspending the territorial rights or claims of the United States, or any of them, or their, or any of their rights or claims to fishing in the American seas, or navigating the American rivers, shall be made, but in cases of the most urgent and extreme necessity, nor shall any such treaty be ratified without the concurrence of three-fourths of the whole number of the members of both houses respectively.

8th. That no navigation law or law regulating commerce shall be passed without the consent of two-thirds of the members present, in both houses.

9th. That no standing army or regular troops shall be raised, or kept up in time of peace, without the consent of two-thirds of the members present, in both houses.

10th. That no soldier shall be inlisted for any longer term than four years, except in time of war, and then for no longer term than the continuance of the war.

11th. That each state respectively shall have the power to provide for organizing, arming, and disciplining its own militia, whensoever Congress shall omit or neglect to provide for the same. That the militia shall not be subject to martial law, except when in actual service in time of war, invasion or rebellion, and when not in the actual service of the United States, shall be subject only to such fines, penalties and punishments as shall be directed or inflicted by the laws of its own state.

12th. That Congress shall not declare any State to be in rebellion without the consent of at least two-thirds of all the members present of both houses.

13th. That the exclusive power of legislation given to Congress over the Foederal Town and its adjacent district, and other places, purchased or to be purchased by Congress of any of the states, shall extend only to such regulations as respect the police and good government thereof.

14th. That no person shall be capable of being President of the United States for more than eight years in any term of sixteen years.

15th. That the judicial power of the United States shall be vested in one Supreme Court, and in such Courts of Admiralty as Congress may from time to time ordain and establish in any of the different states: The judicial power shall extend to all cases in law and equity arising under treaties made, or which shall be made under the authority of the United States; to all cases affecting ambassadors, other foreign ministers and consuls; to all cases of admiralty and maritime jurisdiction; to controversies to which the United States shall be a party; to controversies between two or more states, and between parties claiming lands under the grants of different states. In all cases affecting ambassadors, other foreign ministers and consuls, and those in which a state shall be a party, the Supreme Court shall have original jurisdiction; in all other cases before mentioned, the Supreme Court shall have appellate jurisdiction, as to matters of law only: except in cases of equity, and of admiralty and maritime jurisdiction, in which the Supreme Court shall have appellate jurisdiction both as to law and fact, with such exceptions and under such regulations as the Congress shall make: But the judicial power of the United States shall extend to no case where the cause of action shall have originated before the ratification of this Constitution; except in disputes between states about their territory; disputes between persons claiming lands under the grants of different states, and suits for debts due to the United States.

16th. That in criminal prosecutions, no man shall be restrained in the exercise of the usual and accustomed right of challenging or excepting to the jury.

17th. That Congress shall not alter, modify, or interfere in the times, places, or manner of holding elections for Senators and Representatives, or either of them, except when the Legislature of any state shall neglect, refuse, or be disabled by invasion or rebellion to prescribe the same.

18th. That those clauses which declare that Congress shall not exercise certain powers, be not interpreted in any manner whatsoever, to extend the powers of Congress; but that they be construed either as making exceptions to the specified powers where this shall be the case, or otherwise, as inserted merely for greater caution.

19th. That the laws ascertaining the compensation of senators and representatives for their services, be postponed in their operation, until after the election of representatives immediately succeeding and passing thereof, that excepted, which shall first be passed on the subject.

20th. That some tribunal other than the senate be provided for trying impeachments of senators.

21st. That the salary of a judge shall not be encreased or diminished during his continuance in office otherwise than by general regulations of salary, which may take place on a revision of the subject at stated periods of not less than seven years, to commence from the time such salaries shall be first ascertained by Congress.

22d. That Congress erect no company of merchants with exclusive advantages of commerce.

23d. That no treaties which shall be directly opposed to the existing laws of the United States in Congress assembled, shall be valid until such laws shall be repealed, or made conformable to such treaty; nor shall any treaty be valid which is contradictory to the Constitution of the United States.

24th. That the latter part of the 5th paragraph of the 9th section of the first article be altered to read thus—'Nor shall vessels bound to a particular State be obliged to enter or pay duties in any other; nor when bound from any one of the States be obliged to clear in another.'

25th. That Congress shall not directly or indirectly, either by themselves or through the judiciary, interfere with any one of the States in the redemption of paper money already emited and now in circulation, or in liquidating and discharging the public securities of any one of the States: But each and every State shall have the exclusive right of making such laws and regulations for the above purposes, as they shall think proper.

26th. That Congress shall not introduce foreign troops into the United States without the consent of two-thirds of the members present of both Houses.

Mr. Iredell seconded by Mr. John Skinner moved, that this report be amended, by striking out all the words of the said report, except the two first, viz. "Resolved that," And that the following words be inserted in their room, viz.

This Convention having fully deliberated on the Constitution, proposed for the future Government of the United States of America, by the Foederal Convention lately held at Philadelphia, on the seventeenth day of September last, and having taken into their serious and solemn consideration the present critical situation of America, which induces them to be of opinion, that through certain amendments to the said Constitution may be wished for, yet that those amendments should be proposed subsequent to the ratification on the part of this state, and not previous to it: They do therefore, on behalf of the state of North-Carolina, and the good people thereof, and by virtue of the authority to them delegated, ratify the said Constitution on the part of this state. And they do at the same time recommend, that as early as possible, the following amendments to the said Constitution may be proposed for the consideration and adoption of the several States in the Union, in one of the modes prescribed by the fifth article thereof.

A M E N D M E N T S.

1st. Each State in the Union shall, respectively, retain every power, jurisdiction and right, which is not by this Constitution delegated to the Congress of the United States, or to the departments of the General Government; nor shall the said Congress, or any department of the said government exercise any act of authority over any individual in any of the said States, but such as can be justified under some power, particularly given in this Constitution; but the said Constitution shall be considered at all times a solemn instrument, defining the extent of their authority, and the limits of which they cannot rightfully in any instance exceed.

2d. There shall be one representative for every thirty thousand, according to the enumeration, or census mentioned in the Constitution, until the whole number of representatives amounts to two hundred; after which that number shall be continued or increased as Congress shall direct, upon the principles fixed in the Constitution, by apportioning the representatives of each state to some greater number of people, from time to time, as population increases.

3d. Each state, respectively, shall have the power to provide for organizing, arming, and disciplining its own militia, whensoever Congress shall omit or neglect to provide for the same. The militia shall not be subject to martial law, except when in actual service in time of war, invasion or rebellion; and when they are not in the actual service of the United States, they shall be subject only to such fines, penalties, and punishments as shall be directed or inflicted by the laws of its own state.

4th. The Congress shall not alter, modify, or interfere in the times, places, or manner of holding elections for senators and representatives, or either of them, except when the legislature of any state shall neglect, refuse or be disabled by invasion, or rebellion, to prescribe the same.

5th. The laws ascertaining the compensation of senators and representatives for their services, shall be postponed in their operation, until after the election of representatives immediately succeeding the passing thereof, that excepted which shall first be passed on the subject.

6th. Instead of the following words in the 9th section of the first article, viz. "Nor shall vessels bound to, or from one state, be obliged to enter, clear or pay duties in another." (The meaning of which is, by many deemed not sufficiently explicit) It is proposed, that the following shall be substituted: "No vessel bound to one state shall be obliged to enter or pay duties to which such vessel may be liable at any port of entry, in any other state than that to which such vessel is bound: Nor shall any vessel bound from one state be obliged to clear or pay duties to which such vessel may be liable at any port of clearance, in any other state than that from which such vessel is bound.

This motion made by Mr. Iredell being objected to, the question was put, "Will the Convention adopt that amendment or not?" and it was negatived: Whereupon the yeas and nays were required by Mr.

Iredell, seconded by Mr. Steele, and were, yeas 84.—nays 183.

The yeas on this question are nays upon the concurrence, and the nays, yeas, except Mr. A. Neale, who voted on this question in favor of the amendment, but did not vote on the concurrence, owing to indisposition.

Author–Editor Index
To Bibliographic Essay

Abernathy, Glenn, 89
Adair, Douglass, 70
Adams, Willi Paul, 100n–101n
Allen, W.B., 76–77
Alley, Robert S., 88
Anastaplo, George, 85
Anderson, Alexis J., 100n
Anderson, David A., 85
Antieau, Chester James, 87, 105n
Appleby, Joyce, 71
Arnold, Morris S., 93–94, 108n
Bailey, Raymond C., 89
Bailyn, Bernard, 70
Ball, Terence, 71
Banning, Lance, 71
Barlow, J. Jackson, 101n
Barnett, Randy E., 109
Beard, Charles A., 75, 77
Becker, Robert A., 80
Bedau, Hugo Adam, 95, 108n
Beeman, Richard R., 71, 82, 103n
Bennett, Walter Hartwell, 76
Benton, William E., 73
Berger, Raoul, 94–95, 96, 97, 105n, 108n, 109n
Berns, Walter, 87, 105n, 109n
Bernstein, Richard B., 71, 102n, 103n, 105n
Bickford, Charlene Bangs, 80
Bond, Donovan H., 104n
Borden, Morton, 75–76, 106
Botein, Stephen, 71, 103n
Bowling, Kenneth R., 81
Boyd, Julian P., 70
Boyd, Steven R., 78, 102n
Brant, Irving, 68, 81, 101n, 107n
Brown, Robert E., 77, 102n
Buckley, William F., Jr., 106n

Cahn, Edmond, 101n
Campbell, James S., 94, 108n
Caplan, Russell L., 96, 102n, 108n, 109n
Carter, Edward C., II, 71, 103n
Cartwright, William H., 103n
Chafee, Zechariah, Jr., 66, 84–85, 100n
Clark, Elizabeth B., 104n, 106n
Cohler, Anne M., 71
Colbourn, Trevor, 70
Collins, Ronald K.L., 109n
Commager, Henry Steele, 70–71
Conley, Patrick T., 78, 102n
Cooper, John C., 66
Cord, Robert L., 106n
Corwin, Edward S., 85, 105n–106n
Cress, Lawrence Delbert, 90–91
Cuddihy, William, 91, 107n
Cullen, Charles T., 101n
Cunningham, Noble E., 101n
Curry, Thomas J., 87, 88, 98, 106n
Davidow, Robert P., 101n
DenBoer, Gordon, 80
DePauw, Linda Grant, 79–80, 80
Devlin, Patrick, 93–94, 108n
Diggins, John Patrick, 71
Douglass, Elisha P., 100n
Downey, Arthur T., 105n
Drakeman, Donald L., 107n
Dry, Murray, 75, 102n
Duker, William F., 94, 108n
Dumbauld, Edward, 66, 67–68, 81, 100n, 104n
Dunbar, Leslie W., 96, 108n
Elliot, Jonathan, 74–75
Ernst, Robert, 103n
Farrand, Max, 72, 101n

Feller, Peter Buck, 90
Ferguson, E. James, 103n
Finkelman, Paul, 104n
Foley, Timothy, 95, 108n
Ford, Paul Leicester, 75
Gales, Joseph, Sr., 81
Garvey, Gerald, 105n
Gaustad, Edwin S., 106n
Gillers, Stephen, 95, 108n
Gillespie, Michael Allen, 79
Goldberg, Joyce S., 103n
Goldwin, Robert A., 106n, 109n
Goodman, Mark N., 96, 108n
Gotting, Karl L., 90
Granucci, Anthony R., 94
Greene, Jack P., 71, 100n, 101n, 103n
Griswold, Erwin N., 91–92, 107n
Halbrook, Stephen P., 88–89
Hall, Kermit L., 84, 100n, 102n, 104n
Handlin, Lilian, 71–72
Handlin, Oscar, 71–72
Hardy, B. Carmon, 91, 107n
Hardy, David T., 90
Harmon, M. Judd, 102n
Hays, Stuart R., 89
Heller, Francis H., 93, 108n
Henderson, Edith Guild, 93, 108n
Henderson, Roger C., 103n
Higginson, Stephen A., 89
Hobson, Charles F., 70, 97–98, 109n
Howard, A.E. Dick, 107n
Humphrey, Carol Sue, 105n
Hutchinson, William T., 101n
Hutson, James H., 72, 75, 100n,
    101n, 102n, 103n, 104n
Jameson, J. Franklin, 103n
Jensen, Merrill, 70, 80, 102n
Jillson, Calvin C., 73
Jurow, Keith, 92, 107n
Kalis, Peter J., 95, 108n
Kaminski, John P., 76, 77, 78,
    102n, 108n–109n
Kammen, Michael, 65, 76–77, 99n
Karst, Kenneth L. 83
Kates, Don B., Jr., 90

Kaufman, Art, 106n
Kenyon, Cecilia M., 75–76, 78, 102n
Kerber, Linda K., 72
Kelsey, Knowlton H., 109n
Ketcham, Ralph, 76–77, 101n, 102n,
    107n
Kramnick, Isaac, 72
Kukla, Jon, 83, 91, 103n, 108n, 109n
Kurland, Philip B., 69, 85, 104n, 106n
Lasson, Nelson B., 65, 91, 107n
Laycock, Douglas, 106n
LeDuc, Thomas, 82
Leffler, Richard, 77
LePoidevin, Nicholas, 94, 108n
Lerner, Ralph, 69, 71
Levin, John, 90
Levy, Leonard W., 69, 81, 83, 84–86,
    87, 88, 92, 97, 98, 100n, 101n,
    104n, 105n, 106n, 107n
Lewis, John D., 76
Lienesch, Michael, 71, 79
Lloyd, Gordon, 76–77
Lofgren, Charles A., 97, 105n, 109n
Loss, Richard, 106n
Lutz, Donald S., 101n
McCarrick, Earlean M., 102n, 104n
McCoy, Drew R., 71
McCoy, Ralph E., 104n
McDonald, Ellen Shapiro, 71
McDonald, Forrest, 70, 71, 76, 77,
    102n
McDowell, Gary L., 102n, 109n
McGaughy, Joseph Kent, 76
McLeod, W. Reynolds, 104n
McLoughlin, William G., 106n
McManners, John, 108n
McMaster, John Bach, 102n
Mahoney, Dennis J., 83, 100n
Main, Jackson Turner, 77
Malbin, Michael J., 106n
Malcolm, Joyce, 89, 90
Malone, Dumas, 101n
Martig, Ralph R., 73
Mason, Alpheus Thomas, 75–76,
    104n, 105n

Massey, Calvin R., 97, 108n, 109n
Masugi, Ken, 101n
Masur, Louis P., 108n
Matteson, David M., 81, 82
Mayton, William T., 85, 104n
Miller, Helen Hill, 101n
Miller, William Lee, 106n
Millett, Stephen M., 103n
Mitchell, Lawrence E., 96, 108n
Moore, Terence J., 96, 108n
Morgan, Edmund S., 71
Morgan, Edmund M., 92, 107n
Morgan, Robert J., 107n
Morris, Richard B., 70, 73
Murphy, Paul L., 84
Murrin, John M., 71, 93, 108n
Myers, Denys P., 82
Narrett, David E., 103n
Nelson, William E., 104n, 105n
O'Neill, James M., 87, 105n, 106n
Onuf, Peter S., 103n
Pacheco, Josephine F., 102n
Palmer, Robert C., 86, 105n
Palmer, R.R., 86, 105n
Pangle, Thomas L., 71
Papenfuse, Edward C., 102n–103n
Patterson, Bennett B., 95–96, 109n
Perry, Richard L., 66
Peters, Ronald M., Jr., 101n
Peterson, Merrill, 101n
Pfeffer, Leo, 87–88, i06n, 107n
Pittman, R. Carter, 92, 107n
Pocock, J.G.A., 70–71
Pole, J.R., 76–77
Powell, H. Jefferson, 105n
Prescott, Arthur Taylor, 73
Rabban, David M., 86, 100n, 105n
Rachal, William M.E., 101n
Reams, Bernard D., Jr., 104n
Redlich, Norman, 109n
Reid, John Phillip, 71, 72, 104n
Rice, Charles E., 89
Rice, Kym S., 71
Richards, David A. J., 72, 95, 98, 108n, 109n

Roberts, Edward C., 87, 105
Roeber, A.G., 93, 108n
Rosenberg, Norman L., 105n
Rossiter, Clinton, 73
Rossum, Ralph A., 102n
Rutland, Robert A., 66–67, 70, 79, 81, 89, 100n, 101n, 103n
Sager, Lawrence G., 109n
Saladino, Gaspare J., 76, 102n, 103n
Schaff, Philip, 106n–107n
Schechter, Stephen L., 103n
Schwartz, Bernard, 68, 81, 82, 101n, 103n
Schwartz, Thomas A., 105n
Shalhope, Robert E., 72, 90, 91
Shumate, T. Daniel, 107n
Siegan, Bernard H., 104n, 105n
Sigler, Jay A., 92
Simmerman, Terry A., 103n
Singleton, Marvin K., 107n
Sloan, Irving J., 104n
Sloan, Wm. David, 105n
Smith, Arthur E., 100n
Smith, Don L., 89
Smith, Donald L., 100n
Smith Dwight L., 103n
Smith, Edward P., 79
Smith, Jeffrey A., 86, 105n
Smith, Rodney K., 87, 105n, 106n
State Department, U.S., 74, 82
Stengel, Joseph J., 91, 107n
Stephenson, D. Grier, Jr., 104n
Stiverson, Gregory A., 103n
Stoebuck, William B., 107n
Stokes, Anson Phelps, 87, 88, 98, 106n, 107n
Stone, Frederick E., 102n
Storing, Herbert J., 75, 102n
Sutelan, David K., 96, 108n
Swindler, William F., 101n, 104n
Taylor, Robert J., 91
Teeter, Dwight L., Jr., 104n
Thorpe, Francis Newton, 100n
Tinling, Marion, 81
Treanor, William Michael, 92, 107n

Vaughan, Robert C., 101n
Veit, Helen E., 80, 81
Warren, Charles, 73
Watson, Richard L., Jr., 103n
Weatherup, Roy G., 90
Weber, Paul J., 107n
Webking, Robert, 76
White, G. Edward, 95, 108n
Williams, Stephen F., 92, 107n
Williamson, Rene de Visme, 73
Williamson, Richard H., 94, 108n
Wilson, John F., 104n
Wolfram, Charles W., 93, 108n
Wood, Gordon S., 70, 76, 78, 102n
Wood, James E., Jr., 106n
Yoak, Stuart D., 104n

Index

*See also author–editor index
to bibliographic essay*

Adams, Abigail, 56
Adams, Henry, xiii
Adams, John Quincy, 56
Adams, Samuel, 22
Agrippa, 24
Amendments proposed by state
  ratifying conventions: New York,
  114–23; Massachusetts, 123–25;
  New Hampshire, 125–27; Maryland,
  128–30; South Carolina, 130–31;
  Virginia, 132–38; North Carolina,
  138–46. *See also* Individual rights
Annals of Congress, 81
Antifederalists: demand a bill of
  rights, xii, 20, 21–23; in Pennsyl-
  vania, 26–27, 39; in Massachusetts,
  28–29, 40–41, 56; in Virginia,
  30–35, 41–42, 60; in New York,
  35–38, 42–44; in first federal
  Congress, 45–47; literature on,
  67, 69, 75, 77–78, 79–80, 93–94,
  102n, 103n, 106n
Apportionment. *See Congress*
Arms, right to bear, 114, 127, 134,
  140. *See also* Second Amendment
Army: civilian control over, 136, 140;
  use of foreign troops, 144. *See also*
  Militia; Quartering soldiers;
  Standing army
Articles of Confederation: state-
  federal relations under, 19, 27, 32;
  literature on, 66, 97
Assemble, right to, 116, 134, 140.
  See also First Amendment
Austin, Benjamin, 55
Bail, excessive, 21, 94, 115, 134.
  See also Eighth Amendment
Barron v. Baltimore (1833), xiii, 49

Bible: influence on Bill of Rights,
  5–6, 8, 10
Bill of Rights (U.S.): and Magna
  Carta, x, 3–4, 5, 8, 9; as interpreted by the Supreme Court,
  xii–xv, xvii–xix, 15–16, 49, 87, 94,
  96, 107n, 109n; extended to the
  states, xiii, xvi, xvii; and state
  constitutions and bills of rights,
  xv–xvi, 4, 15; as American contribution to the world, 3; and
  colonial bills of rights, 4, 5, 8,
  66, 68, 84; and common law, 4–5,
  6–7, 9, 92, 93; and the English
  Bill of Rights, 5, 8; religious origins of, 5–6, 8, 10, 11; economic
  origins of, 6; and English political
  thought, 9–12; Federalist comment
  on need for, 12–13, 20, 23–25;
  congressional action on, 13–14,
  44–50; ratification of, 14, 50–61;
  not proposed by Constitutional
  Convention, 19–20; Antifederalists'
  demand for, 20–23; debated in
  Confederation Congress, 21; impact of Virginia amendments on,
  35; as issue in ratification debates,
  26–38; as issue in first federal
  elections, 38–44; general literature
  on, 65–72, 74–75, 77, 80, 82–84,
  99n–101n; literature on ratification
  of by the states, 68, 69, 82. *See
  also* Individual amendments
Bills of rights (state), xv–xvi, 4, 15;
  recent rediscovery of, xviii–xix,
  xxii, 15–16; provisions of, 8–9,
  10, 11; Federalist view of, 12–13,
  20; literature on, 66, 67, 68, 77,
  100n–101n. *See also* Individual states

Bland, Theodorick, 45
Bolingbroke, Henry St. John,
    Viscount, 11
Brennan, William J., Jr., xviii
Brutus, 23
Burke, Aedanus, 47
Carpenter, John, 53
Carroll, Charles, 49
Centinel (Samuel Bryan), 22–23
Charter of Liberties (Pennsylvania,
    1682), 4
Cincinnatus (Arthur Lee), 24
Civil Rights Act (1964), xiv
Civil Rights Movement, xiii, xix
Clinton, George, 33, 35, 51, 53, 54
Clinton, James, 53
Clymer, George, 47
Coke, Sir Edward, 9
Common law: influence on Bill of
    Rights, 4–5, 6–7, 8, 92, 93
Compensation. See Congress, U.S.;
    Judiciary, U.S.
Congress, Confederation: debates
    Constitution, 20–22; calls first
    federal elections, 38; literature on,
    66
Congress, Second Continental, 18
Congress, U.S.: amendment on
    compensation of, 14, 50, 51, 55,
    56; amendment on apportion-
    ment of, 14, 50, 55, 56; first fed-
    eral elections, 38–44; debates Bill
    of Rights, 44–50; literature on
    first federal elections, 80, 103n;
    literature on debate over Bill of
    Rights in, 68, 80–82, 104n
    —amendments concerning pro-
    posed by state ratifying conven-
    tions: regulation of elections, 116,
    117, 118, 120, 121, 124, 126, 129,
    130–31, 137, 143, 145; apportion-
    ment of representation, 118, 124,
    126, 135, 141, 145; power of grant-
    ing monopolies, 118, 124, 126, 143;
    compensation of, 119, 137, 143,
    145; publication of journals of,

119, 135–36, 141; re-eligibility of
    members of, 119; power over fed-
    eral capital, 119, 136, 142; power
    over federal forts, 119; power to
    borrow, 119; power to enact poll
    taxes, 119, 130; war powers of, 119;
    members of ineligible for other
    offices, 120, 129, 135, 141; power
    to grant titles of nobility, 121,
    125, 127; power to pass navigation
    acts, 136, 141; power over com-
    mercial treaties, 136, 141, 143;
    power over rebellions, 142; power
    over paper money, 144; commercial
    powers of, 144, 145. See also
    Taxation
Connecticut: rights in, 4; Funda-
    mental Orders of, 8; ratifies Bill
    of Rights, 14, 54, 82
Constitution, U.S.: interstate com-
    merce clause, xiv; rights in, 12;
    debate over ratification of, 20–38;
    general welfare clause, 27, 32;
    necessary and proper clause, 27,
    32; supremacy clause, 27, 32; lit-
    erature on ratification debate,
    73–79, 102n–13n
Constitutional Convention, 19–20;
    literature on, 72–73, 101n–12n
Constitutions, state: influence on
    Bill of Rights, 4, 15; powers of
    legislature under, 19
Cooley, Thomas M., 83
Corbin, Francis, 30
Courts. See Judiciary, U.S.; Jury trial
Cumberland County (Pennsylvania),
    27
Dane, Nathan, 20–21, 55
Davis, Augustine, xvi, 73–74, 110–11;
    pamphlet of, 112–46
Declaration of Independence, 18–19,
    66, 67
Delaware, 27
Dissent of the minority (Pennsyl-
    vania), 27

Double jeopardy, 115. *See also* Fifth Amendment

Douglas, William O., 94

Duane, James, 52, 53

Due process, 21, 91. *See also* Fifth Amendment

Eighth Amendment: literature on, 94–95, 108n. *See also* Bail, excessive; Fines, excessive; Punishment, cruel and unusual

Elections, 8, 21, 38–44, 133, 138

Ellsworth, Oliver, 49

Everson v. Board of Education, 87

Ex Post Facto Laws, 116

Federal Farmer, 25, 76

The Federalist, xi, xx, xxi, 25, 26

Federalists: views on federal Bill of Rights, xi, 12–13, 20, 24–25; support ratification in Congress, 21; in Pennsylvania, 25–27, 39; in Massachusetts, 28–29, 40–41; in Virginia, 30–35, 41–42; in New York, 36–37, 42–44; in first federal Congress, 44; literature on, 69, 77, 79–80, 97, 106n

Fifth Amendment, xiii; literature on, 91–92, 107n. *See also* Due process

Fines, excessive, 22, 94, 115, 134, 140. *See also* Eighth Amendment

First Amendment: literature on, 83–89, 100n, 104n–107n. *See also* Assemble, right to; Petition, right of; Press, freedom of; Religion, freedom of; Speech, freedom of

Fourteenth Amendment, xvi, xvii, xxi, 15

Fourth Amendment: literature on, 65, 91, 107n. *See also* Searches and seizures

A Free Mechanic (Noah Webster), 46–47

Fundamental Orders of Connecticut (1639), 8

Furman v. Georgia, 94

General Laws and Liberties of Connecticut (1672), 4

General welfare clause, 27, 32

Georgia, 14, 27, 54

Gerry, Elbridge, xvi, 20, 22, 40–41, 47, 72, 75

Gilbert, Ezekiel, 52

Goldberg, Arthur, 96, 109n

Gordon, James, 52

Gore, Christopher, 56–57

Grayson, William, 30, 41, 57, 60

Great Britain: constitution of and political ideas in, x, 4–5, 7, 8–12; Bill of Rights (1689), 5, 8; literature on, 66, 68, 84, 92, 93

Griswold v. Connecticut, xix, 96, 109n

Habeas Corpus, writ of, 115, 119

Hamilton, Alexander, xxi, 12, 26, 111

Hancock, John, 28, 54

Harrisburg Convention (Pennsylvania), 39

Havens, Jonathan N., 52

Henry, Patrick, 29, 41; in Virginia Convention, 30–31, 32, 34

Hitchcock, Zina, 53

Honestus, 40

Hume, David, 5

The Impartial Examiner, 29–30

Impeachment, 120–21, 137, 143

Indictment. *See* Jury trial

Interstate commerce clause, xiv

Iredell, James, 144, 145

Izard, Ralph, 49

Jackson, James, 47, 49

Japanese–Americans, xiv

Jefferson, Thomas: views on Bill of Rights, xi–xii, xx–xxi, xiv; criticizes James Wilson, 25; on Massachusetts' proposed amendments, 29; on Massachusetts' adoption of the Bill of Rights, 56; notification of ratification of Bill of Rights, 61; literature on, 67, 68, 70, 100n, 101n; fires Augustine Davis, 111

Jones, Samuel, 43, 51, 52

Judicial review, 68

Judiciary, U.S.: jurisdiction of, 116, 120, 121, 124–25, 127, 129–30, 136–37, 142–43; salaries of judges, 137, 143

Jury trial, 21, 22, 31, 49, 93; proposed amendments calling for, 115, 116, 124, 125, 126–27, 128–29, 134–35, 137, 139–40, 143. *See also* Sixth Amendment; Seventh Amendment

Kentucky, 30

King, Rufus, 51

Lamb, John, 33, 43

Langdon, John, 49

Lansing, Abraham G., 42

Lansing, John, Jr., 37

Lawrence, Nathaniel, 45

Laws and Liberties of Massachusetts (1647), 4

Laws and Liberties of New Hampshire (1682), 4

Lee, Arthur, 24

Lee, Henry, 30, 60

Lee, Richard Henry: proposes amendments to Constitution, 21, 22; criticizes James Wilson, 25; elected U.S. Senator, 41; opposes ratification of Bill of Rights, 57, 60; as possible author of Federal Farmer, 76

L'Hommedieu, Ezra, 52

Liberty: British view of, 7; American view of, 7, 11; in Virginia Declaration of Rights, 18

Livingston, John, 52

Livingston, Philip, 52

Lloyd, Thomas, 81

Locke, John, 5, 10, 11–12

McCarthyism, 92

McKean, Thomas, 26

Maclay, William, 81

Madison, James: in first federal Congress, xii, xvi, 13–14, 45–49; comments on bills of rights, x–xi, 4–5, 12, 13, 14, 24, 61n; and Augustine Davis pamphlet, xvi, 111;

in debate over ratification, 21; *The Federalist*, 25; on Massachusetts' proposed amendments, 28; in Virginia Convention, 30, 34; and first federal elections, 39, 41–42; on Virginia's reluctance to ratify Bill of Rights, 57–58, 59–60; literature on, 67–68, 69, 70, 78, 81, 86, 87, 88–89, 93, 96, 97, 100n, 101n, 107n, 108n, 109n; notes on Constitutional Convention, 72

Magna Carta, x, 3–4, 5, 7, 8, 9; literature on, 66, 107n

Marshall, John, xiii, 30, 49

Marshall, Thurgood, 94

Maryland: rights in, 4, 8; ratifies Constitution, 29, 73; ratifies Bill of Rights, 50; amendments proposed in ratifying Convention, 128–30

Maryland Toleration Act (1649), 4

Mason, George: and Virginia Declaration of Rights, xv; supports bill of rights in Constitutional Convention, xvi, 20, 72; objects to the Constitution, 22; in Virginia Convention, 30, 32, 33; opposes Madison's amendments, 47; literature on, 66, 68, 70, 75, 89, 93, 101n, 107n

Massachusetts: rights in, 4, 8, 11; colonial compacts, 8; constitution of (1780), xv, 10; ratifies Bill of Rights, 14, 54–57; ratifies Constitution 27–29; amendments proposed by ratifying Convention, 28–29, 34, 82, 123–25; first federal elections in, 40–41;

Massachusetts Body of Liberties (1641), 4, 5, 8

Mayflower Compact (1620), 8

Militia, regulation of, 114, 117, 121, 130, 136, 142, 145. *See also* Second Amendment

Milton, John, 11

Miranda v. Arizona, 107n
Monopolies, 118, 124, 126, 143
Monroe, James, 30, 32, 33, 42
Montesquieu, Charles, Baron de, 5
Morris, Lewis, 53
Morris, Richard, 53
Morris, Robert, 49
Naturalization and officeholding, 118
Nazis, xvi
Necessary and Proper Clause, 27, 32
New Hampshire: rights in, 4; ratifies Constitution, 29, 36, 73; ratifies Bill of Rights, 50; amendments proposed by ratifying convention, 125–27
New Jersey, 27, 50
New York: constitution of (1777), xv; rediscovery of state bill of rights, xviii; rights in, 4; Antifederalists in, 23, 33, 42–43; ratifies Constitution, 35–38, 73; first federal elections in, 42–44; Federal Republican Committee in, 42–43; ratifies Bill of Rights, 50–54; amendments proposed by ratifying convention, 114–23
New York Charter of Liberties and Privileges (1683), 4
Newspapers: print Mason's objections, 22; argument over James Wilson's explanation, 24–25; debate in Virginia, 29–30; debate in New York, 36, 44; debate in Massachusetts, 40; debate on Bill of Rights, 46–47; literature on, 74
Nicholas, George, 30
Ninth Amendment: literature on, 95–97, 108n–109n
Nobility, titles of, 121, 125, 127
North Carolina: rights in, 8; influence of adoption of Bill of Rights on, 46, 50; ratifies Bill of Rights, 50; ratifies Constitution, 73; amendments proposed by ratifying Convention, 138–46

Original intent: literature on, 83, 85, 98–99, 105n
Oswald, Eleazer, 33
Paper money, 144
Paterson, William, 49
Pendleton, Edmund, 30
Penn, William, 6
Pennsylvania: rights in, xi, 4, 6, 8, 10, 11; Antifederalists in call for bill of rights, 22–23; ratification debate in, 25–27; dissent of the minority, 27, 73; first federal elections in, 39; ratifies Bill of Rights, 50; literature on, 74
Petition, right of, 128, 134, 140. *See also* First Amendment
Pilgrim Code of Law (1636), 8
Poll tax, 119, 130
President: reeligibility of, 116, 120, 136, 142; pardoning power of, 120; as commander in chief, 120, 130
Press, freedom of, xiv, 8, 21, 22, 30, 49; literature on, 85–87; proposed amendments on, 116, 130, 132, 134, 140. *See also* First Amendment
Privacy rights, xix. *See also* Fourth Amendment; Ninth Amendment
Private property, 7, 8, 11, 18
Public Accommodations Act (1964), xiv
Punishment, cruel and unusual, 21, 115, 134. *See also* Eighth Amendment
Quartering soldiers, 114–15, 127, 130, 135, 140. *See also* Third Amendment
Randolph, Beverley, 57, 60
Randolph, Edmund, 59, 72, 75, 111; in Virginia Convention, 30, 34
The Ratification of the New Foederal Constitution, 72–73, 111–46
Rebellion, 142
Religion, influence on the Bill of Rights, 5–6, 8, 10, 11; freedom of, 6, 11, 21, 30, 49; literature on

freedom of, 84, 87–89; proposed amendments on freedom of, 114, 127, 129, 131, 132, 135, 140–41. *See also* First Amendment

Remarker, 25

Reserved powers, xvii, 24; proposed amendments on, 114, 121, 124, 126, 130, 131, 132, 133, 135, 137, 139, 141, 143, 144–45. *See also* Ninth Amendment; Tenth Amendment

Rhode Island, 46, 50, 50, 73, 74

Richmond (Virginia), 110–11

Salaries. *See* Congress, U.S.; Judiciary, U.S.

Schuyler, Peter, 53

Searches and seizures, freedom from illegal, 21, 115–16, 129, 134, 140. *See also* Fourth Amendment

Second Amendment: literature on, 89–91. *See also* Arms, right to bear; Militia

Second Convention: proposed, 41, 45, 74, 122–23; literature on, 79–80, 103n

Sedition Act (1798), xii–xiii, 85. *See also* Press, freedom of

Seditious libel, 85–86. *See also* Press, freedom of

Self-Incrimination. *See* Fifth Amendment

Separation of powers, 8, 133, 138

Seventh Amendment: literature on, 93–94, 108n. *See also* Jury trial

Sherman, Roger, xvi, 13–14, 20, 49

Sidney, Algernon, 11–12

Sixth Amendment: literature on, 93, 108n. *See also* Due process; Jury trial

Skinner, John, 144

Smith, John, 52

Smith, Melancton, 37–38, 43, 76

Social compact, 10

South Carolina: ratifies Constitution, 29, 73; ratifies Bill of

Rights, 50; amendments proposed by ratifying convention, 130–31

Speech, freedom of, xiv, 49, 84–87, 130, 134, 140. *See also* First Amendment; Press, freedom of

Standing army: R.H. Lee's proposal on, 21; literature on, 90; proposed amendments on, 114, 118, 127, 130, 134–35, 140, 142

Supremacy clause, 27, 32

Supreme Court, U.S.: interprets Bill of Rights, xii–xv, xvii–xix, 15–16, 49, 87, 94, 96, 107n, 109n

Suspending laws: legislative power of, 129, 133, 139

Talman, Isaac I., 53

Tappen, Christopher, 53

Taxation: direct, 117, 118, 124, 126, 129, 131, 135, 141; excise, 117, 118; poll, 119, 130

Tenth Amendment: literature on, 97–98. *See also* Reserved powers

Third Amendment: literature on, 91, 107n. *See also* Quartering soldiers

Tillinghast, Charles, 43

Treadwell, Thomas, 36–37

Treaties, 136, 141, 143

Tyler, John, 30

Vining, John, 49

Virginia: Declaration of Rights, xv, 4, 18, 33, 66, 67; ratifies Constitution, 29–35, 73; impact on New York, 36; first federal elections in, 41–42; ratifies Bill of Rights, 50, 57–60, 82; literature on, 74; amendments proposed by ratifying convention, 82, 132–38; court system in, 93

Vermont, 50, 61

Walker, John, 60

War powers, 119

Washington, George, 44, 48; 50, 54, 58

Watts, John, Jr., 51

Webster, Noah, 46–47

Whitehill, Robert, 27
Will, Henry, 52
Willett, Marinus, 43
Williams, John, 35–36
Wilson, James, 23–24, 26
Women's Rights Movement, xiii
World War II, xiv
Yates, Abraham, Jr., 42
Yates, Robert, 33, 37, 53
Zenger Case (1735), 86

CONTRIBUTORS

RICHARD B. BERNSTEIN is research director of the New York State Commission on the Bicentennial of the U.S. Constitution. His books and articles on American constitutional history include *Are We to Be a Nation?* (with Kym S. Rice, 1987); *Defending the Constitution* (edited, 1987); *Into the Third Century: The Congress, the Presidency, the Supreme Court* (with Jerome Agel, 1989); *Well Begun: Chronicles of the Early National Period* (co-edited, with Stephen L. Schechter, 1989); *New York and the Union* (co-edited with Stephen L. Schechter, 1990); *New York and the Bicentennial* (co-edited, with Stephen L. Schechter, 1990); and contributions to *Roots of the Republic* (1990). He is completing *"Conven'd in Firm Debate": The First Congress as an Institution of Government, 1789–1791.*

THOMAS E. BURKE was research director of the New York State Commission on the Bicentennial of the U.S. Constitution from 1986 to 1989. His publications include contributions to *New York and the Union* (1990), *Roots of the Republic* (1990), and articles on the colonial history of western New York.

JOHN P. KAMINSKI, Director of the Center for the Study of the American Constitution at the University of Wisconsin–Madison, is co-editor of the *Documentary History of the Ratification of the Constitution and the Bill of Rights, 1776–1791.* His books and articles on the making of the Constitution and the early national period include *The Constitution and the States* (co-edited, with Patrick T. Conley, 1988); *A Great and Good Man* (co-edited, with Jill Adair McLaughlin, 1989); Madison House's *Constitutional Heritage Series*; and contributions to *The Reluctant Pillar* (1985), *Ratifying the Constitution* (1989), *New York and the Union* (1990), and *Roots of the Republic* (1990). His biography of George Clinton will be published in 1990.

DONALD S. LUTZ, Professor of Political Science at the University of Houston, has written or edited several books and articles on American political thought, including *Popular Consent and Popular Control* (1980); *American Political Writing during the Founding Era, 1760–1805* (co-edited, with Charles S. Hyneman, 1983); *Documents of Political Foundation Written by Colonial Americans* (edited, 1986); *The Origins of American Constitutionalism* (1988); and contributions to *Ratifying the Constitution* (1989) and *Roots of the Republic* (1990).

GASPARE J. SALADINO is co-editor of the *Documentary History of the Ratification of the Constitution and the Bill of Rights, 1776–1791* at the University of Wisconsin–Madison. He is the editor of *Empowering the President: The Presidency in the Debate over the Constitution* (forthcoming, 1991), a volume in Madison House's *Constitutional Heritage Series.* His articles and essays on the making of the Constitution and the early national period include contributions to *The Reluctant Pillar* (1985), *Ratifying the Constitution* (1989), and *New York and the Union* (1990).

STEPHEN L. SCHECHTER, Professor of Political Science at Russell Sage College, is executive director of the New York State Commission on the Bicentennial of the U.S. Constitution. He has edited or co-edited several books on the making of the Constitution, among them *The Reluctant Pillar* (1985); *Well Begun: Chronicles of the Early National Period* (co-edited, with Richard B. Bernstein, 1989); *New York and the Union* (co-edited, with Richard B. Bernstein, 1990); *New York and the Bicentennial* (co-edited, with Richard B. Bernstein, 1990); and *Roots of the Republic: Commentaries on American Founding Documents* (1990).